Housing Associations and Housing Policy

5

Also by Peter Malpass:

Housing Policy and Practice (fifth edition) (with A. Murie)
The Housing Crisis (edited)
Reshaping Housing Policy
Implementing Housing Policy (edited with R. Means)
Ownership, Control and Accountability (edited)
Housing Finance: A Basic Guide (fifth edition) (with Henry Aughton)

Housing Associations and Housing Policy

A Historical Perspective

Peter Malpass

First published in Great Britain 2000 by
MACMILLAN PRESS LTD
Houndmills, Basingstoke, Hampshire RG21 6XS and London
Companies and representatives throughout the world

A catalogue record for this book is available from the British Library.

ISBN 0–333–65557–5 hardcover
ISBN 0–333–65558–3 paperback

First published in the United States of America 2000 by
ST. MARTIN'S PRESS, INC.,
Scholarly and Reference Division,
175 Fifth Avenue, New York, N.Y. 10010

ISBN 0–312–23095–8 (paper)

Library of Congress Cataloging-in-Publication Data

Housing associations and housing policy: a historical perspective/Peter Malpass.
p. cm.
Includes bibliographical references and index.
ISBN 0–312–23095–8
1. Housing authorities–Great Britain–History. 2. Housing policy–Great
Britain–History. 3. Housing authorities–Law and legislation–Great Britain. 4.
Housing–Law and legislation–Great Britain. I. Title.
HD7288.78.G7 M35 2000
363.5'0941–dc21   99–050210

This book is printed on paper suitable for recycling and made from fully managed and
sustained forest sources.

10 9   8   7   6 5   4   3   2   1
09 08 07 06 05 04 03 02 01 00

Editing and origination by
Aardvark Editorial, Mendham, Suffolk

Typesetting by T & A Typesetting Services, Rochdale

Printed in Hong Kong

Contents

List of Figures

List of Tables

Preface and Acknowledgements

The initial motivation for this book was the observation that many housing students go on to work for associations, at least for part of their career, and yet there was no good historical account of how associations had developed. There were books on the other main tenure categories within the British housing system, but nothing comparable for housing associations, despite their increasing prominence in recent years. Research for the book began in 1994, with a modest attempt to construct a baseline account of housing association activity in Bristol, identifying and mapping all the associations that owned at least one property in the city. The fieldwork for that project was meticulously carried out by Paul Seville. I was also one of a team (including Stuart Farthing, Christine Lambert, Robin Tetlow, Mark Auchincloss and Glen Bramley) commissioned by the Housing Corporation to carry out three linked projects on land supply for housing associations in England. A separate programme of historical work was launched in 1995, based around a series of case studies of individual associations, chosen with the intention of looking at organisations founded at different times and for different reasons. A number of associations commissioned research on their own organisational histories, and I am grateful to Home HA, the Guinness Trust, the Friendship Group, the Howard Cottage Society and the Octavia Hill Housing Trust for their valuable support. In each case a specific report has been published or is forthcoming (Malpass and Jones, 1995, 1996; Malpass, 1998, 1999a). I am grateful to Coral Jones for her contributions to the fieldwork on three of the case studies, and to Liz Byrne, who worked on one other.

Altogether seven case studies were carried out, on organisations which included three with pre-1914 origins, one from the 1930s, and three established since 1945. In addition to those mentioned above we looked at Bristol Age Care (now Brunel Care) and Knightstone HA. All are distinct and fascinating organisations in their own way, but no claims can be made that they constitute a representative sample; indeed it would be virtually impossible to construct such a sample without including a lot more associations. It would have been fascinating to have extended the list of case studies but a line had to be drawn somewhere. I must record my thanks to all those people involved with the seven case study associations for their help and tolerance.

In the course of the last five years I have learned a lot about housing associations, past and present, from conversations with numerous people but especially Alan Kilburn, Mike Cohen, John Alleston, Richard Best, Ken Bartlett, Chris Holmes, Sam Hood, Stephen Guile, John Crawley, Debby Ounsted, Dorcas Ward, Marjorie Cleaver, Anthony Mayer, Paul Bullivant, Nick Horne, John Newbury and Gareth Lawes. Professor Pat Garside was particularly helpful in gently correcting some of my wilder conclusions and guiding me to fruitful sources of information. My colleague Geoff Winn kindly undertook to read through a draft of the whole book and made many helpful comments; Derek Hawes looked at Chapters 4 and 5 and David Garnett commented on Chapter 10. The wit and wisdom of Jim Allum helped me retain some sense of proportion about the whole project. I record my thanks to all these people, and, of course, to my wife and family. In addition, I am grateful for the valuable assistance provided by staff at the Housing Corporation, the NHF, the Town and Country Planning Association and the local history section of Kensington Library; also Peter Clayton of the Octavia Hill Birthplace Museum in Wisbech.

I must acknowledge the support and encouragement provided by Tony Harrison and Professor Murray Stewart, who both helped to ensure that my workload allowed me sufficient time to write. Finally I must mention Catherine Gray at Macmillan, and an anonymous referee, who wisely insisted that the original draft should be reduced substantially in length.

PETER MALPASS
Bristol

Glossary and List of Abbreviations

ADP	Approved Development Programme, annual investment programme agreed between the HC and DETR
Co-ownership	A form of housing developed in the 1960s and 70s, supported by loans, but not subsidies, from the HC
Co-Partnership Societies	A type of early PUS based on shareholding by tenants
Cost renting	A form of unsubsidised non-profit housing developed in the 1960s
DETR	Department of the Environment, Transport and the Regions, took over from the DoE in 1997
DIYSO	Do It Yourself Shared Ownership, an HC programme in which people identified houses for sale on the open market and then entered into a shared ownership agreement with an HA
DoE	Department of the Environment, central government department with responsibility for housing in England, 1970–97
GLC	Greater London Council, 1964–86
HAG	Housing Association Grant, capital grant supporting new building and major repairs by housing associations, introduced by the Housing Act 1974
HC	Housing Corporation, central funder and regulator for RSLs in England, set up in 1964 and relaunched in 1974
HIP	Housing investment programme
HMP	Housing market package, a time-limited exercise in which HAs were commissioned to buy vacant property to stimulate activity in the housing market in 1992–93
I and P Societies	Industrial and Provident Societies are orgánisations registered with the Registrar of Friendly Societies

LAHAG	Local Authority Housing Association Grant, funding for HA development provided by local authorities (now LASHG)
LCC	London County Council, 1889–1964
LSVT	Large-scale voluntary transfer – refers to transfers of council housing to new landlords
Model Dwellings Co.	Generic term applied to a range of limited profit organisations set up in the 19th century
MoH	Ministry of Health, had responsibility for housing, 1919–50
MoHLG	Ministry of Housing and Local Government, responsible for housing 1951–70
NFHS	National Federation of Housing Societies, 1935–73
NFHA	National Federation of Housing Associations, 1973–96
NHF	National Housing Federation, 1996–. Trade body of RSLs in England, previously known as the NFHA and NFHS
PRO	Public Record Office
PUS	Public Utility Society, generic term for limited profit housing organisations from the 1890s to the 1930s
PWLB	Public Works Loans Board, central government body which made cheap loans available to local authorities, PUSs and later HAs
RSL	Registered social landlord, generic term for housing associations and similar organisations, introduced by the Housing Act 1996
RTB	Right to buy, introduced for council tenants and tenants of non-charitable HAs in 1980
Scottish Homes	Scotland's equivalent to the Housing Corporation, set up in 1989
SHG	Social Housing Grant, replaced HAG following the Housing Act 1996
Tai Cymru	Housing for Wales, Welsh equivalent to the Housing Corporation, set up in 1989

1

Introduction

The growth of housing studies as a distinct field of academic endeavour over the last twenty years or so has seen the publication of a number of good full length historical accounts of the main tenure categories in the British housing system – home ownership (Merrett, 1982), local authority housing (Harloe, 1995; Merrett, 1979) and private renting (Harloe, 1985). However, until now there has been no comparable history of housing associations, despite the fact that they have deep historical roots and occupy a key position in contemporary housing policy. Historical research seems to have slipped out of fashion and favour in housing studies, reflecting the rising popularity of international comparative analysis, and the increasing financial demands on university staff to compete for contract research with its inevitable focus on contemporary policy issues. Nevertheless, it is important to retain a perspective on the past and to remember that alongside change there is often considerable continuity, and vice versa. Some sense of history is particularly necessary in housing where the pattern of location, quality and ownership of the available stock of dwellings is so heavily influenced by the past: a quarter of dwellings in use today were built before the First World War (Mackintosh and Leather, 1993: 20), and much of housing policy in the twentieth century can be understood in terms of attempts to address the overall shortage and poor quality of dwellings inherited from earlier periods.

Throughout the twentieth century housing associations and their predecessors in the field of voluntary housing have played a part, albeit a very small part until quite recent years, in providing for people in need. They represent an attempt to solve the problem of affordability: how can people with low incomes obtain access to housing of a socially acceptable standard at a rent within their means? Historically, voluntary housing providers approached this problem by seeking capital on favourable terms, either as charitable donations or in the

1

form of low interest loans. The obvious weakness of this approach, however, is that since it effectively relies on the willingness of investors to forego some of the interest that they could obtain by lending at the full market rate, it is highly unlikely to raise the volumes of investment necessary to produce sufficient numbers of dwellings. Nevertheless, voluntary housing providers have a long track record of working in some of the poorest parts of large cities, and of pioneering new forms of provision and management. One important strand in the historical evolution of housing associations has clearly been based on religious and philanthropic motivations. In the teeming slums of Victorian London, and in the absence of sophisticated public welfare services, it is easy to understand that some people at least would be spurred to help the least well off, especially those who displayed a wish to improve themselves. Similarly, it is not surprising that some working-class people decided that mutual self-help was the better way forward. But what is more difficult to explain is the persistence of voluntary housing organisations in the twentieth century, alongside the growth of the welfare state and the provision of subsidised public rented housing for the working class on a large scale. And, given the very marginal role played by associations in comparison to that of the local authorities, why did they emerge to prominence by the end of the century?

These are some of the questions to be explored in this book. The overall objective is to develop a new angle on housing and housing policy in Britain by means of a historical account of voluntary housing organisations, from their earliest origins in the medieval almshouses through to their latest manifestation as 'registered social landlords' (RSLs) at the end of the twentieth century. In a sense the book is intended to retrieve the history of voluntary housing from the obscurity to which it has been consigned by academics whose agendas have tended to reflect the changing emphasis of government policy. Although historians of housing and urban issues in Victorian Britain routinely refer to the work of the model dwellings companies and charitable housing trusts, these organisations tend to slip out of sight after 1890, when legislation made it easier for local authorities to build houses. Academic interest then turns to the emergence of council housing. For much of the twentieth century housing societies and associations worked in obscurity, languishing as 'an almost forgotten corner of the housing system' (Harloe, 1995: 290), ignored by both governments and scholars. However, in the early 1960s the government of the day experimented with the model of not-for-profit organisations as a means of reviving investment in non-municipal rented housing, and in 1974 associations were brought within the scope of mainstream housing policy. Although the RSL sector remains the smallest of the main tenure categories, amounting to under 5 per cent of all dwellings, the case for writing at length about it is that, first, it is the fastest growing and most dynamic part of the housing system at the present time, and second, it needs to be re-connected to its historical roots. Thus, within the overall objective there are two more specific aims: to fill in the missing history of voluntary housing between about 1890 and 1974, and to examine the subsequent emergence of housing associations as increasingly important instruments of housing policy.

Curious entities

What are housing associations? Andrew Arden (1983: 3) described them as 'curious entities' because they were neither private trading bodies driven by the profit motive, nor democratically elected public bodies, nor government appointed bodies. More recently the Nolan Committee (1996: 9) included housing associations within the scope of its investigation of local public spending bodies, which it defined as 'not-for-profit bodies which are neither fully elected nor appointed by Ministers, but which provide public services, often at a local level, which are largely or wholly publicly funded'. As such, housing associations are constituents of the wider 'third sector' or 'not-for-profit' sector of the economy, which also includes a diverse range of organisations providing education, health and social services to particular groups. The limits of the not-for-profit sector can be very hard to define with any precision, and so it might be useful to consider the definition of voluntary bodies adopted for a major cross-national study (Kendall and Knapp, 1996: 18). To be included in the study organisations had to be:

1. structured entities with constitutions or formal sets of rules, perhaps, but not necessarily, registered with a public authority or voluntary intermediary body;

2. independent of government and self-governing;

3. non-profit distributing – which means that any budget surpluses must be ploughed back into the organisation, and not used for the personal benefit of the directors or shareholders;

4.   characterised by a meaningful degree of voluntarism in terms of
     money or time through philanthropy or voluntary citizen
     involvement.

It is apparent that British housing associations qualify for inclusion,
although there might be room for debate about whether they enjoy a
meaningful degree of autonomy – an issue to come back to in a
later chapter.

The simplest way to describe housing associations is probably to say
that they are voluntary organisations whose main purpose is to provide
rented housing at affordable rents on a not-for-profit basis. The current
statutory definition of the term housing association is contained in the
Housing Associations Act 1985, Section 1(1):

> Housing association means a society, body of trustees or company established for
> the purpose of, or among whose objects or powers are included those of
> providing, constructing, improving or managing or facilitating or encouraging the
> construction or improvement of, housing accommodation, and which does not
> trade for profit or whose constitution or rules prohibit the issue of capital with
> interest or dividend exceeding such rate as may be prescribed by the Treasury,
> whether with or without differentiation between share and loan capital.

This definition has remained virtually unchanged since it was first set
out in the Housing Act 1935, and that Act built on earlier definitions of
'public utility societies' dating back to the period before 1914. The
definition is very wide since it was framed to embrace a diverse range
of existing organisations, some of which were limited companies
(which voluntarily restricted the dividend paid to share holders), while
others were charitable trusts or Industrial and Provident Societies. This
diversity still obtains, and there is no restriction on the formation of
associations, nor on the use of the labels housing association, society or
trust. However, the key question is whether an organisation qualifies to
be a registered social landlord, the concept introduced in the Housing
Act 1996, to embrace existing registered housing associations together
with other bodies such as local housing companies that were expected
to be formed to receive housing stocks transferred from local authorities. Since the 1996 Act it has been possible for non-profit making
companies registered under the Companies Act to register as social
landlords. It is only RSLs that are entitled to receive financial support
from the Housing Corporation (or in Scotland, Scottish Homes, and in
Wales, Tai Cymru) in the form of Social Housing Grant (SHG). The
role of the Corporation and its equivalents in Scotland and Wales is

discussed later in this chapter, but first it is necessary to look at the constitution of housing associations and the issue of their status as 'voluntary' organisations.

Housing associations do not necessarily employ any staff, nor even provide any houses, but they must have a committee of management, now usually referred to as the board. For the majority of associations that are also registered as Industrial and Provident Societies the minimum number of board members and shareholders is seven, each person holding a £1 share. A requirement of registration is that boards are made up of people with the necessary standing and experience to demonstrate that they can exercise control over the organisation. The legal responsibility for the activities of the association lies with board members, although they do not receive any financial benefit from those activities nor any payment for their service. Historically housing association board members could, and sometimes did, pay themselves fees, and some benefited from contracts for professional advice or building work awarded to them or their businesses. However, this was discouraged after 1974 and prohibited in 1980. Board members are elected by the shareholding members of the association, although there is no absolute requirement that the number of shareholders is greater than the number of board members – the average number of shareholding members among a sample of developing associations in the early 1990s was 64, and the average ratio of shareholders to committee members was 5:1 (Kearns, 1994). In practice, associations vary considerably in their number of shareholders, some pursuing open membership policies while others retain a much more restricted approach. Shares in associations are not tradeable coupons in the way that shares in private limited companies are, and associations have virtually unfettered discretion as to whom they sell shares. Associations which are endowed charities tend not to have shareholding members, and their board members (referred to as Trustees) are appointed according to the terms set out in the original trust deed.

Housing associations have often been described as 'self-perpetuating oligarchies', meaning that control lies with the small group of shareholders on the board, who effectively determine recruitment of new members. Although board members are subject to periodic re-election at general meetings of the associations' shareholders, the fact that boards can control the size and composition of the electorate means that housing associations are open to the charge that they are closed, undemocratic organisations. Contested elections are very rare and most new board members are recruited by invitation. The contrast is often drawn between associations and local authorities, where councillors are elected by the public at large, and where, incidentally, meetings are open to the public. The openness and accountability of housing associations has become more of an issue as they have moved into a position of prominence in relation to housing policy in general, and in terms of the delivery of housing strategies at the local level. Housing associations absorb large amounts of public expenditure, and it is appropriate that they are held to account for their activities. Although they are technically private organisations they rely very heavily on financial support from public funds. Their development programmes are largely dependent on capital grants, supplemented by private loans which are repaid from rental income, a large proportion of which is met by the Exchequer in the form of housing benefit.

Housing associations are curious entities to the extent that their boards occupy a position somewhere between the local authority and private company models of corporate governance. In certain respects, such as the non-payment of board members and the exclusion of senior managers from their boards, housing associations are also different from other third-sector organisations (and different from the Housing Corporation itself). In the case of local authorities it is clear that councillors are elected to represent the interests of identifiable groups of voters, and that in the majority of cases they are members of political party groupings on the council. They exercise the authority of people who have been duly elected, but housing association board members lack any similar form of wider electoral mandate. Equally, housing association board members lack the authority of non-executive board members of private companies whose role is to represent the interests of shareholding investors. This was a role played by housing association board members in the past, when capital was raised from individual investors. In many ways the model of corporate governance in housing associations remains rooted in the voluntary ethos of the small scale philanthropic and self-help organisations of an earlier era, even though the largest associations today are big businesses, some of them with annual turnovers of more than £50 million. There are clearly some important questions to be asked about the governance of housing associations, and these are discussed in greater detail in Chapter 12.

Throughout this book there are frequent references to voluntary housing organisations, and also to the voluntary housing movement, and it is important to clarify what is meant by these terms. In her book on housing associations Helen Cope (1990: 1) makes the distinction between the voluntary, unpaid, work of board members and the notion of housing associations as voluntary organisations in the sense that they are the result of groups of people coming together voluntarily, of their own volition, to take action in relation to a perceived problem. In relation to the first usage the reference is only to the unpaid role of the board, and does not imply that all the work of the organisation is carried out on this basis – indeed, the highest paid housing professionals in Britain are now the chief executives of the largest housing associations. In the second case the term voluntary is used to distinguish housing associations from both statutory providers, such as local authorities, and commercial, profit seeking organisations. In the latter context the term voluntary evokes the values base of housing associations, the idea of service rather than gain. This is regarded as an important principle and one which voluntary board members are determined to preserve; evidence presented to the Hancock Inquiry (NFHA, 1995: 39) showed that a substantial majority of current members were against payment.

To what extent do voluntary housing organisations amount to a 'movement' with shared values and objectives, a sense of common purpose and direction? Cope (1990: 1) asserts that, 'The common aim of the movement is to provide housing and related services for people on low incomes and in housing need'. This is correct, but there are many interpretations of what it means and how best to pursue the common aim. There are numerous differences between associations, reflecting their diverse origins, structures and organisational cultures. In fact, as mentioned above, housing associations are a highly diverse set of organisations (a feature which they do not deny, and, indeed, celebrate as a strength), and their differences are arguably more striking than their similarities. In terms of the historical background it would be quite wrong to talk about voluntary housing as if it constituted a single social movement, and it is safe to assume that activists in the first part of the twentieth century did not think in this way, being well aware of the differences between different types of organisation. It is much more helpful to think in terms of several distinct strands of activity, which have been brought closer together by the effect of government policy in the last quarter of the century. But, having said that, it is also true that the evidence from the 1990s suggests that there is a widening gulf between the 'super league' of large, expanding organisations and the multiplicity of small associations with much less access to development funds. One important aspect of this widening gulf is the increasingly tenuous links between the super league organisations and the traditional values of voluntarism.

It is the function of the trade body of housing associations and other RSLs, the National Housing Federation (NHF) (together with its Scottish and Welsh counterparts), to bind the various parts of the industry together and to promote their interests, in particular by means of public campaigning and, less visibly, by lobbying government on their behalf. The Federation adopted it current title in 1996, having previously been known as the National Federation of Housing Societies (1935–73) and then the National Federation of Housing Associations. The NHF has about 1,400 members, representing nearly two-thirds of all RSLs; on the whole small associations are rather less likely to affiliate to the Federation than large ones.

The shape and composition of the movement

The geography of housing association provision differs significantly from that of local authority housing. Local housing authorities have responsibilities within specified geographical areas, which cover the country with no overlaps and no gaps. With only few exceptions, local authorities built houses exclusively within their own boundaries. Housing associations, on the other hand, tend to be concentrated in urban areas, where there is often considerable overlap and competition, while at the same time there are parts of the country where they are thinly represented. Historically London was the centre of housing association activity, and today a third (440) of NHF members are based in the capital. By contrast, only 27 associations are based in the north-east region, although a further 21 operated there in 1997 (NHF, 1998: 20). Almost every local authority district has at least half a dozen associations operating within it, and large provincial cities such as Bristol and Nottingham have between 40 and 50. Nevertheless, more than a fifth (20.7 per cent) of housing association properties were in London in 1997 – down from a quarter in the early 1990s as a result of increases in other areas due to stock transfers from local authorities.

Mention has already been made of the diversity within the housing association movement: some associations specialise in meeting the needs of particular groups, sometimes on a large scale while others work on a very small scale (Joseph Kaye's Almshouses, for instance, provide 6 houses for women aged over sixty who were born within the city of Sheffield). Other groups for which special associations exist include young people requiring supported housing, people who need homes designed for wheelchair users, vulnerable young lesbian women and gay

men, and a range of minority ethnic groups. There is even an association
serving only retired publicans. Other associations aim to provide for a
wide range of special needs groups, while some of the largest and most
familiar associations combine provision of general needs housing,
supported housing and sheltered accommodation. Some have a history
of concentrating on either new building or rehabilitation, some have a
tradition of working in specific communities, and others have always
operated over a wide area. Associations differ in their constitutional
bases, and in the relationship between the board and the tenants – sometimes, as in the case of co-operatives, the organisation is controlled by
the people living in the properties, while at the other extreme there are
still some associations with no direct tenant representation at board
level. The dimensions of diversity are numerous and it would be
confusing to list any more. However, it is worth saying that there is
probably less diversity among associations now than in the past.

In 1997 there were 2,446 social landlords registered with the
Housing Corporation and its equivalents in Scotland and Wales, but a
much larger number, in excess of 4,000, were listed as housing associations by the Registrar of Friendly Societies. The number and diversity
of RSLs makes some sort of classification both necessary and very
difficult, which is reflected in the different categories used by the
Housing Corporation, the NHF and the Registrar of Friendly Societies.
All three list associations by type, but in a rather arbitrary way. In the
past the Federation distinguished four main types: old people's, self-
build, industrial and general family. To this list were later added cost
rent and co ownership classes. This moved away from defining groups
by users, introducing types of provider organisation as specified in
legislation. Nevertheless these categories (minus cost rent, which no
longer exists) are those still used by the Registrar of Friendly Societies.
The NHF now uses the following five types:

- Housing associations, trusts and societies
- Voluntary transfer housing organisations
- Self-builds
- Co-ownerships
- Co-operatives.

One disadvantage of this list is that a large majority (84 per cent) of
Federation members are in the first category, which clearly acts a kind
of catch-all group, concealing many differences among its members.
For registration purposes the Housing Corporation distinguishes ten

different types, which are shown below, together with the number of associations in each category.

Table 1.1 Organisations registered with the housing corporation by type, 1997

	Number
Almshouses	612
Abbeyfield	353
YWCA	42
Co-operatives	266
Co-ownership	46
LA Co-ownership	13
Letting	548
Letting and hostels	248
Hostels	63
Sale and lease	54
Other	4
Total	2,249

Source: Housing Corporation.

Almshouse charities and Abbeyfields societies both provide exclusively for elderly people and form distinct groupings operating rather differently and independently of the mainstream of the voluntary housing movement. Almshouse foundations differ from mainstream associations in that their residents are not tenants in the legal sense, and the contributions that they pay are not technically rent. The almshouses have their own National Association, which has many more members (about 1,800) than shown in the table – the majority decided that registering with the Corporation was not in their interests. Local Abbeyfields societies are developed by a parent body, the national Abbeyfield Society. Some individual almshouse charities and local Abbeyfields societies affiliate to the NHF.

It is possible to analyse the shape and composition of the movement according to other criteria, such as size, age, legal status and involvement in development activity. Table 1.2 looks at the size distribution of RSLs according to the number of self-contained dwellings owned.

Table 1.2   Size distribution of RSLs, March 1998

Size of association	England	Scotland	Wales
Up to 100 dwellings	1,626	37	60
101–1,000	236	118	13
1,001–2,500	100	37	} 21
Over 2,500	122	6	
Total	2,084	198	94

Sources: Housing Corporation, Scottish Homes and Tai Cymru.

The table reveals the extent to which the majority of associations remain very small. The overall distribution of dwellings is highly uneven: 35 per cent of English associations have no more than 5 dwellings, and 78 per cent have no more than 100. Altogether these 1,600 small associations own less than 3 per cent of the whole RSL stock of self-contained dwellings, while 95 per cent of the stock is owned by just 338 associations. The largest 16 English associations, amounting to just 1 per cent of all RSLs, each have over 10,000 dwellings, and together they control a quarter of the stock. The largest association in 1998 (North British HA) had more than 32,000 self-contained dwellings – considerably more than most local authorities and equivalent to the number of council houses in a city such as Bristol. So at one end of the scale there are large numbers of associations with hardly any properties, and therefore insufficient income to support paid staff (29 per cent of RSLs employed no staff in 1998 (Housing Corporation, 1999: 67)) – these are wholly voluntary organisations. However, most of the stock is owned by associations large enough to employ full-time staff, and at this end of the scale are very large organisations employing several hundred staff – 14 NHF members employ over 500 full-time staff (NHF, 1998: 107). In these associations the day-to-day management and service delivery is in the hands of salaried professional workers, and the role of volunteers is confined to the board.

Associations also vary considerably in the geographical spread of their operations. More than three-quarters (78 per cent) of all RSLs in England operate in just one local authority area, but the larger ones tend to be very spread out and can be regarded as national organisations. In some cases they have operated over a large area for many years, while in other cases geographical expansion has been much more recent, encouraged by the Housing Corporation in the early 1990s. A feature of the growth of housing associations in the 1990s has been the formation of new associations to take over the ownership of local authority housing stocks. By March 1999, 86 English councils had carried out stock transfers to new landlords, in the majority of cases newly formed associations. These new organisations obviously began with all their houses within one district, but some have successfully expanded their field of operations. Altogether the new voluntary transfer associations have added significantly to the number of associations with more than 1,000 dwellings, and therefore they have had a big impact on the composition of the top 150 associations. Although none has yet joined the top 10 all the new associations are in the top 150, and 41 are in the top 100. Voluntary transfer associations form a majority in the group of associations with 3–6,000 dwellings.

One of the main reasons for stock transfer from local authorities has been to increase capital expenditure on both new building and improving existing properties. Thus it is to be expected that the voluntary transfer associations will have substantial development programmes, especially by comparison with the majority of smaller associations. This is not to say that small associations never carry out new projects, but by far the largest proportion of the Housing Corporation's Approved Development Programme (ADP) is carried out by a few large associations. In any one year 5–600 associations receive an allocation of grant from the ADP, although only 3–400 of these contribute to the main rent and shared ownership programmes, and only a much smaller number of associations expect to receive grant aid every year. Thus, whereas the largest associations each receive annual grant allocations measured in tens of millions of pounds, the majority rarely, if ever, receive anything at all, and around half of all registered associations have received less than £1 million in grant over the whole of the period since 1974 (DoE, 1995: 23).

Turning to the age of housing associations, the origins of charitable provision of housing accommodation lie in the distant past, and the oldest member of the NHF is thought to be the St Lawrence's Hospital Charity, founded in 1235. However, the term housing association did not come into regular or official usage until 1935, and throughout this book it is not used with reference to earlier periods. There is an interesting debate about the connections between voluntary housing organisations in the past and RSLs today, but what is clear is that the majority of pre-1914 organisations have not survived as active players on the modern scene. However, some have made the transition, and a few, notably the Peabody Trust and the Guinness Trust, which were established as endowed charities in the second half of the nineteenth century, feature among the top ten housing associations today. One of the historical themes explored in the book is the way that the voluntary housing movement has renewed itself by waves of new formations, in the 1920s and 30s, in the 1960s and 70s, and again in the 1990s. Existing databases do not provide reliable and comprehensive evidence on the age of housing associations, and in this situation the best estimate that can be made, derived from NHF data on the date when associations first took out membership, is that at least two-thirds of the largest 500 associations were set up within the last thirty-five years, since 1963.

The most important legal distinction is between those RSLs that are charities or have charitable status and the rest. The difference between charities and associations with charitable status is that charities (including charitable trusts and companies limited by guarantee) are registered with the Charity Commission, whereas associations with charitable status are exempt, because they are registered with the Registrar of Friendly Societies as I and P Societies with charitable rules. English law docs not provide a strict definition of the term charity, but it has long been established that in order for an organisation to be regarded as charitable in law it must exist for one or more of the following purposes: relief of poverty, education, advancement of religion or benefit of the community. Provision of housing, as such, does not qualify for charitable status, and the argument that housing associations are working for the benefit of the community has not been accepted as sufficient for their work automatically to qualify as charitable. Housing associations qualify as charitable by showing that their activities contribute towards the relief of poverty, and the key phrase that applies in this context is that they are engaged in housing people who are deemed to be 'in necessitous circumstances'. Provision for elderly people or for people with disabilities falls within this definition, as does provision for other people on low incomes. Housing Corporation data indicate that in 1997, 953 RSLs were charities, 697 had charitable status and 595 were non-charitable.

Charitable status confers certain tax advantages, but until now the effect has been masked by the payment to non-charitable associations of a grant to match their tax liabilities. In the mid-1990s the government announced its intention to phase out the grant; this has led non-charitable associations to review their position, and a number have converted to charitable status, and more are likely to do so. Conversion carries with it certain obligations and restrictions (especially in relation to the economic status of tenants), and this in turn has prompted further growth of interest in the creation of group structures, in which associations organise themselves into a number of legally separate entities under a parent body. This gives them the flexibility to pursue both activities that qualify for charitable status and those that do not.

In developing an understanding of housing associations, the diversity within the movement is a key feature, which should be kept in mind, even though their role in relation to housing policy tends to focus attention on registered social landlords, and in particular the subset of larger organisations. Nevertheless, there is a role for small unregistered associations, working in partnership with RSLs. Small specialist organisations often take on responsibility for certain properties (for example, short-life houses) leased from larger RSLs, or act as managing agents, providing for groups of people requiring specific management expertise.

The final point to be made in this section is about a different aspect of diversity. So far the discussion has emphasised the differences between associations, but in recent years there has been a trend towards greater internal diversity. For example, many associations now provide and manage residential care homes as well as conventional tenancies, and some have set up specialist care operations. Another form of diversification away from straightforward rented housing has been the growth of shared ownership schemes, in which the occupier purchases a proportion of the equity in the houses and pays rent on the other part. Here again associations have set up subsidiaries to carry out this sort of work. A third form of diversification comes from involvement in a variety of schemes designed to provide more than just housing for people; examples include local labour and training projects which are intended to provide employment for people living in areas where housing associations are building, and the promotion of credit unions as a method of helping people on low incomes to manage their household budgets. In a sense these 'housing-plus' initiatives are a revival of the sorts of additional activities pioneered by the Victorian philanthropic housing trusts and societies.

The administrative framework

Housing associations spend large amounts of public money, and without capital grants towards their development costs and housing benefit to underwrite their rental stream they would not be able to function on anything like their present scale. The provision of so much taxpayers' money to private organisations in pursuit of government policy objectives requires both a mechanism for distributing resources to RSLs across the country and a clear and effective regulatory regime. This section provides a brief introduction to highly complex systems, which are discussed in rather more detail in Chapters 10 to 12. Since 1974 the Housing Corporation has had responsibility for funding and regulating all registered housing associations in England. Until 1989 it had a nationwide brief, but then separate organisations were created in Scotland and Wales. Scottish Homes was formed by bringing together the Housing Corporation in Scotland and the Scottish Special Housing Association (which was itself a significant landlord with properties throughout Scotland). In Wales the equivalent to the Housing Corporation was Tai Cymru (Housing for Wales), which was absorbed within the Welsh Office in January 1999. In the case of Northern Ireland the scale of housing association activity is much smaller and there is no separate equivalent to the Housing Corporation; instead their activities are funded and regulated directly by the Department of the Environment (Northern Ireland).

The funding and regulatory functions are broadly the same in each country and this account will concentrate on the system in England. The Housing Corporation is a non-departmental body, sometimes referred to as a quango; at the top is a board of sixteen people appointed by the Secretary of State for the Environment, Transport and the Regions. Board members, who work on a part-time salaried basis, are selected for their knowledge and expertise in areas relevant to the business of the Corporation. Since the mid-1990s the Corporation, in common with other quangos, has begun to recruit new members by public advertisement. The staff employed by the Corporation are located in the London headquarters and 8 regional offices around the country.

Working through its regional office staff, who in turn work with the various local authorities in their areas, the Corporation operates a system of annual allocations of grants (now known as Social Housing Grant SHG, but until 1997 Housing Association Grant (HAG)) to support the capital programmes of RSLs. The Corporation's Approved Development Programme (ADP) counts as public expenditure, and it is therefore subject to Treasury control, and the pattern of expenditure within the programme (in terms of the balance between rented, home ownership initiatives and supported housing) is negotiated with the Department of the Environment, Transport and the Regions (DETR). Allocations to individual associations are based on the bids that they have submitted to the relevant regional office and the priorities identified by the local authorities within their local housing strategies.

Turning to the regulatory function of the Corporation, its first task is to ensure that the capital programme is delivered. This means both that the Corporation regional offices have to monitor the progress being made by RSLs, certifying that claims for grant made by RSLs relate to approved projects properly carried out, and that in aggregate terms the budget for the ADP is spent, but not overspent. Going beyond the development programme, the Corporation is responsible for ensuring that RSLs meet the standards of probity and competence expected of them. The Corporation carries out regular performance reviews of all RSLs, and has a detailed list of performance standards against which they are judged (Housing Corporation, 1997a).

The Housing Act 1996, made some important changes to the regulatory framework, allowing small RSLs to deregister, but also strengthening the position of the Corporation in relation to RSLs, including its powers to take action against associations that are deemed to be failing in some way. It should also be remembered that in addition to the formal legal powers of the Corporation, it has considerable influence over the way that associations behave because of its position as their main source of funds for future development.

Perspectives on housing

In a book devoted to one part of the housing system it is important to retain a perspective on the wider context. It is both conventional and convenient to analyse housing in terms of distinct tenures: owner occupation and various forms of renting (from private owners, local authorities and housing associations). But there are dangers attached to dividing such a complex whole into apparently simple categories. First, tenure categories are social constructs which have valuable but limited applicability in contemporary society. In particular there is the risk of diminishing the significance of diversity within tenures, especially in relation to the housing association sector which is perhaps the most artificial category, bringing together quite different organisations. The problem is exacerbated when, as is increasingly the case nowadays, housing associations and local authorities are bracketed together as 'social rented housing'. This term has emerged only in the last ten years, and would have had no meaning for people involved in earlier periods. Indeed, there are dangers implicit in referring to a single housing association or voluntary housing sector much before the 1970s. In earlier periods the differences between housing organisations were often more apparent than their similarities, and it is arguable that it was only after the introduction of the registration requirements of the Housing Act 1974, that it became reasonable to think in terms of a single category. More generally, it can be positively misleading to apply modern ideas of housing tenure to historical situations in which they had no meaning.

Another danger implicit in tenure-based analysis is losing sight of the wider context, and it is important to retain both a cross-tenure perspective and some awareness of the extent to which housing is affected by broader social, economic and political developments. What happens in one part of the housing system clearly influences and is influenced by developments elsewhere. How can voluntary housing be fitted into an understanding of the changing pattern of housing tenure in Britain? One approach is to say that, taking the twentieth century as a whole, changes in the housing system can be seen in terms of the modernisation of the market (Malpass, 1990; Malpass and Murie, 1999; Harloe, 1995). Essentially what has happened is that private renting, which emerged as the dominant form of the housing market in the nineteenth century, has been replaced by owner occupation as the normal tenure for most people. The modernisation process necessarily took many years and generated tensions and problems, some of which were tackled by state intervention, chiefly in the form of rent control and the provision of local authority housing. Initially this served the rather better off working class but increasingly, as home ownership has spread to a wider section of the population, it has been converted into a tenure for the least well off.

Harloe (1995) has argued that this process can be analysed in terms of two main models of social housing, the mass and residual, and four phases since the First World War. The mass model refers to provision for 'a broad range of lower and middle income groups, not just or even mainly the poor' (Harloe, 1995: 72), while the residual model refers to a minimalist approach concentrating on the least well off. He also identifies a third model, the workers' co-operative, which emerged at the end of the nineteenth century but never made much headway in Britain (see the discussion of copartnership societies in Chapter 3). Harloe's thesis is essentially that the mass model predominates only in abnormal times, specifically for limited periods after the two world wars, and that the residual form is the normal mode of provision in normal times. The notion of abnormal in this context refers to the economic disruption caused by large-scale warfare and the politics of the transition from war to peace.

This framework is a very useful starting point, providing a coherent, long-term, cross-tenure perspective on change in the housing system, linking it to wider economic development. It is very useful as a way of understanding the increasing residualisation of local authority housing, but the problem with the modernisation thesis is that it is based on a mis-specification of models of social housing, and relies on an inadequate three-tenure view of the British housing system. As a result it has little purchase on questions about the role of the voluntary sector. It is difficult to incorporate the voluntary sector into the thesis, which therefore provides no help in relation to the problems of explaining why voluntary housing organisations were able to make so little impact for most of the twentieth century, nor why they should rise to prominence in the last quarter.

In relation to the present period there are two processes that need to be explained: the first, residualisation of social rented housing as a whole, can be understood in terms of the modernisation thesis, but the second, the rather more recently begun restructuring (demunicipalisation) of the ownership of social rented housing, requires a different explanation. The starting point is to recognise that whereas the mass and residual models of social rented housing concentrate on the social groups occupying housing, it is necessary to develop a perspective which also takes account of the different organisational forms involved in provision.

Taking the long view it is clear that in the Victorian and Edwardian periods voluntary organisations played a relatively large part in the provision of a range of welfare services. Subsequently the balance within the 'mixed economy of welfare' shifted and the state sector grew much larger, reaching its zenith in the post-1945 welfare state. Now, however, the balance is moving in the other direction and service provision is moving back towards a variety of commercial and not-for-profit organisations (Lewis, 1999: 250). Thus, the changes in housing, both now and in the past, reflect wider trends across other services. Explanations for the fragmentation of state services at the present time would need to include reference to a variety of factors, including the politics of central-local relations, contemporary management theory (the 'new public management') and attempts to control public expenditure (Pollitt *et al.*, 1998; Stoker, 1999). All have pointed towards a reduced role for local government in service delivery. However, this is not to suggest a crude functionalist explanation in which voluntary organisations somehow naturally expand to fill the gaps left by the rolling back of the state. On the contrary, and it is particularly clear in the case of housing, the growth of not-for-profit organisations in recent years has been shaped by government and fuelled by large amounts of public expenditure, in the form of subsidies or payment for services.

This raises the question of the extent to which service providers remain voluntary organisations, and it has been argued (Wolch, 1990) that not-for-profit organisations represent a shadow state apparatus, increasingly steered and influenced by government. On this view voluntary organisations have become little more than agents of the state, and dependence on state contracts and grants makes them more suggestible and less critical of the form and direction of government policy. In a similar vein Hoggett (1996) has argued that managers of decentralised units have little real autonomy, and that decentralisation of operations has been accompanied by increased central control over strategy; this strategy for increased control he refers to as centralised decentralisation. In this perspective, organisational growth and incorporation into the ambit of government policy can be seen as squeezing out, or at least threatening, the traditions of voluntarism: volunteers are displaced by salaried professionals and independence gives way to the need to continue to qualify for state financial support.

The scope and structure of the book

In attempting to analyse the history of housing associations and to construct an understanding of their emerging role in delivering housing policy this book concentrates on the English experience. In terms of the historical narrative this can be justified by the fact that most voluntary housing activity took place in England, and indeed, in the nineteenth century there was very little outside London. In the twentieth century there was some interest in early forms of co-operative housing in parts of Scotland and south Wales, where there was also a certain amount of employer sponsored provision. But generally the impetus behind the growth of housing associations remained in London, although from the early 1970s a distinctive community based approach was developed in Scotland, mainly in association with the improvement of tenement blocks.

The book is essentially chronological, but there are some key themes running through the account. The notions of continuity and change have been mentioned already, and to these may be added diversity, incorporation and transformation: the book seeks to identify the main strands of voluntary housing activity, and to show how much they differed one from another, especially in the past; it is concerned with the long relationship between these various organisations and the developing housing policies of successive governments, and it emphasises the transforming effect on housing associations arising from their ever closer relationship with policy.

The dynamism of voluntary housing organisations and their ability to renew themselves is also a feature of their historical development. This is associated with the idea that various kinds of organisation have been devised in response to different problems and different perceptions at different times. The history of voluntary housing can be understood in terms of a number of waves of new formations, each one renewing and enriching the fabric of the 'movement'. Four main waves of formations may be identified: first there was the pre-1914 diversity, which was followed in the 1920s and 30s by a new and quite distinct set of organisations; in the 1960s and 70s many of these older organisations were making little headway and were easily outflanked by new and more energetic associations focusing on inner-city rehabilitation and the new co-ownership schemes. The latest wave of formations has emerged since 1988 and is based on stock transfers from local authorities; this group of organisations looks set to have an increasing impact on the RSL sector over the forthcoming period.

Alongside the notion of waves of formations is the perception that pre-existing organisations did not evolve into different forms. Often they continued to exist in parallel, retaining their established character and practices, and pursuing their traditional goals. It is only in the last twenty-five years, since the introduction of registration and regulation by the Housing Corporation, that there has been an erosion of differences and a tendency towards convergence. A few organisations dating from before 1914 made the transition to modern housing associations, but most did not.

In writing about the history of housing and housing policy in the twentieth century it is difficult to escape from the influence of the two world wars. They played such a significant part in shaping the development of housing and housing policy, disrupting the market and altering the balance of political power. Any attempt to understand housing must take full account of the impact of the wars, which are generally interpreted as giving housing policy a great boost, breaking down barriers that had previously appeared insurmountable. But an interest in voluntary housing organisations provides a different angle, for they experienced the immediate postwar periods as times of frustration and difficulty. From their point of view it was not until fifteen years after each war that their prospects really improved. For this reason an attempt has been made to get away from conventional periodisation in the choice of break points between chapters.

For mainly presentational reasons the book is divided into three parts. Part I covers what might be seen as the pre-history of housing associations, before the term itself entered common and official usage in the mid-1930s. Chapter 2 traces the origins of voluntary housing back to medieval almshouses, but argues that although there was much new investment in the nineteenth century they remained essentially a solution based on pre-industrial conditions, and that what developed from the 1840s onwards was a variety of attempts to address housing problems of an urban-industrial society. Although the Royal Commission on the Housing of the Working Classes (1885) was scathing in its criticism of their achievements, Chapter 3 shows that the subsequent thirty years proved to be a time of growth and innovation. Chapter 4 deals with the difficult period after the First World War, when the voluntary organisations really struggled to make any progress, despite the obvious need for new and improved housing.

Part II deals with the period from the mid-1930s to the late 1980s, half a century when housing associations progressed from being effectively dismissed by government to being chosen as the main vehicles for the future development of social rented housing. Chapter 5 focuses on the fascinating events in the 1930s, when there were demands for government to set up a strong central body to support housing associations as an alternative to local authority provision. These demands were unsuccessful, but they did raise the profile of the voluntary sector and led to the formation of the National Federation of Housing Societies. Chapters 6 to 8 take the story on through the Second World War and the heyday of the welfare state, with its emphasis on public sector provision of services. Marginalised and struggling to make a visible contribution for fifteen years after the war, housing associations were rescued in the early 1960s by government concern about the decline of private renting. Later, as policy priorities moved on, they were given their own subsidy system and a key role in inner-city rehabilitation.

Part III concentrates on what may be regarded as the contemporary period, since the introduction of major reforms in 1989. These changes, affecting the terms of new tenancies, and the basis on which associations' rents were set, were preconditions of a strategy to bring in private finance to fund development and to shift a substantial

amount of risk onto associations themselves. In this part the chapters
are more thematic, dealing in turn with finance, development and
governance. Chapter 10 examines the development of the financial
regime for housing associations, including the growth of private
finance and the issue of affordability of rents. Chapter 11 concentrates
on how the money has been spent, looking at patterns of development
and ministerial attempts to steer associations into particular types of
activity. Chapter 12 looks at governance in terms of three levels:
national, local and corporate. It concludes with the question: what's
left of voluntary housing?

The final chapter attempts to pull together some of the main themes
of the book and looks forward to the prospects for the new century.

The history of voluntary housing: a summary of events

This summary lists the dates of the foundation of a selection of voluntary housing organisations, together with references to key legislation.

1235   Origin of the St Lawrence's Hospital Charity (the oldest
          member of the NHF)

1830   Society for the Improvement of the Condition of the
          Labouring Classes

1841   Metropolitan Association for Improving the Dwellings of
          the Industrious Classes

1862   Peabody Donation Fund
1863   Improved Industrial Dwellings Co.
1865   Octavia Hill begins her housing work
1866   Labouring Classes Dwelling Houses Act, enabled model
          dwellings companies to borrow at 4 per cent over 40 years

1884–85   Royal Commission on the Housing of the Working Classes
1885   Four Per Cent Industrial Dwellings Co.
1889   The Guinness Trust. Establishment of the London County
          Council

1890   Housing of the Working Classes Act

1898   Ebenezer Howard publishes 'Tomorrow: a peaceful path to real reform'

1900   Sutton Dwellings Trust
1901   Ealing Tenants Ltd – first Co-partnership society
1904   Letchworth Garden City
1906   Samuel Lewis Trust
1909   Housing and Town Planning Act, enabled Industrial and Provident Societies to borrow up to 75 per cent of value of new schemes from Public Works Loans board

1911   Howard Cottage Society
1919   Housing and Town Planning Act: introduced Exchequer subsidies for local authorities, public utility societies and trusts

1924   St Pancras House Improvement Society
1926   Kensington Housing Trust
1928   Liverpool Improved Houses

1933   Report of the Moyne Committee recommends expanded role for public utility societies
1935   National Federation of Housing Societies
1935   North Eastern Housing Association

1947   British Airways Staff Housing Society
1949   Housing Act introduced improvement grants

1952   Coal Board Housing Association
1956   Birmingham Friendship Housing Association

1961   Housing Act, launched cost rent and co-ownership societies
1963   Hanover Housing Association
1963   Notting Hill Housing Trust
1964   Housing Act, set up the Housing Corporation
1965   North British Housing Association
1965   Paddington Churches Housing Association
1966   Launch of Shelter, the campaign for the homeless
1967   Housing Subsidies Act, introduced subsidy on the costs of acquisition and conversion of properties by HAs

1972   Housing Finance Act introduces fair rents for HAs and a new subsidy system. Housing Corporation allowed to support fair rent housing.

1974   Housing Act introduces Housing Association Grant and extends the role of the Housing Corporation to be funder and regulator of all HAs

1975   Knightstone Housing Association

1980   Housing Act introduces right to buy for tenants of non-charitable associations

1987   First big private finance initiative successfully launched by North HA, raising £65 million

1988   Housing Act, introduces assured tenancies for new HA tenants and gives HAs freedom to set 'affordable' rents, new building to be increasing dependent on private finance

1988   Chiltern District Council carries out first successful large scale voluntary, to Chiltern Hundreds HA

1989   Tai Cymru and Scottish Homes take over from the Housing Corporation in Wales and Scotland

1992–93   Housing Market Package

1992–93   Peak year for HA output

1995   NHFA launches the Governance Inquiry

1996   Housing Act introduces Social Housing Grant and widens registration criteria to Registered Social Landlords

1999   Government announces plans to transfer a quarter of Scottish council houses to RSLs and biggest stock transfer programme for England so far.

PART I

2

The Origins of Voluntary Housing, before 1890

Introduction

It is customary to see the origins of modern housing associations in medieval almshouse foundations and nineteenth-century model dwellings providers, but it is important that the precise nature of these links should be demonstrated and not simply taken for granted. This chapter deals with voluntary housing provision in England in the period up to 1890, a cut-off date chosen because, on the one hand, it marks the end of the period during which the voluntary organisations were alone in trying to provide decent, well-managed housing at rents within the reach of the poor, and on the other hand, it has been identified as the beginning of the period in which housing policy emerged as a separate response to urban problems previously seen mainly in terms of public health (Lowe, 1991: 1). Developments in local government, especially the creation of the London County Council in 1889, and the passage of the Housing of the Working Classes Act 1890, signalled the beginning of the emergence of local authorities as serious rivals to the voluntary sector in the provision of housing. Hitherto there were two main forms of charitable or quasi-philanthropic housing, almshouses, derived from medieval foundations, and the model dwellings developed in the Victorian period. In addition there was the housing management approach devised by Octavia Hill, and a number of attempts by enlightened capitalists to provide decent housing for their workers.

The objective of the chapter is to show how the almshouse model was essentially a medieval solution to a medieval problem, and how, although there was a continuing role for almshouses, in the context of

27

the emerging urban industrial city of the nineteenth century there was a need to develop different approaches to tackle new problems. But by about 1890 the new model dwellings solutions were themselves perceived in terms of failure.

Charitable housing in pre-industrial Britain

The previous chapter has shown that almshouses today provide only a tiny proportion of all not-for-profit rented housing, but many almshouse charities are registered housing associations and they represent an important strand in the historical development of charitable housing provision. Almshouses have a long history, stretching back at least to the first half of the twelfth century (Bailey, 1988: 15). The oldest member of the National Housing Federation today is the St Lawrence's Hospital Charity, based in Cirencester, Gloucestershire (Figure 2.1), and originally endowed by Lady Edith Bisset in 1235 for the benefit of two female lepers (Best, 1991: 142; Tickell, 1996: 5). However, the great majority of today's almshouse charities are of much more recent origin – over 30 per cent of all existing almshouses were built during the reign of Queen Victoria (1838–1901) (Howson, 1993: 137).

Today almshouses are thought of as providing exclusively for elderly people, but this is a specialism that emerged only slowly out of a wider range of functions performed by medieval charitable institutions. Clay (1909: xviii) distinguishes between provision for people with leprosy, wayfarers (among whom pilgrims would have been an important group) and what she calls general hospitals, which were not primarily medical institutions but places providing relief for people with a range of needs and conditions. The majority of hospitals were for the support of infirm and aged people, and labels such as hospital, Maison Dieu, almshouse and bedehouse were used indiscriminately to describe those institutions that correspond to the modern almshouse (Clay, 1909: 15). Later writers (Jordan, 1959: 257; Bailey, 1988: 16) have taken much the same view of the evidence, and it seems that many of the charities originally established for lepers ('lazar houses') eventually converted to housing elderly people after the decline of the disease in the fifteenth century.

The giving of alms was encouraged by the medieval church, but it must not be assumed that the provision of almshouses was motivated simply by a desire to help the poor; the benefactors themselves hoped to benefit by their charity to the extent that it would be weighed in the

Figure 2.1 Ancient almshouses in Cirencester, belonging to the St
Lawrence's Hospital Charity

balance in the afterlife. The origins of almshouses, therefore, lie in medieval charitable foundations which were concerned with much more than simply the provision of shelter. On the one hand their concern for the temporal wellbeing of their residents extended to provision of food and drink, and sometimes also small disbursements of cash. On the other hand, almshouse foundations have to be seen in terms of attempts to ensure the spiritual wellbeing of both the residents and the benefactors.

The distribution of hospitals of various kinds in the medieval period was widespread but uneven, reflecting the incidence of wealth and the location of centres of religious observance. There were also important variations in their fortunes over time. Clay (1909, quoted by Jordan, 1959: 258) showed that three-quarters of foundations known to exist in 1547 had been founded before 1350, and both Clay and Jordan refer to the serious decline in charitable institutions that had occurred in the years before 1414. This can probably be explained by reference to the social and economic dislocation caused by the black death in 1348. It must also be remembered that although surviving medieval almshouse charities have endowments that have ensured their durability, a large proportion of early hospitals were not endowed and therefore were much less robust in the face of abuse or neglect.

The Reformation and in particular the dissolution of the monasteries in the 1530s had a considerable impact on charitable housing provision, although Jordan (1959: 259) argues strongly that it is wrong to conclude that the medieval hospitals were destroyed along with the monasteries. Almshouse foundations, he argues, continued to function, but under secular management. The new theology that emerged during the Reformation led to changing attitudes to social relations and the role of charity. Thus Protestant doctrine taught that rich people could not atone for a life of unbridled luxury and indulgence by the simple expedient of alms giving and other good works. Redemption was not so easily attained. Attitudes to the poor also began to change. Protestantism was much less sympathetic to the indiscriminate distribution of alms and much more concerned about the problem posed to society by the idle poor. On the one hand it soon became established that the rich had a personal continuing responsibility for appropriate charitable activity, and legislation passed during the reign of Elizabeth I made it easier for benefactors to set up new endowed charities. On the other hand legislation at the end of the century began to codify a tougher approach to people claiming parish relief under the Poor Law, based on the idea of putting the able-bodied to work. At the same time, however, it was acknowledged that a different approach was necessary in relation to frail elderly people and others who were regarded as the impotent poor (Fraser, 1973: 30). Here lies the origin of the development of residential provision for elderly people by the state, in parallel with the charitable almshouses.

During the first twenty years of the seventeenth century there was a rapid increase in donations to found new almshouses, to the extent that:

> in the early seventeenth century the failure of a London merchant to settle some substantial and conspicuous charitable trust or gift was generally regarded as little short of shocking unless there had been some grievous wasting of the estate because of age, ill-health or commercial misfortune. (Jordan, 1959: 153)

However, by 1650 the disruption caused by the Civil War had brought the flow of funds back to levels seen at the start of the century. New almshouses continued to be established throughout the eighteenth and nineteenth centuries, despite recurrent accusations of widespread abuse in the way that funds were managed. Some of the better endowed charities became very rich indeed as economic growth and the expansion of urban areas increased the value of their property holdings. Owen (1964: 285) reports that in the 1880s the twelve largest City of London livery companies devoted £75,000 per annum of their huge investment income to the provision of almshouses and pensions. However, in less favoured situations the income from endowments sometimes failed to keep pace with changing circumstances.

It is difficult to generalise with confidence about a set of institutions that evolved over such a long time, especially in the absence of good analytical historical research histories of almshouses such as those by Bailey (1988) and Howson (1993) are strong in terms of describing and illustrating individual foundations, but they have little to say on important questions about the relationship between the church and the creation and management of new almshouse foundations. What can be said with confidence is that by the middle of the nineteenth century social and economic change had reached a point where, although there was a continuing role for almshouses, there was also a need to devise new ways of tackling the problem of housing some sections of the poor in the emergent urban industrial society. Whereas almshouses provided for indigent and dependent elderly people, a group who have always been recognised to be deserving recipients of charitable assistance on account of their inability to work for their living, the problem posed by the growth of industrial capitalism and the creation of the urban working class was altogether different, centring on the question of how to provide for the housing needs of younger, able-bodied people, most of whom had some kind of earned income, or at least some earning capacity. Throughout the century the dominant view was that the answer lay in the free play of market forces, and a form of private renting based on weekly letting was evolved to suit the situation of the weekly paid labourer (Englander, 1983).

However, during the nineteenth century neither unfettered market forces nor state intervention was able to remove the link between poverty and poor housing. This failure created the space within which various forms of voluntary housing organisation sought to make some impact.

Philanthropy and 5 per cent

The phrase philanthropy and 5 per cent dates back to at least 1887 (Ashworth, 1954: 67). It has since been employed as a generic label for a variety of organisations set up after 1830 in order to provide accommodation on terms that were affordable to their intended working-class tenants, while satisfying the demand for a rate of return on capital. Investors who agreed to limit to 5 per cent the dividend that they expected to receive could comfort themselves with the knowledge that they were being philanthropic in accepting less than the normal 7 to 10 per cent (Smalley, 1909: 68), while not breaching the principle that almsgiving was demoralising and therefore every project had to be seen to pay its way. The need for a positive rate of return underpinned housing reform throughout the nineteenth century.

The various organisations that constituted the 5 per cent movement have been investigated by a series of researchers since Ashworth (1954), including Owen (1965), Tarn (1973), Gauldie (1974), Wohl (1977), White (1980) and Dennis (1989). As a result the main elements of the story are fairly well-established, although there remain some unanswered – and apparently unasked – questions. Most accounts tend to concentrate on exposing the failure of voluntary housing organisations to make a significant impact on urban housing problems of the nineteenth century, and the alleged influence that this failure had in terms of strengthening the case for state intervention. Owen (1965: 393), for example, is quite explicit:

> Notwithstanding the most creditable of intentions and some considerable accom-
> plishments, year by year the model dwellings agencies were demonstrating that
> they were unequal to the task... their relative impotence in the face of a complex
> and vast problem offered an irrefutable argument for responsible action by
> the state.

However, in the context of an interest in the origins of modern
housing associations, the question to be asked concerns the nature of
any links between these nineteenth-century organisations and the
present. This is an issue that previous contributions have generally
ignored or taken for granted. But if the model dwellings organisations
are accurately presented in terms of failure then this raises interesting
questions about how, and how far, they can be seen as having any claim
to be the forerunners of modern associations.

Model dwellings companies and trusts

It is conventional and convenient to distinguish between two main types
of voluntary housing organisations, model dwellings companies and
charitable trusts, but it is important to remember that there was considerable scope for variation within these categories. The main difference
between them lay in the sources of their development finance: the model
dwellings companies generally depended on raising share capital and
loan stock from private individual investors, and clearly the rate at
which investment flowed in would reflect their ability to generate an
acceptable rate of return. The charitable trusts, on the other hand, had
the task of investing endowments by rich philanthropists who were less
interested in the rate of return than the effective application of the
money. The trustees of charitable trusts generally sought to achieve a
positive rate of return, but closer to 3 per cent than 5. The trustees of the
Peabody Donation Fund sought 3 per cent (Tarn, 1966: 11), while the
Guinness Trust aimed at 3.5 per cent (Minutes of the Trustees meeting,
4 February 1890).

The term 'model dwelling' refers to attempts to 'provide both a standard and example that was worthy of imitation' (Gaskell, 1986: 3).
Model housing was an attempt to demonstrate that the market mechanism could work, even for the poor. It emerged as a response to the
manifest failure of market forces to produce satisfactory housing
conditions in the rapidly growing towns of the early Victorian period.
Emsley (1986: 27–8) argues that, 'landlords were held to be negligent,

builders greedy and tenants destructive and lazy. The proper role of philanthropy was in education – showing the various parties where their true interests lay.' The early companies hoped to show that it was possible to combine quality with profitability in working-class housing, so that a general improvement in living conditions could be achieved. If suppliers were restrained in their pursuit of profit, if the properties were well-built and managed, and if the tenants could be persuaded to lead quiet and sober lives, then the housing problem might be alleviated.

The problem that the various organisations set out to solve was extremely difficult: how to provide satisfactory, sanitary housing for the working class, at rents that were affordable in areas where land values were very high. Acceptance of a limited rate of return was clearly part of the answer, but other compromises were required, principally in terms of form and density, but also, in many cases, amenity standards. The characteristic built form adopted by both companies and trusts was the multistorey block, typically comprising small tenements on four to seven storeys, with upper dwellings reached via stairs and in some cases external access balconies. Although multistorey living was already established in continental Europe, and in Scottish cities, the model dwellings organisations were responsible for introducing the concept to England in the 1840s (Tarn, 1974: 19). Resort to tenement blocks was forced on them by the need to achieve high densities as the only way to generate sufficient income to cover costs and meet the required rate of return from high value sites occupied by poor households each with a low rent-paying capacity.

The first model dwellings organisation is usually said to be the Metropolitan Association for Improving the Dwellings of the Industrious Classes, which was founded in 1841. However, the Society for Improving the Condition of the Labouring Classes (SICLC), which was launched in 1844, traced its origins back to the creation of the Labourer's Friend Society in 1830 (and it later adopted the title of the 1830 Housing Society). The SICLC was the first to actually build model dwellings, at a place called Bagnigge Wells, near Gray's Inn Road in central London, and its purpose remained primarily one of providing demonstration projects intended to inspire others to similar standards. The Society did not confine itself to London (unlike most other model dwellings organisations), but it never built very much, and by 1862 it had built only 127 houses and flats in London, plus five model lodgings houses, and 32 dwellings in Hull (SICLC, 1939).

The Metropolitan Association certainly achieved greater levels of production, ultimately building over 1,200 tenements (Wohl, 1977: 360–1), and it has been said that it had a good deal to do with setting the pattern for semi-philanthropic housing organisations (Owen, 1965: 375). Nonetheless, the Association experienced initial difficulties in raising capital, and in the mid-1850s its investors considered themselves lucky to receive 2 per cent dividend (Tarn, 1968: 45). It was unable to pay a 5 per cent dividend until 1873, by which time its activities were slowing down (Wohl, 1977: 147). The Association built high-density four and five-storey blocks, but it opted for self-contained dwellings (each tenement having its own WC and scullery), which meant that its rents remained beyond the reach of the poor.

The Improved Industrial Dwellings Company (IIDC), established in 1863, also concentrated on building self-contained dwellings. The IIDC became the largest model dwellings company operating in central London, building some 6,000 dwellings on forty-five sites in forty years, although it was overtaken by the Artisans' and Labourers' General Dwellings Company (founded in 1867) which had a policy of developing in rather more suburban locations. The IIDC was set up by Sir Sydney Waterlow, a wealthy London capitalist and politician, who remained involved with the company for over thirty years. He was instrumental in securing an important concession from the Treasury in 1866 when the Labouring Classes Dwelling Houses Act made it possible for limited dividend model dwellings organisations to borrow from the Public Works Loans Commissioners at the preferential rate of 4 per cent over forty years.

The Metropolitan Association, the IIDC and the majority of other significant model dwellings providers were private companies, differing from commercial limited liability companies only in the voluntary restriction on the dividend paid to shareholders and investors. They received no financial assistance from the Exchequer, apart from access to cheap loans. This can be seen as a subsidy, to the extent that it enabled rents to be set at less than the full market price, but it was a form of assistance that merely passed on to the companies the interest rate advantage enjoyed by the government as a secure borrower, and as such was provided at no cost to tax payers. However one looks at these low interest loans they were of real benefit to the model dwellings providers (Wohl, 1977: 147).

Turning to charitable activity financed entirely by rich individuals without any expectation of financial reward, the most notable was the series of gifts by George Peabody, an American capitalist who had settled in London. Between 1862 and 1873 he donated a total of £500,000 (the equivalent of nearly £30 million today) to a charitable trust that he set up for the benefit of the poor of London. He did not specify that the money should be used exclusively for housing and the trustees were given wide discretion to apply the huge resources at their disposal. Owen (1965: 380) describes the Peabody donation as 'perhaps the most dramatic event in the history of Victorian housing', and it is difficult to disagree.

The Peabody trustees chose to apply the money to the construction of tenement blocks on large estates in central London. The first to be completed, at Commercial Road, Spitalfields, was opened in February 1864. It was untypical of later estates in that it was smaller (later estates tended to be in the range 250–525 dwellings), and included some shops on the ground floor, but it established a partnership between the Fund, the architect Henry Darbishire and the builder, Cubitt, that was to last for twenty years (Tarn, 1966: 12). It also set the Fund on a course of building 'associated tenements', which it maintained for even longer. Associated tenements were groups of flats sharing water supplies, WCs and bathing facilities. This form of housing was quite widely used by those organisations which were set up towards the end of the century, and which were most concerned to target the least well-off, such as the East End Dwellings Company (launched in 1884), the Four Per Cent Industrial Dwellings Company (1885) and the Guinness Trust (1889). The latter built over 2,600 such dwellings between 1891 and 1901, while the Peabody Fund built over 5,000. The associated tenement now seems a very primitive form of accommodation, but thousands were built, and many survived until the 1970s.

The Peabody Fund built six estates during the 1860s, but in the 1870s the problem of acquiring suitable, affordable sites in appropriate locations became more serious, and Owen (1965: 384) suggests that there was reason to believe that in central areas it was necessary to acquire land at less than its full market value if working-class housing was to be constructed. After 1870 model dwellings activity in general in London was in decline, but the Artisans' and Labourers' Dwellings Improvement Act 1875, provided the opportunity for companies and trusts to purchase cleared sites at advantageous prices from the Metropolitan Board of Works. The Act required that land cleared of slums should be used for the provision of working-class housing, and this restriction meant that its value was reduced to considerably less than could be obtained for commercial development. Over the next six years the board purchased sixteen sites for slum clearance and sold them on to housing providers, including the Peabody Fund, the IIDC, and the East End Dwellings Company. The Peabody Fund took particular advantage, acquiring six sites on extremely good terms, which the board reluctantly accepted in the absence of other buyers with the Fund's ability to take so much land off its hands. The board seems to have spent over £1.5 million on acquiring and clearing the full set of sites, and to have received a total of only £200,000 for the land.

The sale of land to model dwellings suppliers on these terms represented a considerable, if not widely acknowledged, subsidy, and the scale of the Peabody Fund's involvement led to criticism and to it being described as a 'quasi-public body' by the Select Committee on Artisans' and Labourers' Dwellings in 1882. On the whole the Peabody Fund and the other model dwellings providers were targets for criticism from a number of directions, and much of it was set out in detail in evidence presented to the Royal Commission in 1884. Modern writers, often drawing quite heavily on the report of the Royal Commission, have been equally critical, so it is necessary now to turn to an assessment of the achievements of the various model dwellings providers in the period up to 1890.

Assessing model dwellings

First, in quantitative terms, the model dwellings providers in London were then housing something in excess of 72,000 people (Charles Booth, 1891, quoted by Dennis, 1989: 45), impressive enough up to a point, but not a lot more than the *annual* increase in the capital's population. Altogether there were at least thirty model dwellings companies and trusts operating in London during the second half of the century (Wohl, 1977: 146, 360–1), most of them on a modest scale compared with the likes of the Peabody Fund and the IIDC. The harsh conclusion has to be that the small number of people housed reflected the fact that the companies had failed in their objective of acting as models that would inspire others and attract sufficient capital to make a significant impact on housing supply in London.

Elsewhere activity was 'scarcely noticeable' (Ashworth, 1954: 84). Outside London there are records of model dwellings companies in Newcastle, Leeds, Liverpool, Bristol and Manchester (Ashworth, 1954: 84; Taylor, 1974: 82–3), but the number of dwellings provided remained extremely low in absolute and proportional terms. While the concentration of activity in London is generally noted in the literature, the question of why this should have been the case has not been addressed. It seems that the explanation must lie in the economics of the housing and labour markets at the time, and in the peculiar conditions prevailing in London. Here there was a combination of circumstances that allowed the model dwellings companies to remain viable: high land prices, high concentrations of low paid casual workers and sheer physical size that meant suburbanisation was not a feasible solution until the end of the nineteenth century. It should be remembered in this context that urban growth in English provincial industrial towns in the nineteenth century did not lead to the development of multistorey flats to anything like the same extent as in London (where even some middle-class people lived in blocks) (Sutcliffe, 1974: 13).

Second, the quality of model dwellings can be considered in relation to the standards achieved in the individual tenements and the design of the blocks. The earlier companies seem to have concentrated more on providing self-contained dwellings, while the charitable trusts and later companies adopted the associated tenement. These were generally very small dwellings, most consisting of just one, two or three rooms, in a period when average family size was considerably greater than it is today (Wohl, 1977: 360–1). However, the model dwellings providers' obsession with demonstrating that high density and good sanitary standards could be combined, meant that blocks were kept clean and that tenants probably had access to purer water supply than they could have relied upon elsewhere. Burnett (1986: 179) emphasises the extent to which model dwellings represented an improvement in living conditions when compared with multi-occupied and sub-divided houses, but Ashworth (1954: 85–6) argues that by accepting the twin constraints of high density and profitability the model dwellings designers contributed to a lowering of standards:

> They bestowed the hallmark of sanitary efficiency on high density housing at a time when congestion was probably the most serious of town problems; some of their spokesmen gloried in the huge numbers of people they could house upon an acre.

Some of the estates attained densities that are scarcely imaginable today. Burnett (1986: 178) credits the Metropolitan Association with achieving up to 1,600 people per acre, and although such extreme concentrations were unusual it is important to note that the general effect of model dwellings developments was to considerably increase the population density in the neighbourhoods where they were built.

It is the blocks and their external appearance, rather than the individual tenements, that have been most criticised over the years. English architects had little experience of designing working-class housing, and little to go on in terms of precedent for the type of high-density, multi-storey blocks required. It may be inferred from the quality of the architecture associated with model dwellings that the best architects could afford to eschew the unwelcome challenge of achieving very high densities on a tight budget, but for some the model dwellings became a lifetime's work. Mention has already been made of Henry Darbishire's long involvement with the Peabody Fund, and elsewhere the firm of Joseph and Smithem designed the early schemes for the Four Per Cent Industrial Dwellings company and five of the eight estates built by the Guinness Trust between 1889 and 1901.

The problems facing the architects were severe, since target densities required multistorey blocks, but the need to permit daylight into the ground-floor dwellings put a limit on the height of blocks and the distance between them. Cost constraints meant that ornamentation was cut to a minimum, giving long, high facades a bleak and featureless appearance. White's (1980: 24) description of Rothschild Buildings (designed by N. S. Joseph in the mid-1880s) could apply with equal force to many other estates of the period:

> From the outside the grim, towering buildings, especially when seen from the quarter acre courtyard, starkly stated their purpose of providing homes for the Victorian working class. Their function was to provide the maximum number of sanitary dwellings as cheaply as possible. Ruthless utilitarianism pared away all that was not absolutely necessary to attain that end.

White (1980: 31) goes on to point out that model dwellings sharply divided middle-class opinion, although he says that at best they were seen to be a necessary evil, and their strongest supporters were defensive about them. On the one hand, advocates of model dwellings were engaged in a moral and social project intended to provide 'a controlled environment of enforced respectability' (Wohl, 1977: 164), in which the design of the estate layout, the use of boundary railings and controlled, gated entrances were all deliberate devices to separate the model dwellings from the surrounding turmoil of the slums. On the other hand, concentrating so many people together in such small dwellings, with so much sharing of common spaces and facilities was seen as threatening to family life (White, 1980: 31). It seems that the blocks were also unpopular with the very people who were supposed to be direct beneficiaries of this form of philanthropy, the working class themselves (Jones, 1971: 187). Dennis (1989: 45) quotes a statement from the London Trades' Council submitted to the Select Committee in 1882, to the effect that:

> Dislike to what has been called the barrack-like publicity or gregariousness of the system, and their barrack-like external appearance, has developed into a deep and settled prejudice, which has certainly not been without various and ample ground for its justification.

Working-class objections were grounded in both the appearance of the blocks and the experience of living in them, including the style of management.

> The poor were... not attracted by the prospect of living in model dwellings. The rules, which forbade noise and demanded temperance, regulated the hanging out of washing but insisted on cleanliness, refused house-room for work tools and storage for goods but required regular rent-paying, were too numerous and too repressive for the large majority of the noisy London poor. Certain trades, like coster-mongers, were excluded both by the rules and by the lack of accommodation for their donkeys and carts. But the required standard of virtuousness, docility and respectability excluded many more. (Gauldie, 1974: 235)

The Metropolitan Association employed estate superintendents recruited from ex-military men, and this set a pattern that was adopted by other companies and charitable trusts. The power wielded by the superintendents was potentially considerable, as White (1980: 55) explains:

> The tradition of military (or police) background for the Supers was continued through the long life of Rothschild Buildings, underlining their almost imperialist role, reminiscent of an army of occupation billetted on the people. Certainly the Super had considerable power. All the seventeen rules of the Company were his to enforce as he saw fit. He could choose tenants and he could also deprive them of their homes. He had a duty to 'enquire into the respectability' of each applicant for a flat, so that the mechanics of class control in theory operated from the very beginning of the landlord–tenant relationship.

Although the working class may have developed a 'deep and settled prejudice' against block dwellings, there is no overwhelming evidence that the companies and trusts had serious difficulties in finding tenants. On the contrary, Dennis (1989: 46) reports that both Peabody and IIDC estates were heavily oversubscribed in the 1860s and 70s, although Peabody had difficulties finding tenants for its estate in the east end, at Shadwell, apparently for locational reasons. This suggests either that

there were sufficient people who were not prejudiced against block
dwellings, or that competition for accommodation was enough to overcome their objections.

Having considered the quantity, quality and management of model
dwellings it is necessary to move on to the issues of rents and the
incomes of the people housed. One of the most serious criticisms of
both the companies and the Peabody Fund was that they set their rents
at levels which meant that the poorest households were unable to afford
them. The pattern was set by the Metropolitan Association, which built
to a standard that generated rents too high for people dependent on
labourers' wages (Wohl, 1977: 148).

In contemporary debate the Peabody Fund was criticised for, on the
one hand, failing to set rents at levels within the reach of the poorest
families, while on the other hand, it was accused of unfair trading, and
of poaching tenants from its competitors by its ability to undercut their
rents. It seems that the rents set by the Fund were significantly below
market levels, but that many tenants had incomes above the poverty
level. Charles Booth, the first systematic poverty researcher, defined a
poverty line at £1-1-0 (£1.05) per week in 1887, and there is evidence
that the average income of Peabody tenants at this time was £1-3-8
(£1.18) (Wohl, 1977: 155-6). Average rents in Peabody buildings in
1880 were 4s-4d, but as Stedman-Jones (1971: 185) reports, the very
poor were surviving on irregular earnings of 15s per week, or in some
cases less than 10s. Dennis (1989: 45) quotes figures calculated by
Booth in 1891 showing that only 23.3 per cent of the tenants of philanthropic and semi-philanthropic organisations were within his definition
of the poor or very poor; virtually all the rent fell within Booth's class
of the better paid.

The Peabody Fund probably housed a broader spectrum of incomes
than the more commercial housing companies, but nevertheless, 'It is
true to say that the Peabody buildings were generally housing members
of the regularly employed and better paid labouring class and many artisans and clerks' (Wohl, 1977: 156). Tarn (1974: 102–3) concludes that all
the model dwellings companies eventually deviated from their original
intention to house only the poor. However, it must be remembered that
although this was the conclusion reached by the Royal Commission in
1885 there were then new developments by companies such as the East
End Dwellings Company and the Four Per Cent Industrial Dwellings
Company, which were more determined to reach down to the least well
off. The East End Dwellings Company scheme at Katherine Buildings,
for example, provided single rooms for as little as 1s-6d per week.

Nevertheless, the conclusions reached by most commentators are overwhelmingly negative. The model dwellings companies and trusts are generally seen to have failed in terms of the amount and quality (particularly the appearance) of their buildings, and their failure to accommodate the people most in need. However, a different approach, pioneered by Octavia Hill, did seek to work with the poorest, by concentrating on improving the management of existing houses.

The Octavia Hill system

Octavia Hill (1838–1912) was regarded by her contemporaries as one of the greatest women of the nineteenth century (Darley, 1990), although Owen (1965: 387) expresses the view that, 'Of all the later Victorians few are more baffling to a twentieth century interpreter'. Her name continues to ignite debate, not least among contemporary housing scholars (Brion and Tinker, 1980; Malpass, 1984a, 1999; Power, 1987; Brion, 1995; Clapham, 1997; Whelan, 1998). Her significance in the history of voluntary housing is quite different from that of people like George Peabody, for Hill was very reluctant to set up formal organisations, preferring to emphasise the value of personal contact between individual landlords and their tenants. However, she is a genuinely important figure in voluntary housing primarily because of her approach to housing management and its later influence among people who pioneered the development of housing associations in the 1920s and 30s; indeed some individuals who worked directly with Octavia Hill were still involved in housing management in the 1960s (Malpass, 1999a). Hill's emphasis on the value of the contribution that could be made by individual volunteers, and her opposition to municipal housing, provided the moral and theoretical underinning for an important strand in the development of housing associations after her death, as subsequent chapters will show.

Octavia Hill started her housing work in 1865, and over the next forty five years she built up what was effectively a lettings and management agency for a large number of individual and corporate landlords. She believed in independence through self-help, but also that the rich had a duty to assist the poor towards independence by personal contact and example. Whereas the pre-existing societies for making contact with the poor had depended upon them being willing to receive visitors, Hill's great insight was the realisation that the position of landlord gave her the right of entry to the homes of her tenants, and the opportunity to exercise leverage on their behaviour. It is important to establish that although today Octavia Hill is remembered as the founder housing management as a distinct activity, what she was primarily concerned with was housing management as a form of social work in which the objective was to improve both the houses and the people. Housing management was to her an opportunity for middle-class outreach to the poor, bringing them into personal contact with a different set of values and showing them by example that they could improve their lot.

This approach led to the development of what became known as the Octavia Hill system, which can be seen to have consisted of six central tenets. First, it is worth repeating that she was concerned with housing management for poor people, and she claimed to work with as poor a class as had a settled home; this highlights the social work aspect of the approach – she was not aiming to provide a housing management service to the better off, 'respectable' working class who did not need to be rescued from feckless and dissolute ways.

Second, the approach was based on reciprocity, in which in return for regular payment of rent by tenants the landlord undertook to keep the property in good condition, promptly carrying out necessary repairs. This was a way of both encouraging sober, prudent behaviour from tenants and demonstrating the trustworthiness of the landlord.

Third, however, the system was admitted by Octavia Hill herself to be 'a tremendous despotism' (evidence to the Royal Commission in 1884) in which she was quite prepared to evict tenants who failed to live up to her expectations; she was concerned only with the 'deserving poor', those who showed signs of wanting to improve themselves.

Fourth, the approach went beyond a narrow definition of landlord duties to involve a concern for other aspects of tenants' lives, including outings for the children, organising social events and providing work for unemployed tenants during bad times.

Fifth, the idea of outreach to the poor led to the view that the work should be carried out by middle and upper class women, and the emphasis was placed heavily on the redemptive impact of personal contact.

Finally, the whole undertaking was carried out on business-like lines, guaranteeing investors a return of 5 per cent. From the outset when Hill undertook to provide Ruskin with a 5 per cent return this was seen as one of the keys to the future growth and success of the work. However, the commitment to rewarding investors implied a tolerance of low standards, in the sense that she was quite prepared to accept that whole families should occupy one room if that was all they could afford.

Turning from the principles of the system to the way in which they were put into practice, the work expanded quite rapidly, although the decentralised approach relied mainly on training people to apply the principles and then leaving them to it. The big breakthrough came in 1884 when Octavia Hill was invited by the Ecclesiastical Commissioners to manage 48 houses in Deptford, and this marked the real beginning of a major expansion of her work in south London. Over the next twenty-five years the Commissioners placed increasing amounts of property in Southwark, Deptford, Walworth and Lambeth in Hill's care, to the extent that eventually the majority of her work was south of the river.

All the accounts for the properties of her various owners were kept separately. This is another indicator of the disaggregated and decentralised system. Hill explained to the Royal Commission that she had carried out a decentralisation in 1876, 'and so strongly do I feel about the individual influence and work and relation that I have never formed a society.' The point was also made that, 'We have next to no printing, and next to no stationery; we have no office, and we have no machinery that costs anything.' Finally, to emphasise how decentralised and unstructured her system was Hill insisted that she did not know how many dwellings were managed according to her principles. Her policy was to train workers and then, apparently to give them autonomy, although she seems to have kept a close eye on the finances, for as late as the last months of her life Hill's decentralised managers from all over London would bring their books in for her to check every Thursday after the week's rent collection record had been balanced up (Brion, 1995: 13).

On the question of how the houses and tenants were managed, the approach was summed up by Octavia Hill in one of her letters to fellow workers:

> Each block is placed by me under a separate volunteer worker, who has the duty of collecting, superintending cleaning, keeping accounts, advising as to repairs and improvements, and choice of tenants, and who renders all personal help that can be given to the tenants without destroying their independence such as helping them to find work, collecting their savings, supplying them with flowers, teaching them to grow plants, arranging happy amusements for them, and in every way helping them to help themselves. Of course the weekly visit to collect rent gives a capital opening for all this, and the control of the house itself, judiciously used, gives power for good much greater than that possessed by the ordinary district visitor. (Hill, 1933: 13)

Often dwellings were in a very poor condition when they were acquired, and the approach was to '...put the drains and the water supply and the roofs to rights, and everything else of every sort and kind, is added in proportion to the tenant's own care' (evidence to the Royal Commission).

Although she did not set up formal organisations to carry on her work, Octavia Hill did agree to the establishment of the Horace Street Trust in 1886. This was not a housing association as such, being simply a legal device for holding a small amount of property that had been offered to Hill as a personal gift. However, it endured for a long time after her death, managed by members of her family, and the modern Octavia Hill Housing Trust traces its origins back to the trust (Malpass, 1999a).

Conclusion

This chapter has examined the growth of voluntary housing up to the late 1880s, and has shown how the medieval model of charitable provision represented by the almshouse continued alongside new forms of semi-philanthropic housing that emerged in response to new problems and new ways of thinking. The model dwellings companies of the nineteenth century were not merely a reworked and updated version of the almshouse; they were based on an explicit rejection of charity as the solution for the able bodied poor of the new urban working class, and their origins lay in the theory that the market could be made to provide a sufficient supply of satisfactory housing at affordable levels of rent, even in central London.

A review of the literature has shown that the model dwellings companies and trusts are generally discussed in terms of failure. They failed to stimulate an adequate supply of capital to generate enough new building to make a significant impact on the scale of the housing problem in the capital, and they made almost no impact at all elsewhere. They produced blocks of dwellings that were architecturally unappealing and which their intended occupants apparently disliked intensely. Despite compromises in relation to densities and quality the rents were generally too high for the poor. While the likes of the IIDC could argue that its policy was to aim at the artisan class, the Peabody Fund was most open to attack, because of the fact that its founder had specified that his benefaction should be devoted to the welfare of the poor.

There are two points to be made here about the way that the history of model dwellings has been written. First, Daunton (1983: 1–2, 1987: 40–1) has argued that housing historians have devoted too much attention to the limited achievements of model dwellings organisations, and that the thrust of most accounts is to see the failure of these organisations as leading inevitably to state intervention in the form of council housing. In this vein Owen (1965: 393) has been quoted above, and Gauldie (1974: 235) takes the same line:

> The importance of the model dwellings in the history of working-class housing is limited... Their failures, however, were in themselves important. The fact that these patently admirable, financially respectable, able and determined business men, working on the best commercial principles should fail, had great influence on the future development of government housing policy. The development of social theory running in parallel with the unfolding experience of the model dwellings associations led to a growing belief that state help must be essential for the shifting of the housing problem. The conviction grew that housing should not be left to charitable enterprise but should become a state responsibility.

However, Daunton's case is that this interpretation, with the benefit of hindsight, concentrates on a particular part of the story and fails to give an accurate picture of the range of views held at the time. It is an account that presents as inevitable something that was actually the product of much debate and struggle (see also Byrne and Damer, 1980).

The second point is that most accounts of model dwellings in the nineteenth century rely heavily on the rich source of evidence and opinion represented by the reports of the Royal Commission published in 1885. What is presented, therefore, is essentially a history of the first forty years of their work, and with one or two notable exceptions (White, 1980; Emsley, 1986) the narrative is carried little further forward in time. The fact that most of the model dwellings companies and trusts continued to be active until well into the twentieth century (as the next two chapters will show) is hardly recognised in the literature. While Daunton may be right to argue that too much attention has been paid to the numerically insignificant achievements of the model dwellings organisations in the last century, it is also true that the full story has not been told about their activities in the twentieth.

Taken together, overreliance on the Royal Commission reports and the assumption that failure led to subsidised state intervention, mean that in the history of housing the model dwellings organisations slip out of sight from the end of the 1880s. The creation of the London County Council and the passage of the Housing of the Working Classes Act

1890, provide a new focus of attention. However, it must not be forgotten that not only did the established organisations carry on but new ones were being set up. The Four Per Cent Industrial Dwellings Company and the East End Dwellings Company, for example, were set up at the time of the Royal Commission, while the Guinness Trust came four years later. Moreover, Octavia Hill's work was on the brink of expansion in 1884, when she began to manage property for the Ecclesiastical Commissioners.

A further point here is that by not carrying on the account of model dwellings organisations, historians have left unasked the important question of the putative links between these organisations and modern housing associations. A number of writers even use the term housing association anachronistically and inaccurately in relation to nine-teenth-century organisations, thereby implying (or at least allowing the inference of) a degree of continuity which has not been demon-strated. But at the same time, by presenting the model dwellings organisations in terms of failure these same writers invite scepticism about any link between nineteenth-century voluntary housing and today's housing associations. All this adds up to the conclusion that it is necessary to construct a fuller and longer term account of the devel-opment of voluntary housing. This needs to be an account based on a questioning approach to the notion of links between model dwellings and housing associations.

3

Multiple Visions of Housing Reform, 1890–1914

Introduction

The period covered by this chapter, from the Housing of the Working Classes Act 1890, to the outbreak of the First World War in 1914, was a time when the housing question was being tackled in a number of different ways. One of these was council housing, but in terms of the numbers of dwellings produced it was not the most important and it was certainly not clear at that time that local authorities would soon emerge as the major providers of new rented homes. Among the various non-municipal organisations there were some cross linkages but there was no overall coherence and no conception of a single voluntary housing movement.

The story is essentially one of innovation, experimentation and growing diversity, but not large scale. The 1890s and 1900s were decades when some exciting and visionary ideas about housing design, layout and tenure were being actively pursued by new types of provider, alongside the continuing work of the established organisations. Such is the dominance of the focus on the emergence of local authority housing in existing accounts of the history of housing in Britain that although model dwellings, the work of Octavia Hill, employer sponsored model villages and the garden cities movement are routinely mentioned, they tend to be treated as isolated historical curiosities or discussed in relation to council housing rather than to each other. An objective of this chapter, therefore, is to construct an account that explains the connections and recognises the distance between these various strands of activity, rescuing them from the shadow of council housing.

Policy developments before 1914

In the twenty-four years from 1890 to 1914, successive governments edged, albeit ever so reluctantly, closer to the formulation of genuine housing policies designed to increase the supply of houses at rents affordable to working-class families. This can be explained, at least in part, by reference to the growth of political power among the urban working class, whose activists saw housing as an issue around which to build support for the newly formed Labour Party after the turn of the century. Debate about housing took place alongside campaigns for reform of land ownership, for the introduction of town planning schemes, and for entirely new settlements to be built on 'garden city' lines. It is also important to locate developments in housing in the context of the wider social reform programme of the Liberal governments from 1906 onwards (Hay, 1975; Fraser, 1984).

The importance of 1890 is that it marks the start of the emergence of local authorities as large scale providers of rented housing, but it was not until after 1918 that they actually achieved significant levels of production. The 1890 Act did not represent a great step forward in terms of powers or principles; it was essentially a consolidating measure, restating powers that had grown up over the previous forty years. But the effect of consolidation was to simplify the legislation, making it much easier for local authorities to understand and use their statutory powers. It is this that makes the Act the most significant piece of pre-First World War housing legislation (Morton, 1991: 16). However, the Act would have made much less impact had it not been for the fact that at the same time the government was in the process of creating a new system of local government, which was capable of implementing housing policy. Hitherto the voluntary organisations were effectively on their own as providers of limited profit rented housing; local councils had made virtually no use of their powers to build. The Local Government Act 1888, created the county councils, including the London County Council, which quickly adopted a much more active approach to housing than had been displayed by the old Metropolitan Board of Works. Further legislation meant that by 1894 there was a coherent set of general purpose local authorities across the whole country, and that there was, therefore, an infrastructure of local government with at least the potential to develop an effective housing service. The final development came in 1899 when London's vestries (which had been a barrier to effective housing action) were replaced by the Metropolitan Borough Councils, with housing powers (Young and Garside, 1982).

The 1890 Act was in three parts. Part I was a consolidation of the Cross Acts (the Artisans' and Labourers' Dwellings Improvement Act 1875, as amended in 1879 and 1882) dealing with the clearance of areas of unfit houses. The new Act did not challenge the presumption that it was better for rebuilding on cleared sites to be carried out by the private or voluntary sectors. Part II represented the consolidation of the Torrens Acts (the Artisans' and Labourers' Dwellings Act 1868, as amended in 1879 and 1882) dealing with the closure and demolition of individual unfit properties. Part III referred to working-class lodging houses, and was effectively a restatement of the Lodging Houses Act 1851, which had given local authorities the little-used power to build houses for general need, separate from the removal of existing dwellings. In the different situation prevailing in the latter part of the century and beyond, this part of the Act became the basis of the initial expansion of council housing. However, the Act should not be seen as a strong signal from the centre that councils should now start to build:

> After 1890… it was legally possible for an enlightened local authority to pursue an enlightened housing policy, possible but not very much more possible than it had been since at least 1875 and, arguably, since 1851. The Act was very far from being imperative. (Gauldie, 1974: 294)

Local authorities did not rush to build houses, and in the case of rural district councils there was virtually no activity until 1912–14 (Gauldie, 1974: 324). Altogether there were only 24,000 local authority houses and flats in the whole of Great Britain by 1914 (Merrett, 1979: 26). This should be seen alongside the 50,000 or so built by the various model dwellings companies and trusts. Moreover, most council housing was built towards the end of the period, nearly half of it after 1909 (Ministry of Health, 1921: 57), that is, at a time when the majority of voluntary organisations had ceased new building. In some cases the low level of local authority building reflected the control of the council by property interests, in particular people who were themselves landlords of working-class housing, and who were most unlikely to use ratepayers' money to develop houses that would compete with their own. Elsewhere, even when councils were enthusiastic about house building the continued lack of financial support from central government meant that the whole of any loss would fall on the rates.

However, some councils did build, and among them were the major cities of Glasgow, Birmingham, Leeds, Manchester and Sheffield

(Morton, 1991, Burnett, 1986). The London County Council did most to establish local authority housing before the First World War, building some 9,272 dwellings, plus 1,856 bed spaces in lodging houses, by 1912 (LCC, 1913: 103). By 1914 the Metropolitan Boroughs had built a further 3,300 dwellings (LCC 1915), so that half of all municipal housing built before 1914 was in greater London. At first the LCC built tenement blocks, not unlike those of the model dwellings companies, although the standard of design was generally considered to be higher. The Council set up an architects' department which attracted some talented designers and helped to establish a reputation for better quality than had come to be expected of model dwellings. The first large scheme was built on a slum clearance site inherited from the Metropolitan Board of Works at Boundary Street, Bethnal Green, in 1895. The Boundary Street estate consisted of 1,044 dwellings, but the layout represented an attempt to get away from the barrack like appearance of block dwellings, and it has been generally well-received in the literature. However, in terms of the accommodation provided it must be pointed out that nearly eight out of ten dwellings consisted of just two or three rooms (Burnett, 1986: 185), and that some flats had shared facilities (Gaskell: 1986: 63). After the turn of the century the LCC also built suburban cottage estates, first at Totterdown Fields, Tooting, and then at White Hart Lane, Tottenham, and Old Oak, Hammersmith. Other cities, including Birmingham, Manchester and Sheffield, adopted the same policy of developing on cheaper land away from city centres as improvements in public transport made decentralisation easier. These suburban estates reflected contemporary developments in thinking about planning.

In view of the emphasis which has come to be attached to the Octavia Hill system of housing management it is worth noting that the LCC seems to have modelled its management style more on that of the model dwellings companies and trusts (LCC, 1913: 103). In 1901 the Council set up a centralised department under the control of a male Housing Manager, and each of the larger estates had its own resident superintendent. On these estates, as was the case with the companies and trusts, tenants were required to pay their rent weekly at the estate office. On the smaller estates there was a resident caretaker, and rents were collected weekly, door to door.

Mention must now be made of the Housing and Town Planning Act 1909. This was significant for the development of voluntary housing in two ways. First, it improved the terms on which public loans were available to limited profit organisations, and it introduced the term 'public utility societies' to cover those bodies registered as Industrial and Provident Societies under the Friendly Societies Act 1893, which were in future entitled to higher percentage loans, two-thirds rather than one-half. Second, the Act gave a boost to the principle of low-density suburbs, and the public utility societies that were associated with their development. Under the provisions in Part II of the Act, covering town extension schemes, councils were given powers to define the way in which land on the urban fringe should be developed, including the zoning of industrial, residential and leisure land uses, the form and height of buildings and the overall density of development (Gaskell, 1981: 42). As a result 'the garden suburb became synonymous with town planning' (Gaskell, 1981: 41).

In terms of housing policy the Housing and Town Planning Act has been seen as a considerable advance in so far as it signalled greater central government support for house building by local authorities, but its real significance may be that it served ultimately to demonstrate that no progress would be made without financial assistance from the Exchequer (Wilding, 1972: 7–8). In the years immediately before the war there were growing demands for the introduction of Exchequer subsidies in the face of a housing shortages and falling private sector output, especially in rural areas. One factor blamed for the decline in house building was the imposition of a tax on increases in land values, introduced by the Finance Act 1910, a measure which has to be understood in the wider context of the Liberal government's policy on land and taxation (Offer, 1981). However, there were other factors at work, in particular the higher returns available at that time from investments in companies competing in the international arms build-up. During 1912–14 a number of private member's Bills were introduced in Parliament with the intention of securing housing subsidies but none progressed beyond a second reading debate (Wilding, 1972: 9). In this period the government could withstand demands for subsidy, despite widespread recognition of the problems facing low paid workers. The case for subsidy was by no means universally accepted, and respected liberals such as Seebohm Rowntree argued that the problem of the affordability of rents should be addressed through action to lower the price of land and to raise wages rather than provide benefits to employers by means of subsidised prices (Rowntree, 1914).

Housing trust activity

The history of voluntary housing in the twenty-five years up the First World War is particularly rich and interesting. Before looking at the innovations of the period it is necessary to consider the continuing work of established organisations and the emergence of three new heavily endowed charitable trusts. The previous chapter discussed the widely held view that the model dwellings movement had failed, and was seen to have failed, by the time of the Royal Commission in the mid-1880s. However, not everyone shared this perception nor were they deterred by it. Established organisations carried on managing their extensive estates, and a number went on building, as Table 3.1 shows.

Table 3.1   New building by selected model dwellings companies and trusts, 1890 to 1914

Organisation	Number of dwellings built
Improved Industrial Dwellings Co.	500 (by 1910)
Artisans' and General	more than 2,000 (by 1915)
East End Dwellings Co.	2,200 (1885–1905)
Four Per Cent Industrial Dwellings Co.	1,913 (1885–1905)
Peabody Donation Fund	more than 1,500
Guinness Trust	more than 2,500 (1890–1903)
Sutton Dwellings Trust	1,783 (1909–18)
Samuel Lewis Trust	443 (by 1911)

Sources: Artisans, 1967, Pearman, 1985; Malpass, 1998; LCC, 1913; Garside and Morris, 1994.

This is by no means an exhaustive list, but it does indicate the level of activity among the largest housing organisations, and that approximately 13,000 dwellings (possibly more) were built after the critical conclusions of the Royal Commission in 1885. In addition to the continued activity among long established organisations, a newer generation of model dwellings providers such as the East End Dwellings Company and the Four Per Cent Industrial Dwellings Company made their mark. There is a case for presenting this period as the era of the charitable trusts, because of three major endowments: the Guinness Trust, £250,000 in 1889, the Sutton Dwellings Trust, £1.5 million in 1900 and the Samuel Lewis Trust, £400,000 in 1901. Whatever the Royal Commission's view of model dwellings, it is clear that at least three hugely successful capitalists felt that it was worthwhile to devote very large amounts of money to the cause of housing the working class. In the case of Guinness, the Trust Deed made explicit reference to the founder's hope that others would follow his example. A point worth noting about these later organisations is that they were more determined to reach the poor. In the case of the East End Dwellings Company this was achieved by building to very low specification, while the Guinness Trust aimed for 3.5 per cent but settled for a rate of return of only 3 per cent, and the Sutton Dwellings Trust looked for only 1.5–2 per cent. It may therefore be argued that this was an implicit acceptance of the failure of philanthropy at 5 per cent.

The Guinness Trust became the most active voluntary sector builder after 1890 – indeed it claimed to out-build the LCC in the period up to 1897 – and it is therefore appropriate to look in a little more detail at its early development. This will help to illustrate how far Victorian charitable housing trusts differed from modern housing associations. In 1889 Sir Edward Guinness was one of the wealthiest people in the country, having been the sole owner of the family brewing business until turning it into a public company in 1886. The sale of shares produced a cash mountain in excess of £4 million, as well as a controlling interest in the business (Martelli, 1956: 13). Unlike George Peabody, who modestly declined the honours offered to him by the Queen (Owen, 1965: 380), Edward Guinness led a princely lifestyle, cultivating his position in the upper reaches of English society, and actively seeking a peerage (Martelli, 1956: 119). However, this is not to suggest that Guinness was cynically buying himself a title by good works, for he remained actively involved with his Trust right up to his death in 1927.

The Guinness Trust was based on a Trust Deed, drawn up to Sir Edward's specification, setting out that £200,000 should be allocated to 'the amelioration of the condition of the poorer of the working classes' of London, the remaining £50,000 to be used for the same purpose in his home city of Dublin. Edward Guinness appointed three trustees to administer his gift, reserving to himself the sole right to appoint further trustees during his lifetime. The first trustees were David Plunket, MP (an old friend and political ally of Edward Guinness, he later became Lord Rathmore), Lord Rowton (former secretary to Disraeli, a prominent Conservative and adviser to the Queen; founder of a number of men's hostels known as Rowton Houses), and the Rt Hon Charles Ritchie, MP (in 1889 he was President of the Local Government Board, and as such he was responsible for taking through Parliament both the

Local Government Act 1888, and the Housing of the Working Classes Act 1890; he was later Home Secretary and Chancellor of the Exchequer, and elevated to the Lords as Lord Ritchie).

These three trustees, all drawn from the social and political elite, were joined by Edward Guinness himself in 1891. They were clearly an influential and well-connected team, illustrating the top-down nature of voluntary housing organisations in this period. Initially the trustees met very frequently, but later they settled into a less frenetic pattern of two meetings per year. The staff appointed to help them consisted of 'a clerk and a boy' (both of whom stayed for forty-five years), who were managed by the secretary (or chief executive in modern parlance). There is no evidence to suggest that any of these people had a background in housing work. This small team relied heavily on consultants, especially the various architects who helped to identify sites for development as well as producing the designs and overseeing the construction process.

Between 1891 and 1903 the Trust completed eight estates, seven of which were close to central London, although the last to be built was a little further out, at Fulham Palace Road, Hammersmith (Figure 3.1). The average number of dwellings per estate was 325, all of which were associated tenements, with shared sinks and WCs on the landings, and separate communal bathhouses. Individual flats were essentially simple suites of rooms, with a range for heating and cooking, but no water, gas or electricity. Like the Peabody Buildings the majority of Guinness Trust tenements had just one or two rooms. The adoption of the associated tenement reflected the Trust's objective of reaching a class of tenant poorer than had been reached by other organisations such as the IIDC and Peabody. Accordingly the trustees instructed staff to give preference to 'working men earning about 20/- a week'; information about actual incomes is rather scarce, but it appears that in 1891 the average household income among tenants on the first estate, at Brandon Street, Walworth, was 18s-5d. Rents at Brandon Street varied between 1s-6d per week for one room on the fourth floor, to 5s for three rooms on the ground floor (rents were lower on upper floors). In addition there was what would today be called a service charge of up to 6d per week for baths, hot water, window blinds, club room, chimney sweeping and 'boiling water supply for tea pots' – the last was a centrally dispensed service believed to be unique to the Trust.

The firm of Joseph and Smithem produced five of the first eight estates, and established a relationship with the Trust that lasted into the 1930s. Nathan Joseph was a leading figure in London's Jewish community and had been one of the group brought together by Lord Roths-child to set up the Four Per Cent Industrial Dwellings Company in 1885 (Pearman, 1985: 26). As the architect to that company he had some experience of designing high density model dwellings, and his work for the Guinness Trust built on that expertise. Tarn (1973: 105) is relatively positive about the design of Trust's estates:

> It is possible to find the traditional tenement block planning arrangements at Guinness Trust estates; for example in Vauxhall Walk, Lambeth, [which was not designed by Joseph] where the blocks are still regimented in closely spaced parallel rows with barren concreted areas between them. But the architecture was less harsh and uncompromising, the choice of brick more mellow, and the effec-tive height was minimised by treating the top floor as an attic; all these were architectural devices, designed to reduce the scale and the effect of sheer physical bulk, qualities usually inherent in working-class dwellings. The Lever Street Buildings [by Joseph] were a good example of the real care which was taken in order to achieve pleasing modelling and decorative effect; the result justified the effort, for buildings such as these showed that tenement blocks need not appear 'barrack-like'.

The Trust acquired sites from a variety of vendors, at less than full market price (Emsley, 1986: 60), and in one case an acre of ground in Chelsea came as a gift from Lord Cadogan. However, in marked contrast to the way that before 1890 slum clearance sites had been disposed of very cheaply to the Peabody Trust and other organisations, the Guinness Trust failed to establish a good relationship with the LCC and acquired no sites from this source until after the Second World War. The Trust came close to buying a site from the LCC at Cable Street, Stepney, in the early 1890s, but the deal fell through because the trustees were not prepared to accept the Council's insistence that it should approve the plans before building started (the story of the wrangle is told in detail by Emsley (1986: 55–66), drawing on LCC records). In those days (in sharp contrast to today) the trustees could afford to take a firmly independent line and not to worry about culti-vating a good relationship with the council.

Endowed with great wealth the progress of the Trust was not slowed by its fruitless negotiations with the LCC, but the construction of the first six estates used up Edward Guinness' donation and in order to carry on building a bank loan of £140,000 was raised in 1897 – an early example of the sort of private finance that is so important to housing associations today. However, unlike present practice, the trustees adopted a policy of consolidation, preferring to repay their loans before embarking on further new building. The result was that it was not until

Figure 3.1 The Guinness Trust Buildings, Fulham Palace Road, Hammersmith, as they looked at the time of their opening in 1901

the end of 1912 that they were ready to build again, and in fact nothing more was achieved before the outbreak of the war.

The evidence presented so far in this section suggests that the model dwellings companies and trusts did not build much after about 1905, although the Sutton Dwellings Trust and Samuel Lewis Trust were only just beginning to develop at that point. The first Sutton estate was completed in Bethnal Green in 1909, to be followed by a large estate in Chelsea in 1913. The EEDC built twelve estates between 1885 and 1905, but nothing thereafter until 1935. The Four Per Cent Industrial Dwellings Company also began a thirty-year period of quiescence in 1905 (Pearman, 1985: 85).

The expanding empire of Octavia Hill

The distinctive approach to the housing of the very poor developed by Octavia Hill has been referred to already in Chapter 2. The purpose of this section is to note the continued expansion of her work up to her death in 1912, and to look in a little more detail at an organisation set up by some of her friends, to develop her work in a notorious area of north Kensington (Malpass, 1999a).

After 1884 the Ecclesiastical Commissioners, who were ground landlords of some of London's worst slum districts, placed increasing numbers of their properties in Southwark, Deptford, Walworth and Lambeth under Octavia Hill's management, to the extent that eventually the majority of her work was south of the Thames. In her later years Hill was involved with a large scheme in the Walworth area carried out by the Commissioners on an estate where the leases had fallen in and where the Commissioners decided to undertake the redevelopment themselves. Initially Hill and her co-workers took over the management of 5–600 rundown, multi-occupied houses, and then advised on their redevelopment into an estate that Darley (1990: 296) describes as 'in many ways the embodiment of Octavia's ideas upon housing the poor'.

Octavia Hill was also involved in overseeing the management of the property developed by the East End Dwellings Company, which was set up by friends of hers, Rev. Samuel and Mrs Henrietta Barnett. One of the women employed to manage the company's first estate was Beatrice Potter – the future Beatrice Webb, who later wrote vividly of her experience of the work and her contact with Octavia Hill (Webb, 1971).

However, in terms of the longer term development of voluntary housing, Hill's work in Notting Hill, which started as late as 1899, was of greater significance. She was invited by the local vicar to take over the management of five houses in St Katharine's Road, Notting Dale. St Katharine's Road was one of a small cluster of streets that was designated as a special area because of its high crime rate. Hill described it in these terms:

> The neighbourhood seems corrupt, not poor; only too much money seems to reach the inhabitants from the rich people of Kensington. This district is filled with beggars and others who feed on the lavish alms of the ignorant or careless donor. Vice seems rampant and whole streets are let in furnished lodgings, an extravagant form of tenure, not likely to attract the steady workman, and lending itself to the loafer, and the shiftless or vicious. (Hill, 1933: 41)

Notting Dale was, therefore, fertile ground for Hill's redemptive style of housing management (Figure 3.2). Some of the houses managed by Hill were purchased by her friends, Dr and Mrs Schuster, who later formed the Wilsham Trust to hold these properties. Other houses were taken into the ownership of the Horace Street Trust, set up by Hill in 1886 as a vehicle for owning a small amount of property in her management. It was noted in Chapter 2 that Hill was not herself interested in founding formal organisations to manage working-class houses, and in that sense she was not a pioneer of modern housing associations. The Wilsham and Horace Street Trusts carried on in a small way and it was not until many years later that they merged and converted into a modern housing association (Malpass, 1999a). However, another, quite different type of organisation, also set up by friends of Octavia Hill to work in Notting Dale can be seen as a precursor of the societies set up in the 1920s and 30s, and which played an important part in establishing the National Federation in 1935.

The Improved Tenements Association (ITA) was a limited company (not an Industrial and Provident Society), set up in 1900 in order to purchase properties in Notting Dale and to place them under Hill's management. The initiative came from a small group of wealthy people from south Kensington, including Reginald Rowe (chairman for forty four years, and first chairman of the National Federation). The ITA differed from the Wilsham and Horace Street Trusts in that it sought to raise capital from shareholders and purchasers of loan stock. This gave it much greater growth potential than the Trusts which effectively depended on income surpluses and donations from trustees. There is no evidence that Octavia Hill was personally very closely involved with

Figure 3.2 Kenley Street, 1904, in the Notting Dale 'Special Area', where Octavia Hill had recently begun to expand her work

the ITA; she never bought any shares or loan stock and she never attended any meetings. However, she was responsible for overseeing the management service, which was provided by one of her workers on a commission basis (5 per cent of rents collected).

In marked contrast to the great endowed trusts such as Peabody and Guinness, the ITA had very modest ambitions, and concentrated on acquiring houses in small batches or singly. Typically the properties purchased were rundown, multi-occupied houses; for example, the first four (now buried under the Westway) consisted of 13 two-room tenements. The company's purpose, in keeping with the Octavia Hill system, was to improve the properties and the tenants together, or as Rowe put it in his address to the annual general meeting of shareholders in 1905:

> Our aim is merely to replace a bad landlord with a good one. We leave rents much as we find them, and do not meddle at all with the economic conditions, while as far as possible we encourage in our tenants thrift and the simpler virtues.

In some cases the directors came to regret their purchases, because although in terms of their social objectives the worst houses with the most difficult tenants were a priority, they also cost most to repair and yielded least in rents. The company managed to pay a dividend of 4 per cent every year up to 1909, but for the next ten years the dividend was lower. As a result the work developed only slowly, so that by 1917 the company's total stock was only 29 houses, but its significance lies in the longer term, as a model for the proliferation of similar organisations after the First World War, and as the platform for Rowe's contribution to the creation of the National Federation.

The garden cities movement and copartnership housing societies

So far this chapter has dealt with organisations operating exclusively in London – of those mentioned only the Sutton Dwellings Trust had a brief to work outside London. In this section, however, attention turns to organisations inspired by a rejection of the noise, congestion and smokey atmosphere of the city. The romantic idea that life could be better in the country has been around for a long time – Offer (1981: 351) refers to 'rural nostalgia' in the first half of the nineteenth century, and it was a widely held view later in the century when, for example, Octavia Hill helped to found the National Trust. The garden cities movement drew on a number of strands of thought – radicals, utopians and socialists came together with enlightened capitalists and Liberal politicians to promote an idea which was always about much more than just the design and layout of residential neighbourhoods. The garden cities movement features heavily in the history of planning (Sutcliffe, 1981, Hardy, 1991, Ward, 1992), but in housing histories it is recalled chiefly for its influence on the design and layout of interwar council estates (Swenarton, 1981). What needs to be remembered is that for Ebenezer Howard and other leading advocates of the garden cities idea it was about creating entirely new types of settlement, based on the common ownership of land, and it was about promoting a whole way of life. This included the belief that working men who had substantial vegetable gardens to attend would be less likely to spend their evenings drinking beer; it was suggested in 1901 that 'More air and less alcohol' should be the motto of the Garden City Association (Day, 1981: 173). It was also argued that workers who could grow some of their own food would be better able to support themselves and their families during periods of unemployment (Rowntree, 1914). Some have seen the broad support for garden cities as arising from the way that the concept could appeal to both people like Howard, who envisaged a gradual replacement of capitalism, and others who saw it as the best way to preserve capitalism (Fishman, 1977: 65).

In terms of an interest in the development of voluntary housing in Britain, the garden cities movement deserves attention because of its close association with a particular type of public utility society (the tenants' copartnership societies), and because the Garden Cities and Town Planning Association made an important contribution to the creation of the National Federation in 1935. It is also interesting as a movement, unlike the earlier manifestations of voluntary housing, to which people from the left of politics (such as Howard, Raymond Unwin, the dominant architectural figure of the movement, and, in a more detached way, the socialist playwright and critic George Bernard Shaw) were attracted. Swenarton (1981: 5) has suggested that the garden cities movement should be seen as embracing at least three distinct strands of activity, which he identifies as: the model villages developed by three leading capitalists (Lever, Cadbury and Rowntree), the garden city itself, as advocated by Ebenezer Howard, and the garden suburbs. This provides a convenient framework for present purposes, although an objective of the following discussion is to show the links between these various strands.

William Lever, millionaire soap manufacturer, developed a delightful model village for his workers at Port Sunlight on the Wirral peninsula in Cheshire in the years after 1888. Lever's action was self-interested: to ensure himself of a happy and productive workforce by giving them a healthy and pleasant residential environment, and he never sought to generate a rate of return on his investment. Port Sunlight was in many ways a late-nineteenth-century version of the sorts of employer village previously built by the likes of Ackroyd and Salt, and it has more in common with them than with the subsequent development of voluntary housing organisations. Of greater interest are the villages developed by the Quaker chocolate magnates, Cadbury and Rowntree. George and Richard Cadbury moved their cocoa and chocolate business from central Birmingham to the then rural setting of Bournville in 1879. Some years later, in 1895, work started on a 140 acre site for residential development according to principles set out by George Cadbury with the intention of improving on the typical urban by-law street layout. Sites were leased for others to develop, provided that plans were approved by the estate architect. It seems that by the end of the decade the project had evolved into a plan to create a garden village, and in 1900 a further important step was taken when the Bournville Village Trust was established (Henslowe, 1984).

Bournville Village Trust was set up with an endowment of 330 acres of land and 313 houses, rather than with a large cash sum. Although it differed in many ways from the Guinness Trust, the new Trust's deed echoed that of Edward Guinness in that the purpose was, 'To ameliorate the conditions of the labouring classes...' (Henslowe, 1984: 6). The Trust's role was to develop the land, and in doing so it built some houses for rent, but it also leased sites to other agencies, including public utility societies. In this sense the Trust acted in a way that was very similar to Howard's idea of how garden cities would be developed. Although the Cadbury family made up a majority of the trustees, the village was never intended to be reserved for company employees, and the trust deed provided for rents to be set at a level producing a 4 per cent return. In this sense, too, Bournville represents a step away from the tradition to which Port Sunlight belonged.

The third garden village project was that developed by Joseph Rowntree at New Earswick, outside York, from 1901, and constituted as the Joseph Rowntree Village Trust in December 1904 (Day, 1981: 168–73). This project is of interest chiefly because the architects employed to design the layout and the first houses were Raymond Unwin and Barry Parker, who were soon to win the competition to produce the layout for the first garden city, at Letchworth (Figure 3.3). Their work at New Earswick can be seen as a testbed for ideas that were developed further at Letchworth (Miller, 1993: 46). Both the Joseph Rowntree Village Trust and the Bournville Village Trust still exist as active registered housing associations.

Letchworth: the first garden city

Letchworth was the first garden city to be based on the principles set by Ebenezer Howard in his book, *Tomorrow: a Peaceful Path to Real Reform*, published in 1898, and republished in 1902 as *Garden Cities of Tomorrow*. Howard made his living as a shorthand writer and had no professional training in architecture, surveying or planning, but he was an effective and passionate advocate of the garden city idea. Howard was the originator of the garden city concept and of the idea that the land of the city should be held in perpetuity on behalf of the community, but he was also part of a wider campaign for reform on aspects of housing, land and taxation, and when the Garden City Association was formed in 1899 it was closely allied to the Land Nationalisation Society (Hardy, 1991: 16). It is clear from what has been discussed above that Howard was able to draw on existing ideas and experience, and he enlisted a number of influential supporters, including William Lever, George Cadbury and Seebohm Rowntree.

A company was formed to buy land on which to develop the city, and in 1903 nearly 4,000 acres of farmland in Hertfordshire were purchased. Raymond Unwin and Barry Parker won a competition to design the overall plan for the city, and they subsequently also designed some of the houses and exercised considerable influence over the design of others. However, for present purposes the organisations that built the early schemes at Letchworth are more interesting than the houses themselves. The company developing the town, First Garden City Ltd, was not in a position to undertake the building work itself, and the intention had always been that it would lease sites to others. It proved to be easier to attract businesses to the area than to secure houses for their workers, but in 1904 Garden City Tenants Ltd was set up as a copartnership society (see below), with Howard, Cadbury, and Lever on its board. It quite rapidly built over 300 houses using Unwin's designs. However, copartnership societies required tenants to become investors and so it was difficult to provide for lower paid workers with no savings. Accordingly, in 1907 First Garden City set up Letchworth

Figure 3.3 Rushby Mead, Letchworth, pre-1914 houses built by the Howard Cottage Society, showing the design influence of Raymond Unwin and Barry Parker

Cottages and Buildings Ltd as another vehicle for building working-class housing. This company built a further 200 houses by 1911, using Public Works Loans Board loans to cover 50 per cent of capital outlay and raising the remainder from shareholders.

The effect of the Housing and Town Planning Act 1909, was to make higher percentage loans available to organisations registered as Industrial and Provident Societies, and so First Garden City then set up, in 1911, the Howard Cottage Society, specifically to take advantage of the Act. It is appropriate to look at the Society in a little detail, because it occupies an important place in both the early development of the first garden city and in the wider history of modern housing associations. The first set of directors included Ebenezer Howard and two others who were also directors of First Garden City Ltd. The Society raised capital in the form of shares at £5 each, yielding 5 per cent, and loan stock yielding 4.5 per cent. The largest single investor was George Bernard Shaw, who bought £5,000 of loan stock by 1914. The Society was successful in securing a series of loans from the Public Works Loans Board, although there were some tough negotiations over certain design details and over the question of whether loans should be calculated according to valuation (as the Office of Works insisted) or cost (as the Society wanted).

In its first five years the Society built 395 cottages, making it the main provider of housing in the garden city until the newly formed local authority started building in the 1920s. The very close relationship with First Garden City meant that it could rely on sites becoming available on affordable terms, and all sites were obtained on 99-year leases for around £20 per acre. The cottages were built at twelve to the acre, and most had three bedrooms, fixed baths and piped hot water – a very much higher specification than the almost-contemporary Guinness Trust blocks in London. From the outset the Society employed staff to manage its affairs, including Frederic Osborn, who went on to become one of the leading figures in British town and country planning (Cherry, 1981).

The Howard Cottage Society was not only the main contributor to early residential development in Letchworth, but also a prototype housing association. Mention has been made above of the Improved Tenements Association as an organisation which prefigured the development of housing associations, and the Howard Cottage Society deserves to be seen in the same terms. Although they operated in very different contexts, one concentrating exclusively on rehabilitation in inner London while the other did only new building on greenfield sites, in financial and organisational terms they proved to be more successful than other models then in vogue. The Society carried on after the First World War, becoming a founder member of the National Federation, and it continues today as an active, expanding association. Garden City Tenants, however, was taken over and the individual houses were eventually sold off (Birchall, 1995: 353).

The copartnership societies and garden suburbs

Copartnership housing societies flourished briefly before the First World War and feature in histories of planning because of their close association with the development of garden cities and suburbs. But, as Birchall (1995: 330) has pointed out, housing historians have almost completely ignored them. This is probably because they made little impact after 1918 (although a few still exist and are members of the National Federation), and they cannot be easily tied into accounts dominated by the growth of council housing. However, in the context of the history of voluntary housing they need to be considered, as an indicator of the diversity of models available, albeit in this case one that failed to maintain its early momentum. The copartnership societies are interesting because, in contrast to the top-down character of the majority of voluntary housing organisations, they represented a bottom-up, workers' co-operative, form of provision (Harloe, 1995: 6).

The idea of copartnership housing societies originated in the 1880s, and a pioneer society, Tenant Co-operators Ltd. was set up in 1888 (Jackson, 1973: 348). The leading figure in the development of copartnership housing was Henry Vivian, who in 1890 became secretary of the Labour Association for Promoting Co-operative Production Based on Co-partnership of Workers (not surprisingly this is generally referred to as the Labour Association). He later became chair of Garden City Tenants, a Liberal MP and council member of the Garden Cities and Town Planning Association. Vivian founded General Builders, a labour copartnership, and it was from this that the first successful copartnership housing scheme was developed by Ealing Co-partnership Tenants Ltd. in west London. He has been described by Skilleter (1993: 128) as the most significant figure in the early development of housing associations in Britain, a judgement which is, however, open to some debate.

The basis of the copartnership housing societies was that tenants were required to be shareholders, and in the case of the Ealing society the amount was set at £50, payable by instalments. Investment was open to non-tenants, and at first voting rights were not related to the size of investment. Ealing Tenants Ltd had a majority of tenants on its management committee, but this did not last long and soon the power of outside investors overtook that of tenants. However, elsewhere it seems that the ideals of co-operation survived longer in more favourable circumstances. Birchall (1995) describes copartnership as a unique form of tenure, combining features of a tenant co-operative and a limited dividend company, but clearly its relevance was restricted to people who could afford the cost of the investment.

The sharing, co-operative aspect made copartnership attractive to Ebenezer Howard, but the concept made most impact in the development of garden suburbs rather than at Letchworth. The best known garden suburb is at Hampstead in north London, which was founded by Henrietta Barnett (previously mentioned in connection with the East End Dwellings Company). Hampstead Garden Suburb, started in 1906, was designed by Raymond Unwin (as were most of the others), and developed by a series of separate copartnership societies. Elsewhere at least 52 garden suburbs were developed in Birmingham, Manchester, Liverpool and a number of other places in England as well as schemes in Wales and Scotland (Ashworth, 1954: 163). For the first time, therefore, voluntary, limited profit housing organisations were established on a nationwide basis. A factor in the spread of copartnership was the creation in 1905 of a central organisation, Co-partnership Tenants Housing Council, with Unwin, Vivian, Howard, Lever and Cadbury involved. This was followed in 1907 by Co-partnership Tenants Ltd, which was both a federal body and a promoter of new societies. In Wales an equivalent role was played by the Welsh Town Planning and Housing Trust. The close links with the Garden Cities and Town Planning Association must have helped too. 'By 1913, Vivian had become a member of the Council of the GCTPA, and the interests of copartnership became increasingly merged with those of the Association' (Hardy, 1991: 90). Altogether, by 1914 there appear to have been at least forty societies, which built more than 7,000 dwellings (Birchall (1995: 344).

Conclusion

Three main points emerge from this chapter. First, although the conclusions of the Royal Commission of 1884–5 have often been interpreted subsequently as a demonstration of the failure of the model dwellings companies and trusts, these organisations continued to expand in the period 1890–1914. Far from council housing becoming inevitable it was just one of several ideas for tackling contemporary housing problems, and it has been shown that there were a number of other quite different and distinct approaches.

Second, it is the diversity of voluntary organisations, rather than their similarity of outlook, that is most striking. In particular, the more recently formed model dwellings companies clearly targeted the poor, while the copartnership societies aimed at a significantly better-off section of the population. The model dwellings organisations represented essentially a conservative, top-down response by wealthy people, whereas copartnership was clearly more progressive and bottom-up. The model dwellings organisations reflected acceptance of the dominant social, economic and urban-industrial framework, while the garden city offered a different vision of a utopian alternative, rejecting existing urban forms. Taken together the various strands of activity provided opportunities for participation by people from both the left and right of British politics.

Third, the differences among the various voluntary organisations meant that they had no shared identity as a cohesive social movement. Indeed they were more likely to recognise their differences than their similarities.

A final point has to be that none of the models was able to overcome the central problem of how to generate sufficient capital to make a significant impact on the housing shortage without sacrificing quality or affordability.

4

False Dawns, 1914–33

Introduction

Historians have seen the outbreak of the First World War in August 1914 as marking the boundary between the social, economic and political framework of the nineteenth century and the new world order of the 'short' twentieth century (Hobsbawm, 1994). The war had an effect at many different levels, including the development of housing policy in Britain and other belligerent countries (Harloe, 1995: 75–149). Although it emerged on the winning side, Britain's economic power was substantially weakened by the war effort, and its overseas markets eroded by competition. On another level British society was permanently changed by the war; for example, the vital role played by women ensured that at last they were given the vote. At the end of the war it was clear that there would have to be some kind of settlement to secure peace at home, and housing was at the forefront of public debate about the creation of a better Britain. The war created conditions which meant that it was possible to break through barriers that had hitherto seemed solid, and in the case of housing this took the form of government acceptance of Exchequer subsidies; stoutly resisted before 1914, they became inevitable by 1916 (Byrne and Damer, 1980, but see also Wilding, 1972).

The title of this chapter, False Dawns, reflects the fact that both immediately after the war and again in the early 1930s there were heightened and ultimately unfulfilled expectations as to the contribution of voluntary housing organisations. After the Armistice of November 1918 the emphasis was placed on the need to build houses rapidly and in quantity, and the public utility societies were expected to play a significant part in meeting urgent needs. In practice it was the local authorities which emerged as the main providers of new rented housing for the working class, eclipsing the contribution of the voluntary sector. Nevertheless, by the early 1930s there was renewed momentum behind the cause of non-municipal housing organisations. Having originally evolved in the era of *laissez-faire*, and having operated for decades in the absence of government policy on housing, the voluntary organisations had seen themselves sidelined by emergent housing policy, but by 1933 they appeared to be on the brink of a breakthrough to greater recognition as one of three legs on which government policy was to stand (the others were the local authorities and the commercial private sector (Garside, 1995: 99).

Housing and housing policy on the brink of the First World War

The situation in 1914 was that house building had been in decline since 1906, following the boom of the late 1890s and early 1900s. Some writers refer to the housing problem of this period in terms of a crisis of overproduction (Byrne and Damer, 1980: 63–70), and there is evidence to support this view, for example, Octavia Hill wrote in 1911 that, 'The demand for rooms in London is nowhere near what it once was...' (Malpass, 1999a: 29). Nevertheless, by 1914 the slump in building led to growing shortages in some areas, both in overall numbers and more especially in terms of affordable housing; as a result there remained a considerable problem of overcrowding among the poorest households. In the years after the Housing and Town Planning Act 1909, output by local authorities increased to a much higher rate than hitherto. However, the level would undoubtedly have been much higher if the Exchequer had been willing to bear some of the cost. In the absence of Exchequer subsidies revenue losses were borne by local ratepayers, and in the years immediately before 1914 there were attempts to introduce subsidies. These were unsuccessful, largely because, 'State subsidised social housing was advocated by relatively few and uninfluential voices' (Harloe, 1995: 40). Without financial support for rent subsidies there was very little prospect of council housing growing on a significant scale. The Liberal governments in office from 1906 were opposed to subsidies on principle, and defeated a series of attempts by back bench MPs from 1912 to 1914 to promote Bills proposing housing subsidies, preferring instead to seek affordability through land and taxation reforms. The Liberal government's resistance to housing subsidies should be seen as contrasting with their reformist agenda in other areas of social policy, notably old-age pensions and national insurance.

It should also be noted that, rather than encouraging council housing, policy immediately before the war favoured the channelling of high percentage loans (up to 90 per cent) to public utility societies to meet both the needs of government employees and rural workers (Swenarton (1981: 45). The Housing Act 1914, provided for up to £2 million to be lent for housing government employees (mainly those employed at the recently established Rosyth Dockyard in Fyfe).

The war and after

This section looks at the development of housing policy during the First World War and the implementation of the Housing and Town Planning Act 1919, The period from 1914 to 1919 was a major watershed in the development of British housing policy and has been the subject of considerable attention among housing scholars. The intention here is not retell the whole story but to concentrate on those aspects which had an impact on voluntary, limited profit housing organisations. There are three key aspects of housing policy development during the war, all of which had implications for limited profit housing organisations: the introduction of rent control, the programme of building for munitions workers, and the negotiations over subsidies to be paid towards the cost of new houses to be built after the war.

At the outbreak of the conflict the government introduced a number of measures designed to ensure that it had access to all the resources needed to prosecute the war to a successful conclusion. Among these were restrictions on the issuing of new debt, and this had serious implications for capital intensive activities such as house building. However, new building did not stop immediately, and although general needs housing did grind to a halt by 1916 there continued to be a certain amount of construction to meet the needs of munitions workers throughout the war. At Letchworth, for example, Howard Cottage Society continued to build right up to 1916, completing at least 100 houses after the outbreak of the war, despite difficulties in obtaining loans from the Public Works Loans Board. Some of these new houses were allocated to Belgian refugees and others engaged in munitions work. The need to produce vast amounts of weaponry, ammunition, uniforms and all sorts of other equipment meant not only that there were large increases in the total number of workers engaged in this work, but that some areas experienced such great influxes of population that existing accommodation was quickly overcrowded. In some places, most notably in Glasgow but also elsewhere, the arrival of thousands of munitions workers tilted the housing market in favour of the city's landlords, who responded by increasing rents, thereby fuelling the resentment of tenants who saw such action as profiteering. At a time when thousands of young men were losing their lives in the trenches of France and Belgium, and munitions workers themselves were labouring under difficult conditions, the spectacle of landlords increasing their profits in this way was highly provocative. During 1915 rent strikes broke out in munitions areas across the country and mass demonstrations were staged (Orbach, 1977; Damer, 1980; Melling, 1980). In the context of a war on the scale of 1914–18 the government was highly sensitive to the mood of the workers on whom the fighting forces depended. Social unrest at home would not help the war in Europe, and so, in December 1915 the government passed emergency legislation (the Rent and Mortgage Interest (War Restrictions) Act 1915) to fix rents and mortgage interest rates at the levels that had prevailed in August 1914. This had the desired effect of calming the situation, although Englander (1983) has shown that the Act was flawed and often evaded. Rent control applied to virtually all but the highest value properties, and therefore included the whole of the voluntary sector, where organisations faced increased costs due to wartime inflation without the ability to increase income.

In places where there was no possibility of existing housing absorbing the whole of the additional workforce, the government undertook a limited programme of new building, in which public utility societies played a significant part. At the Woolwich Arsenal, for example, the workforce increased from under 11,000 in 1914 to over 74,000 in 1917, and in the remote village of Gretna, in Dumfrieshire, the government built an explosives factory which required accommodation for 13,500 people (Swenarton, 1981: 50, 58). Altogether, 10,000 permanent houses were built, on garden city lines, on 38 estates around the country, together with 2,800 temporary homes and hostel places for 20,000 workers (Swenarton, 1981: 51). A few of these schemes were developed by the local authorities, and some were carried out directly by the Ministry of Munitions. The majority, however, were undertaken by private employers, in conjunction with public utility societies.

Whereas the struggle for rent control had been highly visible, the negotiations over housing subsidies were conducted behind closed doors between the Treasury and the Local Government Board, the Ministry of Reconstruction and later the Ministry of Health. From the spring of 1916 onwards it was recognised within the government that it would be necessary to ensure that house building resumed in earnest as soon as the war was over, and that it would be necessary for the Exchequer to make some kind of contribution towards the cost of an emergency programme. The reasoning was that there would be a severe housing shortage, that private enterprise could not be relied upon to build anything like enough houses (or indeed any at all), but that it was politically necessary to ensure that houses were built in quantity and let at rents that were affordable. Private enterprise could not be relied upon for three reasons: first, falling returns on working-class house building before the war had contributed to the decline in building, and unless rents were substantially increased the necessary investment would not be forthcoming, but, second, rents could not be increased because it was politically impossible to remove rent control until housing supply had increased:

> Increases in rents staved off in deference to public opinion during the war could scarcely be regarded as an appropriate form of peace celebration. (Bowley, 1945: 9)

And, third, whatever line was adopted on rents, it was widely expected that the significant price inflation that had taken place during the war would continue, at least for a while, before prices settled back to normal. Given this expectation the prudent course of action for investors in housing would be to hold off until normal conditions returned, otherwise they would be saddled with high cost investments on which it would be impossible to secure a commensurate rate of return in competition with lower cost houses built once prices had returned to normal.

Thus, for a combination of economic and political reasons the government was effectively forced to concede that, at least during the immediate postwar period, it would be necessary to provide some kind of subsidy for house building. The issues to be resolved concerned the nature of the subsidy, and who would build the houses. For present purposes it is not necessary to rehearse in detail the full story of the negotiations surrounding the housing policy eventually adopted after the war (Swenarton, 1981: 67–87), but it should be noted that what emerged was significantly different from the policy as it had stood in August 1914. This was a direct reflection of the growing concern in government circles that there was a revolutionary situation in the country after the armistice of November 1918, and that this could be defused through the programme of building 'homes fit for heroes'. The four important differences were, first, the large scale of the programme: in marked contrast to the very limited building programme envisaged in 1914, the plan was to build up to 500,000 houses within three years of the end of the war; second, the local authorities, not the public utility societies, were to be the main providers; third, there was to be a generous Exchequer subsidy covering the majority of losses incurred under the scheme, and fourth, garden city standards of design and layout were to be adopted.

The local authorities became the main providers of subsidised rented housing after the war because the scale of the planned programme was too great for the public utility societies to be relied upon, and because the alternative of subsidies to commercial private builders was regarded as politically unacceptable. The public utility societies were few in number, they lacked the nationwide coverage provided by the local authorities, and they lacked the financial strength of local authorities which could raise large amounts of capital secured against their ability to raise income through the rates. There were then over 1,800 local authorities as against approximately 128 societies (of which only 106 had actually built any houses) (Ministry of Reconstruction, 1918: 4). However, the societies were included within the scope of the planned housing programme from the outset, as were the charitable trusts. In May 1917 Seebohm Rowntree wrote an influential report for the Housing Panel of the Ministry of Reconstruction, in which he concluded that it would have to be the local authorities that built most of the proposed houses (Swenarton, 1981: 69), but the Housing Panel and the President of the Local Government Board also expressed support for public utility societies (Ministry of Reconstruction, 1918: 5). Swenarton (1981: 84) reminds us that, 'In 1914 [the public utility societies] had occupied a central place in the housing policy of the Liberal government and during the war their interests continued to be well represented in Whitehall, largely through the influence wielded at the Ministry of Reconstruction by the Garden Cities and Town Planning Association'.

In October 1918, just a month before the end of the war and when it was already clear that victory would soon be achieved, the Housing (Financial Assistance) Committee of the Ministry of Reconstruction produced a report on help for public utility societies (Ministry of Reconstruction, 1918). It recognised that the local authorities were unlikely to build sufficient houses to meet the postwar emergency, and that help for public utility societies was required. The report made a series of recommendations, the most important of which concerned higher percentage loans (increased from 66 per cent to a maximum of 80 per cent of estimated value) from the Public Works Loans Board, at the lowest rate of interest at which the state could borrow. Loan periods were recommended to be increased from forty years to fifty (local authorities were allowed to repay over sixty years). On the all-important question of subsidy, the report recommended a capital grant of three quarters of the difference between the actual approved cost of construction and the estimated value. This, of course, meant that societies would not be compensated for the whole of any loss incurred, and the argument for this was that since the government was not proposing to cover the full loss on local authority schemes it would be wrong to treat the societies more generously.

The report made a series of other recommendations concerning conditions that should be attached to any offers of assistance. Interestingly, in view of subsequent events, at the top of the list were recommendations concerning the right of tenants to become shareholders in the society, and the right of tenants to elect a Tenant Members' Committee, which would have the right to appoint a quarter of the Board of Management. It was also recommended that tenants should have security of tenure (recognised as an important protection in the context of employer-promoted societies).

Just after the publication of the report on public utility societies another, much better known, was produced by a committee on technical aspects of house production, chaired by the Liberal MP Sir John Tudor Walters (1918). Its content was largely the work of Raymond Unwin, who seized the opportunity of the proposed state housing programme to promote his ideas for design and layout on garden city principles, as previously pioneered at Letchworth, a series of garden suburbs and the wartime housing programme of the Ministry of Munitions. Swenarton (1981: 190) has argued persuasively that the high quality of subsidised housing produced after the war was as important as the quantity, for it was through a demonstration that the future was going to be better than the past that the government hoped to manage the transition from war to peace. It was precisely because the garden city standards had been seen as too expensive for local authority housing before 1914 that they were adopted after the war, as proof of the government's commitment to producing a land fit for heroes to live in.

The Housing and Town Planning Act 1919

The legislation needed to turn the vision into reality was passed as the Housing and Town Planning Act 1919. In the turbulent months immediately after the armistice, when fears of revolution were strongest, the government conceded to local authorities a subsidy system which restricted their liability to the product of a one penny rate, and all other revenue losses were covered by the Exchequer. However, councils (except the smallest) were expected to raise the necessary capital themselves. This was to lead to problems for both the local authorities and for the public utility societies, who were in competition for the same funds. As far as public utility societies were concerned, they were offered a subsidy expressed as 40 per cent of the loan charges on the 75 per cent of costs that they were permitted to borrow from the Public Works Loans Board – this equated to a subsidy of 30 per cent of total loan charges (in an attempt to boost output the rate was subsequently increased in 1920 to 40 per cent overall, for the period up to 1927; the Housing Act 1923, extended the period of 40 per cent subsidy to cover the whole period of the loan). The societies were given a better deal than the local authorities to the extent that they had access to capital raised by the Loans Board, at lower interest rates than they could have secured on their own account. It should also be recorded that the Loans Board was empowered to lend money to public utility societies for the purchase of existing houses which could be made suitable for working-class families (Ministry of Health, 1939: 14), but there is very little evidence on the extent of subsequent action.

The 1919 Act gave local authorities, for the first time, powers to assist voluntary housing societies. They were empowered to assist in the promotion of public utility societies, to give them grants or loans, and to subscribe to share or loan capital; they could also provide guarantees of loan repayments.

In order to administer the scheme the Local Government Board (which was soon to hand over to the newly created Ministry of Health) set up a series of eleven District Housing Commissioners for England. The board also issued a *Manual on the Preparation of State-aided Housing Schemes* (Local Government Board, 1919), which clearly stated that,

> It is the intention of the Government that the housing schemes to be carried out with State assistance should mark an advance on the building and development

which has ordinarily been regarded as sufficient in the past, and that the houses to be erected should serve as a model or standard for building by private enterprise in the future (paragraph 7).

The Manual embodied the principles of the Tudor Walters Report, setting out the expectation that estates should be developed to no more than twelve houses per acre in urban areas and eight in rural areas.

The story of the implementation of the 1919 Act, of how prices rose to around £1,100 per house (compared with an average of under £250 in 1909–14), of how the total number of houses built with subsidy fell short of half the original target of half a million, and how the whole programme was cut short in the summer of 1921, has been told by writers such as Swenarton (1981) and Merrett (1979), and there is no need to repeat it at length here. However, existing accounts concentrate on the performance of the local authorities and little has been written about the role played by the public utility societies. In one sense this is not surprising, because the societies built only 4,545 subsidised houses under the 1919 Act (Ministry of Health, 1925: 52), compared with 170,000 council houses and 39,000 private enterprise houses subsidised under the Housing (Additional Powers) Act 1919. Nevertheless, there remain the interesting questions of which organisations actually built the 4,545 houses, and what connection, if any, they have to modern housing associations, and, more importantly, why there was not more activity by public utility societies.

The question of which organisations built houses under the 1919 Act remains shrouded in uncertainty. Societies eligible for assistance under the Act were defined in general terms: they must be registered under the Industrial and Provident Societies Act 1893; they must include within their objects the provision of houses for the working class; their rules must prohibit the payment of dividends above the rate set by the Treasury, and they must comply with the regulations concerning the conduct of business (these regulations were based on the recommendations of the Committee on financial assistance to public utility societies, as discussed above). It was also possible for the charitable housing trusts to receive loans and subsidy under the Act, although they were not I and P Societies, and were not required to give tenants places on their boards of trustees. The Guinness Trust, for one, took advantage of the opportunity to develop its site at Kennington Park Road, south London, that had been delayed by the war, but the details of the activities of other similar trusts are unknown. The Guinness Trust was initially denied subsidy by the London Housing Board because its proposals for five-storey blocks of associated tenements in the established Guinness mode were out of tune with current expectations. After reducing the storey height to four, and introducing a bath for each flat, approval for subsidy was obtained and the 160 dwelling estate was completed in 1921. This was the only occasion until after the Second World War that the Trust built with Exchequer subsidy. The estate was also unusual in a wider sense, because even in London, with its history of high-density flatted accommodation, in general 1919 Act developments conformed to the garden city model of two-storey houses.

Elsewhere, there is only patchy evidence of who built what. Swenarton (1981: 184) refers to 110 cottages being built by a public utility society at New Earswick, York, and Skilleter (1993: 152) reports that in 1921 there were six societies building at Welwyn Garden City. He also lists two at Bournville. It is also known that a total of 271 1919 Act houses were built in South Wales by the Rhiwbina Garden Village, Cardiff, Barry Garden Suburb and Burry Port Garden Suburb (NFHS, *Bulletin*, no. 1, April 1936: 12). A piece of negative evidence, which may reflect wider difficulties being experienced by limited profit housing organisations at that time, is that the Howard Cottage Society, which had been the main provider of working-class housing in Letchworth before the war, built nothing at all under the 1919 Act. At the end of the war the Society's finances were not in a strong condition, depleted by the need to increase expenditure on the backlog of repairs and the inability to raise rents. 1919 was the only year when the directors were unable to pay a dividend to shareholders. Meanwhile, the newly formed Letchworth Urban District Council built 700 1919 Act houses.

The first Annual Report by the Ministry of Health (1920: 36) says that 136 schemes had been submitted by public utility societies for approval, but by the following year the report's authors commented that, 'the response to the Government's offer is smaller than might have been expected' (Ministry of Health, 1921: 69). The lack of detail available makes it difficult to say very much about any links between the active societies immediately after the First World War and modern housing associations, but it is reasonable to conclude that, apart from the larger trusts, very few indeed of those bodies participating in 1919 have survived into the 1990s. Birchall (1995: 350–2) also implies that the copartnership societies which had flourished to an extent before 1914 never really recovered from the impact of the war, and he identifies several that never built again. It is probable that many of the houses built in 1919–21 by public utility societies were eventually sold for owner occupation or commercial renting.

The very limited contribution of the public utility societies to the postwar emergency housing programme was clearly not due to a lack of official support for them; a circular on financial assistance to public utility societies issued by the Local Government Board in March 1919 said that:

> the Government desire to encourage Public Utility Societies... The Government are satisfied that much can be done to meet the urgent housing needs of the moment by Public Utility Societies formed or to be formed for the provision of working-class houses. (Local Government Board, 1919: 48)

However, the circular went on to refer to the hope that 'many industrial organisations' would form new societies, and expressed confidence that employers were aware of the advantages of having a well-housed workforce. Swenarton (1981: 84) quotes sources indicating that it was believed in Whitehall that the 'great majority' of public utility societies would be promoted and managed by employers of labour, and it seems there was a proposal from the housing committee of the Federation of British Industry to set up an organisation for the promotion of societies in all districts where housing was needed (Ministry of Reconstruction, 1918: 5). The involvement of employers in sponsoring some of the houses built for munitions workers during the war may also have contributed to the expectation that employer-based public utility societies would flourish afterwards. But it did not happen. The first Annual Report of the Ministry of Health lamented the lack of interest shown by employers:

> It would appear that employers have not to any large extent realised the advantages which indirectly accrue to business and production from a good housing scheme, while it is possible that the requirement that full security of tenure be given to tenants tends to prevent some employers from providing houses. (Ministry of Health, 1920: 33)

Tudor Walters (1927: 13) later explained this in terms of employers' reluctance to commit capital to the building of houses for their employees when it was more urgently needed for the more profitable development of their businesses. The housing programme in general suffered from difficulties of raising sufficient capital, and although the public utility societies had access to Public Works Loans Board loans they still had to raise a quarter of their capital from other sources, while being restricted in the dividend that they could offer investors (Industrial and Provident Societies had been restricted to 5 per cent, although after the war the ceiling was lifted to 6 per cent).

Looking back at the very low number of houses built by the public utility societies under the 1919 Act, especially in comparison with the output of the local authorities, the inescapable conclusion is that their poor performance was of considerable long-term significance. Although Garside (1995: 85–6) has argued that the leading role of local authorities in housing provision was contested throughout much of the interwar period, the fact that the public utility societies had made such a tiny contribution during the period of greatest urgency must have influenced official and public opinion. From that time onwards the societies faced an uphill struggle to establish their claim to be able to play a significant role in tackling housing problems. Whereas before 1914 the voluntary organisations had built more than twice as many houses as all the local authorities, within three and a half years after the armistice the local authorities owned twice as many as the voluntary sector. The local authorities had shown that they could deliver, and the fact that they had become established as landlords put them in a much stronger position than the small voluntary organisations in later debates about who should do what.

Voluntary housing in the 1920s and early 1930s

This section concentrates on the period from the premature ending of the housing programme under the 1919 Act to the appointment of the Moyne Committee in March 1933. Throughout much of this time the various voluntary housing organisations found themselves working in difficult economic circumstances and in a policy framework which, if not actually hostile, gave them little scope to expand their work on a large scale. Overall it was a period when the voluntary sector made very little impact in terms of the number of houses built or acquired – although there are no reliable aggregate statistics. Nevertheless, it is clear that there was a marked increase in activity measured in terms of the number of new organisations coming into existence to tackle housing problems. It will be argued that these new societies, trusts and associations formed after the war amounted to a second wave of voluntary housing providers, and that by the early 1930s they had begun to generate significant impetus.

The political and economic context can be briefly sketched in. Immediately after the war there was a brief economic boom, which collapsed in 1920, leading to a steep rise in unemployment, which was to remain high for virtually the whole of the remainder of the interwar period.

Establishment worries about Bolshevism and revolution, which had been acute (if not actually well-founded) in the weeks and months following the armistice, faded away, and although labour militancy continued up to the debacle of the General Strike in 1926, unemployment reduced the power of the unions. After the collapse of Lloyd George's coalition government in 1922 the Conservatives were in office for the remainder of the decade up to May 1929, apart from ten months in 1924.

Conventional economic theory prescribed cuts in public expenditure as the remedy for recession, and the postwar housing programme was a major victim of the retrenchment policies introduced by the coalition government. However, there remained a severe housing shortage, and there was still little prospect of sufficient unaided private sector production. In this situation two policies were pursued: first, rent control was maintained, although in 1920 landlords were permitted to increase rents by up to 40 per cent of their 1914 levels. This remained the basis for controlled rents throughout the period up to 1939 (Holmans, 1987: 390–1), although in 1923 there was some relaxation of control insofar as rents became decontrolled at the next change of tenant. The second aspect of policy was the decision to introduce a new subsidy, of £6 per year for twenty years (or a single payment of £75). The Housing Act 1923, was passed by a Conservative government which was concerned with encouraging building by private enterprise more than by local authorities, and councils were only allowed to build with the new subsidy where they could show that there was a demand that was not being met by the private sector. The 1923 Act subsidy was available until 1929, and voluntary housing providers were eligible on the same terms as other private builders.

In early 1924 the first Labour government took office, and although it lasted less than a year it passed an important Housing Act which some people have seen as the real basis of the long term role of local authorities as large scale providers of rented housing. Whereas the 1919 Act can be seen as essentially a short-term reaction to the postwar emergency, and the 1923 Act was mainly about encouraging the private sector, the 1924 Act embodied a much longer vision for the development of a major municipal housing service, to the extent that the continuation of subsidy was conditional upon councils and builders meeting predetermined output targets up to the mid-1930s (Merrett, 1979: 46). The scale of the proposed local authority building programme was huge, amounting to 2.5 million dwellings over fifteen years (Jarmain, 1948: 78). Although the Labour government fell, its

Housing Act remained in force until 1933, alongside the 1923 Act, and local authorities and voluntary providers could choose which Act to operate. The key differences between them were that the 1923 Act had a lower rate of Exchequer subsidy, but from the point of view of local authorities there was no mandatory rate fund contribution; the 1924 Act subsidy was 50 per cent higher and lasted longer (£9 per year for forty years), but there were conditions attached to the rents that could be charged. The level of subsidy under both Acts was subject to periodic review, and houses completed after September 1927 were eligible for assistance at a reduced rate, reflecting falling construction costs. The 1923 Act subsidy was removed altogether in 1929, but further planned cuts in the 1924 Act subsidy were rescinded by the minority Labour government which had come into office earlier that year. In addition to the Exchequer subsidies, local authorities could make revenue contributions from their own resources, they could subscribe to shares or loan stock and they could provide guarantees for loans (the latter enabled societies to obtain up to 90 per cent loans from the Public Works Loans Board). There is no systematic evidence on the scale of such help from local authorities, although it generally assumed to have been on a very small scale.

Throughout most of the 1920s it was necessary to concentrate on adding to the total housing stock in order to reduce the overall shortage, and little energy was directed to clearing away or improving existing poor quality housing, of which there was huge amount. Only about 15,000 buildings were demolished with slum clearance powers in the whole of the period 1919–30 (Ministry of Health, 1931: 106). By the general election of May 1929 the housing debate was turning to the question of what to do about old and unfit housing, with the Conservatives tending to favour limited intervention in the form of 'reconditioning', while Labour supported clearance and redevelopment. The new Labour government passed legislation in the form of the Housing Act 1930, which introduced both a new housing subsidy, calculated according to the number of people rehoused from slum clearance areas, and powers to enable local authorities to declare improvement areas. In such areas it would become compulsory for owners to bring their properties up to a specified minimum specification. Basement dwellings could be closed, overcrowding had to be abated, every tenant given a separate water supply, sink and ventilated food store and every house had to have a WC above basement level.

Turning to the impact of these policies, local authorities built a total of 75,000 houses with the 1923 Act subsidy, compared with over

360,000 by private enterprise. Under the 1924 Act local authorities built 505,000 houses by the time the subsidy was withdrawn in 1933, and private enterprise built just 16,000 (all figures refer to England and Wales (Bowley, 1945: 271)). In addition, there were over 930,000 unsubsidised private houses built between 1919 and 1933. In this context the numerical achievements of the voluntary organisations are undeniably trivial, but also much more difficult to quantify accurately. The problem is that official statistics record only those public utility society dwellings that were directly subsidised by the Ministry of Health, while those that were subsidised via the local authorities or were not subsidised at all are not separately recorded. There is no way of calculating an accurate estimate, but it is certain that the number was very small in relation to the achievements of the local authorities and capitalist builders.

According to the Ministry of Health (1933: 101) total recorded (centrally subsidised) output by public utility societies between 1919 and 1933 was only 18,161 (including the 4,545 1919 Act houses referred to in the previous section), but this 'in no way' represented the total number, because 'in the normal course' societies obtained aid through the local authorities. (A later estimate put the total number of centrally subsidised dwellings at 29,000 (Ministry of Health, 1939: 6). It must also be remembered that there was no state aid towards recon-ditioned houses and so that whole area of work went unrecorded. The total number of new and reconditioned houses owned by the voluntary organisations may have been two or three times the number that were centrally subsidised, but it is unlikely to have been any more. And if this estimate is correct then the societies produced in fourteen years roughly the average annual output of local authorities in the same period.

In the absence of reliable aggregate statistics it is necessary to gauge the overall level of activity from what is known about individual organ-isations. A review of the some of the evidence will help to illustrate the wide diversity of organisations involved at the time, and also provide an opportunity to refer to the origins of some associations that have become well known in the present period. By far the largest single builder in the period under consideration was the Industrial Housing Association, which built 12,000 houses between 1922 and 1927 in mining areas in South Yorkshire, Derbyshire, Nottinghamshire and South Wales. The Association was initiated by Lord Aberconway and managed by Sir John Tudor Walters (who had conveniently lost his seat at the general election of 1922 (Tudor Walters, 1927)). It was described as a co-operative of mining employers and its purpose was to provide good quality, garden city style houses for miners on a non-profit basis. In 1922 a number of colliery companies combined to form the Association as a limited company paying no dividend on share capital. Loans were raised from the Public Works Loans Board, together with additional private borrowing, and once built the houses were leased to the colliery companies for their employees at rents which reflected the value of the subsidy available under the 1923 Act.

Another example of an employer based initiative was the Great Western Railway Company's offer in 1923 to assist its workers to provide houses for them at various rail centres (*Garden Cities and Town Planning*, April–May 1932). The Welsh Town Planning and Housing Trust was involved in the formation and management of the seven public utility societies which were set up in London, Cornwall and South Wales, and by 1931 1,297 houses had been built, with the help of 90 per cent loans from the Railway, supplemented by share capital subscribed by tenants and other investors. Housing subsidies were arranged through the local authorities. There were other employer based housing initiatives during the 1920s and 30s, although the nature and extent of such projects has not been systematically written up in the academic literature. Nevertheless, it can be said that such initiatives failed to make the kind of impact that was apparently expected of them at the end of the war.

A rather different kind of initiative from this period deserves a mention, as an example of direct government involvement in the establishment of housing providers. Faced with recession in the Scottish steel and shipbuilding industries, a number of manufacturers proposed to build steel houses, and with the support of the Scottish Office a company, Second Scottish National Housing Company, was set up (as a subsidiary of the original SNHC, which had been established in 1914 to build houses at Rosyth). Between 1926 and 1928 over 2,500 steel houses were built in Glasgow and other cities (Begg, 1996: 33–4).

Among already established organisations it seems that the 1920s was experienced as a difficult decade; rent control, high interest rates and uncertainty about when the market would return to normal made it difficult for them to undertake new projects. For example, following its one 1919 Act estate in 1921, the Guinness Trust built only one more scheme, of 160 flats on King's Road, Chelsea, before the mid-1930s. This scheme was made viable by the fact that the Borough Council offered the site to the Trust at a peppercorn rent. The Sutton Dwellings Trust, which had built nearly 1,800 houses and flats before the war, built nothing more until 1926. The Victorian model dwellings companies, too, seem to have remained inactive after the war. At Letchworth the Howard Cottage Society built one small scheme of a dozen dwellings in 1924, but this was an isolated project promoted and financed by two individuals, and nothing more was built until the mid-1930s. The directors of one of the oldest voluntary housing societies outside London, the Oxford Cottage Improvement Society, noted in 1927 that they were unable to build, despite high demand in the area (Mole, 1987: 20). The directors of the Improved Tenements Association seriously considered winding up the company at the end of the war, so bad was the financial situation and so bleak was the outlook. No dividend was paid in 1920, but from 1922 onwards the Association showed renewed energy: new investment was actively solicited and by 1926 the stock of houses had grown from under 30 to 115 with continued growth thereafter.

Having emphasised how difficult it was for voluntary organisations to make much impact on the housing situation in the 1920s, it is important to note that in the second half of the decade a considerable number of new societies and associations were established. To understand why there was this wave of formations it may be relevant to recall that local authority housing during the period was in practice helping the rather better off among the working class (Bowley, 1945: 129), and that the lack of municipal action on slum clearance meant that the poor were effectively abandoned in ever worse conditions. In London there was a proliferation of new organisations, of which the St Pancras House Improvement Society (1925, now the St Pancras Housing Association) has been claimed as the first (Barclay, 1976: 17). This Society was one of several promoted by Father Basil Jellicoe, an Anglican priest working at Somers Town Mission in Camden. He toured the country addressing fund-raising meetings, and enlisting the assistance of a number of very wealthy people to serve as committee members (Barclay, 1976: 22). The St Pancras Society started by purchasing and improving rundown houses, but it was soon decided to concentrate on new building. Given the heavily built-up nature of central London, this meant acquiring and demolishing existing houses, which in turn meant the decanting of tenants from the old houses into new flats – a difficult and complex task for a small organisation lacking the powers and resources of the local authorities. However, the Society was able to undertake its first project of this kind in 1926, and to open its first new built flats in 1927 (Barclay, 1976: 26).

Following soon after the St Pancras Society came the Kensington Housing Trust, which, like the Improved Tenements Association, was the product of concern among wealthy residents of the Borough of Kensington for the plight of the poor of the area. The chairman of KHT was Lord Balfour of Burleigh, who was also a member of the Borough Council and went on to be a leading figure in the National Federation of Housing Societies. Kensington was unusual in that the Borough Council announced in 1925 that it did not intend to become a large scale landlord, and it displayed a more supportive approach towards voluntary providers than was generally the case elsewhere. Nevertheless, there were new organisations springing up in different parts of London.

In view of the way in which capital was raised mainly from individual investors, the new societies tended to grow quite slowly and to remain small. This meant that it was not possible to employ full-time staff, and the societies were very lean organisations by modern standards, unburdened by bureaucracy and overheads. The voluntary committee members were the heart of the organisation, acting on the one hand as fund raisers and providers of accommodation, and on the other hand as purchasers of professional services from a variety of private consultants. An important difference between organisations such as the St Pancras Society and the Improved Tenements Association and the charitable trusts was that the small societies bought in their housing management service from independent managers. The management of the Improved Tenements Association properties continued to be provided on a commission basis by former colleagues of Octavia Hill, and the Association had no offices or salaried staff until 1935.

The situation in London in the early 1930s was summed up by Quigley and Goldie (1934: 116), who reported that 5,993 public utility society houses had been provided in the capital between 1920 and 1931, although they do not say whether that figure included reconditioned houses. They also say, (p. 119):

> Most of the public utility societies are of quite recent growth and their record of houses built is, on the whole, meagre. Up to last year [1933] the Lambeth Society had housed 24 families; Bethnal Green 49; Chelsea 64; the Stepney Housing Trust 16; St Marylebone 79 and Wimbledon 2.

Meanwhile, in a number of towns and cities around the country groups of concerned people were also coming together to raise capital in order to tackle the worst housing problems; new organisations were set up in Newcastle upon Tyne, Birmingham, Southampton, Salford, Bristol, Exeter, Plymouth and Nottingham, as well as many other places. Evidence presented to the Moyne Committee in 1933 by the Town and Country Planning Association listed 106 societies across England and Wales and affiliated to the Association (*Town and County Planning*, March 1934: 47–9). Some of these organisations were pre-1914 copartnership societies, but the majority had been set up since the war, and mostly since 1925. In Birmingham, for example, in 1925 a conference was held which led to the formation of the Birmingham COPEC House Improvement Society (COPEC was taken from the initials of the Conference on Politics, Economics and Citizenship; the society is now part of Focus Housing Association). The objective was to acquire and improve decaying houses in the Birmingham's inner area, and by 1936 19 reconditioning schemes were prepared, embracing 355 dwellings (Fenter, 1960).

In Liverpool in 1928 people associated with the Personal Service Society formed Liverpool Improved Houses (later Merseyside Improved Houses and now Riverside Housing Association). The association concentrated on acquiring and renovating dilapidated old houses, starting with a group of fifteen in Edge Hill (MIH, 1988: 8), but over the next few years growth remained slow, reaching only 120 dwellings by 1936, although by then it also managed an estate of over 600 properties for Lord Salisbury (NFHS *Bulletin* No. 1, April 1936). Small-scale was the defining characteristic of the voluntary housing organisations set up after the war: of 169 organisations surveyed in 1936, the average number of dwellings was 94, and the largest had 930 (NFHS, *Bulletin* No. 1, April 1936).

Conclusion

The story of voluntary housing organisations in this period is one of growing diversity, frustrated ambition and raised expectations. On the issue of diversity, the old model dwellings companies and large charitable trusts appeared to have ground virtually to a halt, and were being overtaken by newer, more energetic organisations. These new societies saw themselves as different from the pre-1914 organisations, being more inclined to the Octavia Hill approach, committed to small-scale activity, mostly involving reconditioning of rundown old houses. But in terms of how they were financed, by individual investors buying shares and loan stock, they were actually very similar to the old model dwellings companies. The copartnership societies and employer sponsored public utility societies represented a quite different approach, targeting a different section of the population.

On the point about frustrated ambition, the questions to be asked concern why the promise of the pre-1914 period was not fulfilled afterwards, and why was there so little new building by voluntary housing organisations in the period 1919–33? Different answers apply to different groups of providers, although all were affected by high prices and interest rates during the early postwar years. In the case of the old model dwellings providers there is doubt about how far they still had unfulfilled ambitions. They were saddled with ageing and unpopular housing stocks that required repair and modernisation, but were subject to rent control. Diversification may have been a theoretical possibility, but Emsley (1986: 43) refers to the 'extreme financial conservatism' of the trusts, and the evidence referred to above confirms that the Guinness trustees were still trying in 1920 to build associated tenements when public demand was for cottages. In the case of the copartnership societies, it may be inferred that a reason for their lack of progress after 1918 lay in the fact that the local authorities, with better access to capital, had usurped their role of building garden-suburb-type housing for precisely the better-off workers that they had previously served. As Daunton (1987: 52) has put it: 'The aesthetic of the garden city movement survived, but not the institutional form'.

The most dynamic group of organisations in the period was the Octavia Hill societies, and here it is important to remember that the Octavia Hill system was essentially qualitative rather than quantitative. The emphasis was on middle-class outreach to the poor, rather than on the creation of large organisations for housing provision. The proliferation of small organisations committed to the Octavia Hill system reflects the nature of the social project involved. In the context of a state housing policy which emphasised large-scale house building for the relatively better-off within the working class, there was plenty of scope for well-meaning middle-class people to form societies to reach the poor left behind in the slums.

The final point concerns the idea of raised expectations. As has been mentioned above, by the end of the 1920s there was agreement that something had to be done about the huge amounts of unfit and nearly unfit housing in Britain's cities. Garside (1995: 97) argues that, 'Local authorities it appears did not relish the task nor were they well fitted for it'. Redeveloping the slums was a quite different, and more difficult activity than building suburban estates for well-off skilled workers. Slums were conceived as having social as well as economic causes, and therefore remedial action required more than physical redevelopment. In any case, the scale of the problem meant that there were strong arguments for a reconditioning strategy alongside clearance. And in this context the voluntary organisations, especially the Octavia Hill societies, were recognised as having a role to play. Thus it was that in March 1933 the Minister of Health appointed a departmental committee under the chairmanship of Lord Moyne, with the task of looking at the potential of 'public utility societies or other similarly constituted bodies' in relation to overcrowded and rundown houses that were not yet suitable for clearance.

PART II

5

An Unequal Struggle, 1933–39

Introduction

The previous chapter finished with the appointment of the Moyne Committee in March 1933, an event which appeared to portend a much expanded role for voluntary housing organisations in pursuit of the government's policy objectives. However, over the next two years there ensued a lively debate between the advocates of non-municipal and technocratic approaches and the defenders of local authorities as key actors in housing provision. Although its significance is barely recognised in the literature, this was in fact a crucial period in the development of housing policy in Britain, for although it helped to bring the various strands of voluntary housing together and led to the creation of a national federation, it also marked a defeat for voluntary housing and a triumph for local government.

Before looking in detail at the Moyne Committee and its report it is necessary to sketch in a little of the wider context of the time. The economy was suffering from the Depression, which had brought down the Labour government in 1931, precipitating a period of so-called National Government, with a Conservative majority and a Labour prime minister (Clarke, 1996: 174–81). The worst effects of the Depression were felt in the regions such as South Wales, Yorkshire, the north-east of England and central Scotland, which depended most heavily on coal mining and heavy engineering. In these areas male unemployment reached unprecedented levels, and the overall rate peaked at more than 20 per cent of the insured workforce in the early part of 1933 (Hobsbawm, 1994: 92; see also, Ward, 1988).

The appointment of the Moyne Committee has to be seen in the context of the retrenchment policies adopted by the government in the wake of the economic crisis. Public expenditure on housing came under renewed scrutiny, and the Committee on Local Expenditure (comprised of local authority representatives) concluded that, 'the time has come when the normal provision of working-class houses (by whomsoever undertaken) shall cease to be a charge on the public purse' (Local Expenditure, 1932: 68). The Committee's principal recommendation on housing was that the 1924 Act subsidy for general needs provision should be abolished. There then ensued what Merrett (1979: 55) has called a stunning switch in housing policy, with the result that local authorities were effectively removed from general needs building while being required to produce new five-year plans to remove slums remaining in their areas. The stated intention was that all slums would be removed by 1938, although this was based on a hopelessly inadequate understanding of the scale of the problem. There was also the question of what was to be done about the huge numbers of ageing and rundown houses that would inevitably remain outside the clearance programme.

The decision to appoint the Moyne Committee was a response to critical public debate about the inadequacies of government housing policy. Sir Raymond Unwin, for example, called for support for public utility societies operating in that part of the housing market between the slums and the types of houses that could be produced by private enterprise. This was followed by a series of articles in the *New Statesman and Nation* (28 January–25 February 1933) by leading public figures criticising the government's approach and advocating the creation of a national housing board or corporation. Unwin argued that it was necessary to set up an agency to work with and alongside local authorities in tackling both slum clearance and reconditioning. He favoured a National Housing Board working with a series of local public utility societies. He also proposed that the government should provide a guarantee for the capital borrowed by the board, in order to ensure low rates of interest. Criticism of the government's policy was intense, with influential support for a national housing board and an expanded role for public utility societies. Appointing a committee to inquire into the possibilities was a conventional way of deflecting criticism – it was a positive response which nonetheless allowed the Ministry of Health to concentrate on its priority of progressing the Housing Bill through parliament. This decision was welcomed by *The Times* (9 February 1933):

> The idea of a corporation financed by investors with or without some form of guarantee... is so attractive that an immediate answer is required to the question whether it is practicable.

The Moyne Committee: taking housing out of politics?

The Departmental Committee on Housing under the chairmanship of Lord Moyne has been very widely ignored by housing scholars. Only Garside (1995) seems to have paid any attention to it, and most established accounts of the development of housing policy in Britain fail to mention it at all. The lack of attention given to the Committee is unfortunate, because although its report did not lead to major changes in housing policy, it was nonetheless significant as a key element in a prolonged and lively public debate about the relative merits of elected local authorities or non-elected specialist organisations at central and local levels. At one level this can be seen in terms of a struggle between the defenders of democratic accountability and the advocates of a more technocratic model of policy implementation.

The Moyne Committee deserves attention because of its exploration of potentially radically different approaches to housing, and because of the ultimate rejection of those ideas. The importance of the report of the Committee is that it precipitated a struggle which effectively marked the triumph of the local authorities as the main providers of new rented housing for the working class, with the result that the voluntary organisations remained on the margins of housing policy for the next forty years.

The Committee consisted of nine MPs, plus Lord Moyne, who had recently been elevated to the Lords after more than twenty years as a Tory MP. Moyne was undoubtedly a figure of some political standing, with ministerial experience; a vastly wealthy member of the Guinness family, Moyne was also a trustee of the Guinness Trust, and so he had some knowledge of voluntary housing. The Committee's terms of reference were:

> To consider and report: (a) What, if any, further steps are necessary or desirable to secure the maintenance of a proper standard of fitness for human habitation in working-class houses which are neither situate in an area suitable for clearance under Part I of the Housing Act 1930, nor suitable for demolition under Section 19 of that Act; and (b) What, if any, further steps are necessary or desirable to promote the supply of houses for the working classes, without public charge, through the agency of public utility societies or similar bodies subject to similar limitations operating in particular areas or otherwise.

The first part of the terms of reference dealt with the work of societies in reconditioning, while the second part dealt with new building. The Committee interpreted its brief to exclude consideration of slum clearance. In addressing its task the Committee heard evidence from 'a roll call of those with an interest in the housing questions of the day' (Garside, 1995: 100). Included among those who gave evidence were Unwin, Sir Edgar Bonham Carter (of First Garden City Ltd and Howard Cottage Society, Letchworth), Reginald Rowe (on behalf of the Improved Tenements Association) and Lord Balfour of Burleigh (Kensington Housing Trust). Unwin submitted proposals for a national housing board, and similar ideas were put forward by Lord Eustace Percy and two liberal MPs, J Rees and R Nicholson. The Town and Country Planning Association submitted evidence and made recommendations, including support for a national Housing Finance Board, which would be charged with promoting and lending to public utility societies; unlike the long-established Public Works Loans Board, the Housing Finance Board would consist of people with a special knowledge of housing, and it would have a more positive, promotional role. The Association's evidence concluded with the following statement which effectively summarised the sentiments of the pro-society lobby:

> There are many advantages in encouraging Public Utility Societies. They are free from local political influences, they enlist the help and support of people of all classes and all opinions who are interested in housing, and represent the only unofficial channel through which can be directed the large amount of goodwill which is prevalent in the interests of slum clearance and re-housing work. (*Town and Country Planning*, May 1933)

The Committee's Report (Ministry of Health, 1933), which was published in August, indicating a certain sense of urgency, discussed the various proposals put forward and made a total of 32 recommendations. All but one of these recommendations related to part (a) of the terms of reference, and the only recommendation under part (b) was rejection of proposals for a national housing board. The Committee took the view that if its recommendations under part (a) were implemented then the need for action under part (b) would be greatly reduced.

With slum clearance ruled out of consideration by the terms of reference the Committee concentrated on the question of reconditioning and on ways of enhancing the role of public utility societies in this work. The basis of this approach was that where private landlords neglected their responsibilities it was necessary to take action, but that the local authorities were not best suited to, nor interested in, taking on the management of scattered properties in working-class areas. The recommendation, therefore, was that local authorities should have compulsory powers to acquire working-class houses in need of reconditioning and which could be given a life of at least twenty years, but that as a rule such houses were to be acquired on behalf of PUSs which would carry out the necessary work and manage them along Octavia Hill lines. Where societies did not already exist local people should be encouraged to form them, and where this proved impossible then the local authority would be expected to appoint Housing Management Commissioners; only in exceptional circumstances would local authorities themselves take on the work of reconditioning and managing property. Local authorities were to be encouraged to make use of the proposed powers of compulsory purchase for reconditioning, and where they declined to do so, or showed undue delay, then the Moyne Committee proposed that PUSs whose activities were being frustrated should have a right of appeal to the Minister, who could vest in such societies the compulsory purchase powers of a local authority.

It was recognised that many of the houses in need of reconditioning would be overcrowded, the Committee accepted that there would be a need for a certain amount of new building to rehouse existing occupants, and it was proposed that there should be a subsidy available to PUSs for the relief of overcrowding, but that reconditioning work should not be subsidised. However, evidence put to the Committee by people such as Reginald Rowe emphasised the difficulties faced by societies in raising the necessary capital for the acquisition and improvement of rundown houses. Rowe outlined a typical scenario for the Committee:

> The housing society, faced with the need of a loan of £50,000, on which the utmost it can pay is 3 per cent (if it is to house the poorest), meets with the following experience. After much propaganda it arranges a big meeting with... the Minister of Health, and an ex-Prime Minister, or others equally eminent, among the speakers. By this means, and with the aid of further propaganda, it raises £20,000 at 3 per cent in a year. Then, as subscribers complain that nothing is being done and hint at the return of their money, the Society takes a plunge and during the next year (in which, with luck, it raises a further £10,000) builds the 80 flats. It is thus left with a debt of £20,000, which it finances somehow, but at a greater cost than 3 per cent, so that the rents have finally to be put above the average of, say, 4s. per room, including rates, originally aimed at. This is not an exaggerated case but about normal. (Ministry of Health, 1933: 28–9)

Responding to this type of evidence the Committee recommended that approved societies should be given access to loans of up to 100 per cent of the cost of acquisition and improvement, provided that the full cost of loan repayments could be met from rental income. Where this was not the case, or where societies wished to provide additional facilities then they would be responsible for raising the balance of the capital required.

In order to ensure both an adequate supply of capital and that it was directed only to properly constituted and competent societies the Committee made two key recommendations. First, there was to be a Central Financing Authority, the powers of which were to be vested directly in the Minister of Health rather than the PWLB, and second there was to be a Central Public Utility Council, which would be responsible for approving both societies and their individual projects. In terms not dissimilar to the way that the Housing Corporation over- sees housing associations today, the Committee explained that:

> Assistance will only be given to Societies approved by the Minister on the recom- mendations of the Central Council, who before making any such recommendation will pay special attention to the qualifications of the managing personnel, and will satisfy themselves not only that the Society has been formed with the single purpose of service, but that the managing committee includes persons able to carry out our proposals with businesslike efficiency. (Ministry of Health, 1933: 34)

Recognising the lack of experience of societies, the Committee attached special importance to the role of the Central Public Utility Council. In terms of its constitution, composition and role this was to be a body which prefigured the Housing Corporation, which was not actu- ally set up for another thirty years: it was to consist of not more than five people, who would be appointed by the Minister of Health, and paid on a part-time basis. The principal functions of the Council were to be to stimulate the formation of new societies and to supervise their activities, advising the Minister on funding applications. It was also to advise on best practice in relation to reconditioning and housing management. The Committee suggested that the Council might consider the promotion of what it called a non-statutory housing associ- ation for the purposes of propaganda and as a forum for municipal and voluntary workers interested in housing. It proposed that the Minister should be empowered to make a small grant to such an organisation.

The proposal for a Central Public Utility Council has to be seen alongside the Committee's rejection of suggestions for a National Housing Board. The role of the Council was restricted to facilitating the activities of PUSs, whereas the various proposals for a National Board went much further, implying a direct role in house building and the partial or complete replacement of the local authority role in housing provision. The standing of the supporters of the National Board was such that the Committee took the matter very seriously, devoting six pages of their report to explaining their reasons for rejecting the idea. The private builders' representatives advised the Committee that competition from the board would effectively prevent them from re-entering the field of working-class housing. The Committee observed that the government had only recently adopted a policy of encouraging private enterprise back into building for the working class, and it was too soon to consider such a radical alternative: 'We decline to play the part of undertaker at a premature burial' (Ministry of Health, 1933: 47). Additionally, it was clear that the leaders of the local authorities were not at all keen on the proposed National Board, and in a gesture of support the Committee said that, 'if private enterprise should fail, we are not satisfied on the evidence which has been brought to us that the appropriate remedy would not be found in the provision of unsub-sidised houses by the local authorities, whose skilled staffs and organi-sations are actually in being' (Ministry of Health, 1933: 47).

The Committee's report received a generally favourable response both in parliament and in the country at large (Garside, 1995: 110). However, the view within the Ministry of Health was rather different:

> The Minister said that the provisional conclusions which he had formulated upon the report of the Moyne Committee, were that in legislation implementing the report the first object of policy should be to strengthen the hands of local authori-ties by increasing their powers to deal with reconditioning... The practical value of the Committee's recommendations relating to the Public Utility Societies seemed to him to be more doubtful, but he thought it would be essential to deal with Public Utility Societies in the Bill. There were one or two aspects of the Committee's recommendations which seemed to him to be open to serious objec-tion. In the first place, he did not think it would be possible to enable the Public Utility Societies, aided by the Minister, to take administration out of the hands of the local authorities willy-nilly. This would mean setting up rival authorities, a proposal which could not be contemplated... (PRO, HLG 29/213)

In this stance Sir Hilton Young was warmly supported by Sir Arthur Robinson, his top civil service adviser, who welcomed the Minister's willingness to depart from the Moyne Committee's recommendations, and was disparaging about the housing societies:

> He felt strongly that the contribution which Public Utility Societies could make to the housing problem was a very small one. They might achieve something in London, but ten years of experience showed that they were bodies neither effi-cient nor easy to deal with, as their members were not normally men of affairs. He considered, therefore, that they had only a very small contribution to offer at the price of much inconvenience. (PRO, HLG 29/213)

The tone was thus set for the prolonged process of negotiation which led from the Moyne Report of August 1933 to the Housing Act 1935. Moyne's recommendation that societies should be given, in certain circumstances, powers to compel owners of property in need of reconditioning to sell to them was rejected from the outset, partly on the grounds that the societies were not capable of carrying out the work on the scale required, and partly because to empower them in this way would 'anger and discourage the local authorities'. Nevertheless, most of the rest of the Committee's proposals seemed, at first, to be accepted. The Minister felt it would be impossible to avoid setting up a Central Public Utility Council, and it was accepted that a central funding body should be established.

However, as negotiations on a draft Bill proceeded the local authorities made clear their strong reservations about an expanded role for PUSs and their firm opposition to any suggestion that they be compelled to establish local housing management commissions (equivalent to stock transfer associations or local housing companies today – see Chapter 12). Meanwhile, the supporters of a National Housing Commission had not given up their campaign, and a somewhat pretentiously titled document, 'A National Housing Policy' was published by the self-styled National Housing Committee (1934). This committee included among its membership Sir Raymond Unwin, Lord Balfour of Burleigh, Seebohm Rowntree and Sir Edgar Bonham Carter. While accepting much of the Moyne Report's emphasis on reconditioning the Committee emphasised the need to build a million new houses at low rents over the coming ten years, and argued that speculative builders could not be relied on to build for lower paid workers. They favoured a planned approach in which the Housing Commission would assess need and co-ordinate construction work, in collaboration with the local authorities and PUSs. Underlying the proposal was the notion that housing should be freed from the vicissitudes of politics at both central local government levels, a view that was most unlikely to find much support among elected representatives.

'The local authorities strenuously defended their position, forming alliances not only with private landlords but also appealing to the self-interest of civil servants. It proved to be an overwhelming combination of forces' (Garside, 1995: 108). Having conceded from the start that PUSs would not be put in a position to override the wishes of local authorities, the Ministry of Health proceeded to retreat further from the Moyne Report, in terms of both its detailed recommendations and its overall emphasis on reconditioning. The focus on PUSs faded, and as it did so attention moved away from reconditioning to the related but distinct questions of overcrowding and the redevelopment of old, congested inner urban areas. The Moyne Committee had recognised that there was a responsibility to reduce overcrowding in houses acquired for reconditioning, and that this implied a certain amount of new building. The Committee recommended the introduction of a new subsidy, specifically for houses and flats built to relieve overcrowding, and overcrowding subsequently became the main target of the Housing Bill. Reconditioning was to remain an unsubsidised activity, in line with the terms of reference given to the Moyne Committee.

Before leaving the Moyne Committee it is appropriate to return to the question posed at the start of this section: was it about taking housing out of politics? While at one level it is impossible to take housing out of politics, it is clearly possible to vary the degree of direct involvement of democratically elected bodies such as local authorities. There are various ways of looking at what was going on the mid-1930s. The softest interpretation would be to say that advocacy of PUSs was a pragmatic response to the fact that the government had effectively confined local authorities to slum clearance activity. In the absence of subsidy for reconditioning, the limited profit PUSs represented the only realistic way forward in relation to the huge problem of how to improve existing working-class housing.

A rather stronger interpretation would be that for some people the promotion of PUSs was in conscious preference to the involvement of local authorities, and it is worth remembering the politics of the situation; on the one hand there was a strongly paternalistic, top-down, thread running through many of the housing organisations inspired by the memory of Octavia Hill. To the extent that they identified with political parties at all, the people running organisations such as the Improved Tenements Association and the Kensington Housing Trust in the 1930s were Conservatives. On the other hand, the Labour Party was a growing power in local government in many major cities, especially London (Garside, 1995), and tended to be seen as 'introducing politics'. Taking housing out of politics meant, therefore, handing it over to organisations controlled by middle- and upper-class Tories.

A third interpretation would be that for some people the notion of taking housing out of politics was primarily about improving technical efficiency. For this group it was important to take responsibility for housing policy action away from the Ministry of Health as well as out of the hands of the local authorities. In this context it is worth recalling

Bowley's criticisms of the performance on both central and local government between the wars:

> the local authorities have been given powers which they are only partially willing to exercise, and duties many of which they are in fact unwilling to perform. In the absence of any effective central control, the local authorities can flout policies approved by Parliament, and the local councils can, and do, in practice, relegislate as to the extent to which they will carry out, or accept, a national policy

> There is no doubt that the organisation of the provision of working-class houses through the local authorities has not been satisfactory. Although there has in practice been little attempt to control their activities, there is no evidence at all that the Ministry of Health would be competent to do so. (Bowley, 1945: 258)

The Housing Act 1935

Introducing the second reading debate on the Housing Bill in January 1935, Sir Hilton Young presented it as an attack on overcrowding. He said that the reconditioning proposals were based on the Moyne Report, but that it was clear that town centre redevelopment had to be handled by the elected local authorities. He went on to say that, '…what we are contemplating is nothing less than the reconstruction, to a large extent, of the bad old cores of the inner areas of our great towns' (*House of Commons Debates*, vol. 297, col. 368, 30 January 1935). The Minister said little about the role of housing societies, but he was careful to praise their achievements and to explain that the government was proceeding on the basis of encouraging co-operation between them and the local authorities. He acknowledged that it was in reconditioning that some of the most useful and characteristic work of the societies had been done, but he did not want to limit them to this area in future. Despite the retreat from Moyne over the previous eighteen months, he presented the Bill as 'a kind of charter' for the voluntary sector.

Responding from the Labour benches Arthur Greenwood (a former Minister of Health) said, among other things, that his party took 'very considerable exception' to the proposals inviting local authorities to farm out their housing responsibilities to housing associations, and to hand over their own estates to housing management commissions. He attacked the notion that such moves would take housing out of politics; on the contrary, he saw it as handing over responsibility to organisations dominated by Tory views, and it is important to recognise that much of Labour's opposition to housing associations both then and later was based on this perception.

The official version of the role of housing societies in the new housing policy was that,

> The new Bill is designed to provide opportunity for a considerable increase in the scope of the operations of these bodies. It includes provision enabling Local Authorities to enter into arrangements with Associations (1) to provide rehousing for persons displaced by slum clearance action, (2) to provide rehousing for persons displaced by the abatement of overcrowding, (3) to carry out the whole or part of the work involved in the redevelopment of a congested area, and (4) to undertake the reconditioning and management of houses bought by the Local Authority for that purpose. (Ministry of Health, 1935: 102)

To assist them in their work voluntary housing organisations were entitled to receive the overcrowding subsidies on the same terms as the local authorities, except that any rate fund contribution was to be at the discretion of the authorities. Evidence put to the Moyne Committee had emphasised the difficulty that societies faced in raising the capital to undertake building and reconditioning work, and the Act restated the power of local authorities to make loans to societies and to subscribe to their share capital. It also increased the proportion of costs that could be borrowed from the PWLB. The board could lend up to 75 per cent of the value of houses to be built, and, where the local authority guaranteed loan repayments, up to 90 per cent. However, the Act did not introduce the central funding authority, vested in the Minister of Health, as proposed by Moyne.

The Act made two further provisions relating specifically to the voluntary sector. It introduced the generic term housing association to apply to a range of societies, companies and trusts providing rented housing on a non-profit basis, or which undertook to restrict dividends offered to shareholders to a limit set by the Treasury. However, the Act did not set up the central public utility council envisaged by Moyne; instead it established a Central Housing Advisory Committee (CHAC), with a brief to advise the Minister on a range of matters, including local authority housing.

Overall, then, the outcome of the Moyne Committee in terms of changes in policy was much less than had appeared likely in the spring and summer of 1933. The debate on the Moyne proposals led to a consolidation of the entrenched position of the local authorities, and a defeat for the housing societies, which were left in a position where the positive-sounding statements coming from the government were tempered by the fact that although local authorities were encouraged to co-operate with the voluntary sector, there was no real pressure on them to do so. The subordinate position of housing associations was summed up in a report published by the CHAC in 1939:

> It is left to the discretion of each individual local authority to decide whether or not the co-operation of any housing association operating in their area should be sought. Moreover, the statutory power to initiate schemes of slum clearance and for abating overcrowding rests solely with the local authorities. They are the only bodies who, by their right to make clearance or compulsory purchase orders and submit them to the Minister for confirmation, are able to set in motion the large scale operations with effective powers for demolishing the old houses and removing the tenants; they are the only bodies empowered to acquire rehousing sites by compulsory purchase; they are the only bodies who can make available to housing associations any Exchequer contributions payable in respect of the provision of houses eligible for such contributions. So that housing associations are dependent upon the goodwill of local authorities in the fulfilment of the functions which the legislature has seen fit to entrust to them. Quite clearly, therefore, housing associations can only function if they and the local authorities work together in a friendly spirit of mutual help. (Ministry of Health, 1939: 5)

While most of the Moyne Committee's proposals were accepted in principle, and several were implemented via the Housing Act 1935, the combined effect of local authority defence of their primary role in the delivery of housing policy and civil service scepticism as to the capacity of housing societies meant that key proposals were rejected. The rejection of the power for societies to take action on poor quality housing where the local authority declined to do so, and the decision to set up neither a central public utility society council nor a central funding authority marginalised the voluntary organisations, leaving them heavily dependent on the discretionary co-operation of the elected local authorities. Eligibility for subsidy, for example, was made subject to associations agreeing to enter into an agreement (later referred to as 'authorised arrangements') with the local authority (Section 94 of the Housing Act 1936). The provisions of the Housing Act 1935, demonstrated that the local authorities had effectively seen off any challenge to their position posed by the societies. However, the Act did implement the Moyne Committee's proposal that the Minister should have power to make an annual grant (of £1,000 for five years) to support the work of a representative body of housing associations, should such a body be brought into existence.

The formation of the National Federation of Housing Societies

Reference has been made in Chapter 4 to the growth in the number of housing societies from the mid-1920s, with most of the action being concentrated in inner-city areas which had been effectively ignored by postwar housing policy, and whose inhabitants had not benefited from the growing supply of new council houses. The great majority of these societies were very small and survived on meagre funds. Although there was contact among them at a personal level there was no central co-ordinating body, and therefore they lacked the power and influence that they might have been able to exert by collective action. This was undoubtedly partly a reflection of the diversity of aims and objectives of the different types of organisations. It must be remembered that there were important distinctions between the copartnership societies, which generally provided for the rather better off within the working class (and sometimes for people who could not be regarded as working class at all), and the inner-city societies such as the Improved Tenements Association whose tenants were drawn from among the poorest. In this situation the Garden Cities and Town Planning Association, which had a long association with the copartnership societies, acted as the national mouthpiece of voluntary housing in general until the mid-1930s (Hardy, 1991: 203). In the absence of any other central representative body it was the Association which organised a national conference on PUSs in February 1932, at which both the co-operative and philan-thropic societies were represented (*Garden Cities and Town Planning*, April–May 1932: 75–9). In September 1934 the Association staged a second national conference on PUSs, at which proposals for a National Federation were outlined and approved unanimously (*Town and Country Planning*, March 1935: 45).

Discussions about the formation of a National Federation proceeded in parallel with the legislation enabling the Minister to provide grant aid to such a body. In the spring of 1935 four regional conferences were held to garner support, and the National Federation of Housing Societies (NFHS) was formally incorporated on 22 June 1935. The Federation aimed to carry on the sort of work that had been done at the GC & TPA, namely to help existing societies with advice on schemes and raising capital, and stimulating the formation of new societies. It was also envisaged from the outset that the Federation would have a lobbying role in relation to central government. At the GC & TCPA this work had been largely carried out by Alfred Pike, who became the first Secretary of the National Federation. At first the GC & TCPA and the NFHS occupied offices at the same central London address (Hardy, 1991: 205).

The Federation was run by an elected council of sixteen members, plus the chairman (Sir Reginald Rowe). Societies from across England, Wales and Scotland were represented on the council. Some 75 societies joined the new Federation on its formation (*NFHS Annual Report*, 1964), but within a year membership had risen to 92 out of an estimated 226 active societies (*NFHS Bulletin*, No. 1, April 1936). There are several interesting features of the composition of the societies that joined the NFHS in its first year. First, the list of names is quite unfamiliar to the modern observer; only about a third of the 92 organisations listed as members in 1936 are readily identifiable from the National Housing Federation *Directory of Membership 1997*, although mergers and name changes make it difficult to make confident statements about lack of continuity. Nevertheless, some of today's well-known associations were founder members, including Swaythling HS, Cambridge HS, St Pancras House Improvement Society (now St Pancras HA) and Kensington Housing Trust, although very few have become large players: only three original members (COPEC (now part of Focus HA), Liverpool Improved Houses (now Riverside HA) and Church Army HA)) were represented among the largest fifty associations in the late 1990s. The average size of the 170 societies surveyed by the Federation in 1936 was just 93 dwellings, and the largest single society (the Great Western (London) Garden Village Society) had 930 dwellings. Further interesting aspects of the composition of the original membership were, first, that only about a dozen seem to have been garden village societies, and only three copartnership societies joined at the start (Birchall, 1995: 337–9).

Even more noticeable by their absence were the long-established almshouse trusts and the model dwellings companies and trusts. Although it is known that the model dwellings companies such as the Society for Improving the Condition of the Labouring Classes and the Artisans, Labourers and General Dwellings Company were still building in the mid-1930s, and the Improved Industrial Dwellings Company continued to manage its several thousand dwellings, neither these nor any of the thirty Victorian companies listed by Wohl (1977: 360–1) joined the Federation before the start of the Second World War (and the great majority never joined). An exception was the Four Per Cent Industrial Dwellings Company, which became the Industrial Dwellings Society (1885) Ltd, and joined the National Federation in 1951. Notably absent from the Federation in its early days were the four great pre-1914 housing trusts endowed by Peabody, Guinness, Sutton and Lewis, although they were all actively building in the 1930s.

Explaining the absence of these organisations requires speculation, for there is very little hard evidence to suggest either that they were deliberately excluded by the Federation, or that they refused to join. It is possible that the old model dwellings companies saw themselves as having nothing much in common with the organisations making up the majority of the new Federation, and it is important to remember that although the Federation *subsequently* became the main voice of a growing voluntary housing sector, at the time of its formation the societies had just been dealt a severe blow to their aspirations by the government's decision not to implement key recommendations in the Moyne Report. Thus, what later became the mainstream of the 'housing association movement' was not readily identifiable in such terms in the mid-1930s. For their part, the members of the Federation may well have taken the view that they did not want to be associated with the model dwellings companies. As has been discussed in Chapter three, the garden city movement was at least partly inspired by opposition to the kind of high density urban form exemplified by the blocks built by the model dwellings companies. And the wider unpopularity of the dwellings provided by the companies and trusts may be seen as grounds for the members of the Federation wishing to keep their distance. If the block dwellings and associated tenements were unpopular before 1914, by the mid-1930s expectations had risen to an extent which only intensified the perceived inadequacies of this sort of accommodation. While tenants in the old block dwellings continued to share basic facilities and relied on gas lighting into the 1930s (and in some case beyond), post-1919 council houses had their own baths, WCs and electricity.

The Federation sought to establish itself by organising events for members, and by publishing a quarterly bulletin, which first appeared in April 1936. It also lobbied the government on issues including the difficulties encountered by associations in negotiating loans from the PWLB and the case for providing subsidy for reconditioning. Despite bombarding the Ministry with letters on the latter point, the Federation was unable to break down government resistance (PRO, HLG 52/810 and HLG 37/16).

Housing associations in the late 1930s

Speculative house builders enjoyed boom conditions during the five-year period 1934–38, when output exceeded 250,000 dwellings per annum. Local authority production also rose, and by 1939 completions stood at over 121,000, more than double the total for 1935 (Merrett, 1979: 320). As mentioned above, there are no reliable aggregate statistics for housing associations before the Second World War, but compared with the level of activity in the speculative and municipal sectors their achievements were numerically insignificant. However, the generally favourable market conditions encouraged individual associations to undertake new building; at Letchworth, for example, the Howard Cottage Society, which had built virtually nothing for nearly twenty years, raised sufficient capital to start building again, and completed 281 houses by 1938. The Guinness Trust completed two large schemes in London during the 1930s, including the 398 dwelling estate at Loughborough Park, Brixton, in 1938. Neither of these organisations built with subsidy or rate-fund contributions at this time. However, a number of housing associations began to forge agreements with local authorities to co-operate in slum clearance activity and the relief of overcrowding. It can be assumed that under such deals Exchequer subsidy was provided, but it is less clear whether local authorities made rate-fund contributions equivalent to those that would have been required for council houses; the LCC, for example, routinely provided a rate-fund contribution of only half the amount due for council houses (PRO, HLG 52/810). In London as a whole by 1938 34 associations had agreements with 40 local authorities to produce 7,697 houses (Ministry of Health, 1938: 104). Among individual local authorities, Kensington was the most supportive of voluntary organisations, notably in the form of a large scheme involving both the Peabody Trust and the Sutton Dwellings Trust. Reference has been made earlier to the activities of societies promoted by the Welsh Town Planning and Housing Trust, but in Scotland the development of housing associations was slower; when the NFHS held a conference in Edinburgh in June 1937, only six societies were represented. A Scottish contributor to the *NFHS Bulletin* (July 1937) complained that while the councils in Edinburgh and Aberdeen were co-operative, Glasgow and Dundee councils refused to facilitate the work of housing societies.

It is not clear from available sources whether these figures included the activities of the North Eastern Housing Association (NEHA, now Home HA), which had agreements with 20 local authorities to build over 7,000 houses. The NEHA deserves a special reference, because of both the scale of its building programme and the peculiar circumstances surrounding its creation in 1935. The north-east of England, specifically the industrialised parts of Durham and Northumberland, had inherited from the nineteenth century a severe housing problem, with high levels of overcrowding. The area was very badly affected by the Depression of the early 1930s, leading to heavy rates burdens on domestic ratepayers. There was thus a situation in which there was an acute need to build large numbers of houses, in areas where the local authorities could ill-afford the additional cost to the rates. In 1934 the government passed the Special Areas Act, which established commissioners for the areas worst affected by unemployment and industrial decline. The commissioners were given powers to provide financial support for certain types of expenditure, but not including assistance to local authorities to build houses. A solution was found by setting up a housing association, the NEHA, which would be entitled to housing subsidies just like any other association, and which the commissioner would be able to assist. The arrangement was that the equivalent of the rate fund contribution would be paid from the budget of the commissioner for the north-east special area.

The story behind the creation of the NEHA provides a fascinating insight into aspects of housing policy including the hostility of local authorities to any perceived threat to their position, and the Ministry's attitude to both local authorities and housing associations (Malpass and Jones, 1995, 1996). It is clear from evidence in the Public Record Office (PRO, HLG 30/50) that the Ministry of Health initially hoped, and tried, to keep housing off the agenda of the commissioners for special areas, but that the situation in County Durham in particular was so bad that this proved to be impossible. Nevertheless, the Ministry was able to withstand demands that the new Housing Bill (which became the Housing Act 1935) should make special provision for the circumstances of depressed areas to enable local authorities to build in quantity. Within the Ministry the view was expressed that if large numbers of houses were to be built then

> it would be necessary to consider the carrying out of the work directly by the State as past experience shows that unless they have some direct financial interest local authorities are not likely to operate efficiently or economically. Direct State action would, however, give rise to the difficulties which have led the Minister in recent months to resist the suggestion for a National Housing Board. (PRO, HLG 30/50, paper dated August 1934)

Figure 5.1 Deckham Hall estate, Gateshead, under construction in 1937. The estate was started by Gateshead Borough Council but taken over and finished by the North Eastern Housing Association

The intention to set up an association was made public by the Minister of Health in March 1935, but it was not until November that the NEHA was properly constituted. In the meantime it was necessary to secure the co-operation of the Ministry of Labour and the Treasury, to agree an appropriate legal basis for the organisation, to prepare the ground with the local authorities and to find people willing to serve on the board of directors. On the constitution of the association, it was registered under the Companies Act 1929, not as an Industrial and Provident Society. This meant that the NEHA differed from other associations in that it had only seven shareholders (the members of the board) and it did not depend on raising capital from individual shareholders or investors. This was an advantage in financial terms, but it also meant that in the case of this association the local authorities were neither encouraged nor permitted to subscribe to the share capital of the association, and therefore they could not exercise the normal powers of shareholders over the membership of the board and the policies that were adopted. In a situation where the local authorities were known to be generally hostile to the principle of a housing association taking over their role this was clearly an important structural point.

The local authorities carried on a sustained campaign of opposition to the NEHA, accusing it of being set up in order to usurp their housing powers. There is some force to this argument, and the association was effectively run as an outpost of the Ministry of Health. However, the local authorities were in a difficult position: they opposed the principle of the association, but nevertheless it offered them the only realistic way of getting substantial numbers of houses built at no cost to the ratepayers. Moreover, the association was pledged only to build in areas where it was invited by the local authority, so those councils who remained implacably opposed were not forced to compromise their principles. Some authorities, such as Newcastle, refused to co-operate with the association (this was a position maintained by Newcastle until 1974), while others, such as Gateshead, co-operated from the start (Figure 5.1).

It has been argued (Malpass and Jones, 1996a) that the NEHA can be seen as an experiment by the Ministry of Health, which was generally dissatisfied with the performance of local authorities and sceptical of the capacity of existing voluntary housing societies. In the context of debate about how affordable rented housing should be provided, including the idea of a national housing board, it is not unreasonable to speculate that from the point of view of the Ministry the creation of the NEHA represented an opportunity to explore the potential for the development of organisations that would be independent of the local authorities and more effective than the generally small-scale housing societies of that period.

In 1937 the Ministry of Health in Scotland set up the Scottish Special Housing Association (SSHA), on lines very similar to those of the NEHA (Begg, 1996: 43). Like the NEHA, the SSHA was registered under the Companies Act 1929, it had no share capital, and no membership beyond the nine appointed members of the Council of Management. It was set up by the Commissioner for Special Areas in Scotland to build 5,000 houses in the Special Areas (its scope was widened to the whole of Scotland in 1946).

On the issue of the stance adopted by local authorities towards housing associations, the north eastern councils might be seen as unrepresentative of the country at large, and certainly nowhere else in England and Wales faced the same sort of provocation. However, by 1939 no local authority had yet used the powers provided under the 1935 Act to buy rundown houses on behalf of associations and to transfer them at cost (Ministry of Health, 1939: 7). In January 1936 the House Management and Housing Associations Sub-Committee of the CHAC had been given a brief similar to that given to Moyne (Ministry of Health, 1939: 3). But on this occasion the Sub-Committee was packed with people with local government experience, and there was obviously much less sense of urgency, because the report took three years to emerge. Moreover, the report contained no recommendations of any substance, although it did say that:

> It is... essential, if the associations are to be allowed to co-operate on a bigger scale, that there should be the fullest possible collaboration between them and the local authorities. This cannot be emphasised too strongly and we recommend that the matter be brought to the local authorities' notice. (Ministry of Health, 1939: 7)

The local authority representatives on the Sub-Committee had been lukewarm about this exhortation and would have preferred to see it excised (PRO, HLG 36/6). In any case the increasing expectation of war with Germany meant that housing policy action was unlikely in the near future. Nonetheless, in May 1939 the Minister did issue a circular to local authorities, endorsing the Sub-Committee's statement about the need for local authorities and housing associations to co-operate with each other.

6

Voluntary Housing and the Welfare State, 1939–61

Introduction

Whatever ambitions housing associations might have had in the late 1930s were put into abeyance by the outbreak of war in September 1939. Like the war of 1914–18, the Second World War had an immediate and far-reaching impact on British economy and society. It also led to fundamental changes in social policy as the government managed the transition from war to peace after 1945. This chapter looks at the impact of the war and the subsequent establishment of the welfare state from the point of view of voluntary housing organisations.

As has been discussed earlier, the First World War helped to create the conditions which led to the introduction of housing subsidies and launched large-scale provision by local councils. Then housing was the main focus of the demands for reform and social improvement in the period of postwar reconstruction. After the Second World War the terms of the settlement between capital and labour were much broader, including a commitment to full employment and fundamental improvements in a range of welfare services. On this occasion reforms in the health service, education and social security were more far reaching, but housing was clearly an important part of the new welfare state as the government tackled the worst housing shortage of the century (Holmans, 1987: 93). In the longer term it can be argued that much of the development of housing policy since 1945 has to be understood in terms of responses to the measures adopted in the period of reconstruction. During that part of the postwar period covered by this chapter the emphasis was on high output, with local authorities making a substantial contribution, and with housing associations unable to make a significant quantitative impact. However, associations continued to be

113

active in a small way; many new organisations were established, and new sorts of services were pioneered, particularly for elderly people.

Coping with total war

The war was such an important watershed in the twentieth century, and its impact on social policy was so great that it provides an almost irresistible break point in most historical accounts. However, some of the best histories of housing (Merrett, 1979; Harloe, 1985) ignore developments during the war itself, apart from noting the virtual cessation of new building, the impact of bombing and the growth in the number of households requiring accommodation. These were all key factors deepening the housing crisis facing the newly elected Labour government in 1945, but it is important to remember that planning to deal with postwar reconstruction had been going on for several years before the military victory was finally achieved (Addison, 1977; Hennessy, 1992).

There is also a story to be told about how housing organisations were directly affected by the war itself. The mobilisation of millions of young men and women into the forces, and the evacuation of women and children caused massive disruption to established ways of life. Right at the start of the war there was a huge evacuation of women and children, mostly from London but also from other large cities where heavy bombing was expected. The poor organisation of the exercise, coupled with the absence of bombing raids during the first months of the war meant that nearly everyone drifted back home, but there was then a second and more effective evacuation. From the point of view of landlords evacuation created problems of rent arrears, which added to the management problems of letting certain types of dwelling (mainly flats on upper floors) in view of the fear of bombing. Managing housing in places such as inner London must have been a very stressful activity throughout the war – the Guinness Trust, for example, lost 13 per cent of its stock as a result of bombing.

In order to prosecute the war effectively the government took a wide range of powers to manage the economy and to direct resources and activity into the war effort. Britain became a highly controlled society, with high levels of taxation and restrictions on all sorts of things, from petrol to food. One new property-based tax faced by housing associations was imposed by the War Damage Act 1941, which created a fund from which to compensate victims of bombing. Just before the start of the war the government passed the Rent and Mortgage Interest (War

Restrictions) Act 1939, freezing all rents (except those for local authority dwellings) at their September 1939 levels, thereby removing the freedom of landlords to raise income in line with the inevitable wartime inflation in wages and prices. However, the impact of this problem was much reduced by the introduction of controls on expenditure on new building and repairs and maintenance. Schemes under construction were finished off, but from October 1940 to March 1945 fewer than 50,000 new houses were built (Ashworth, 1957: 36). Restrictions on repairs expenditure meant that some organisations, including housing associations, accumulated budget surpluses, which, in the case of non-charitable associations, then became liable to 'excess profits tax' under wartime revenue raising legislation. This became a matter of great concern to some associations and was taken up on their behalf by the NFHS. The Inland Revenue refused to make an exception of housing associations, but a solution was found in the form conversion to charitable status. A number of associations, including the Howard Cottage Society, Pancras House Improvement Society and Kensington Housing Trust, converted during the war years.

Planning for postwar reconstruction began surprisingly early in the war, well before victory was assured. At the national level, as early as 1940 Sir John Reith, the Minister of Works, set up a panel of experts to advise on postwar planning, and in January 1941 the prime minister, Winston Churchill, set up a Reconstruction Committee under the chairmanship of Arthur Greenwood. Reith also commissioned a plan for the development of London, and set up two committees to consider the future of the countryside (Scott Report, 1942) and questions of compensation and betterment (Uthwatt Report, 1942). The best known of all blueprints for postwar Britain was of course the Beveridge Report (1942), which laid out the basis for the development of the welfare state.

Housing organisations themselves contributed to the planning process. For example, in 1941 the Bournville Village Trust published a book outlining ideas for planning and building in Birmingham after the war, but somewhat curiously the authors eschewed direct references to housing tenure and so there is nothing about housing associations as such. In July 1942 the NFHS wrote to members about postwar planning, and in May 1943 a further circular to member societies sought feedback on relations with local authorities, because the Federation had been consulted by the Ministry of Health about the role that associations could play after the war. Early in 1943 Beveridge opened an exhibition in London about rebuilding Britain after the war, the Institute of

Housing organised a conference on postwar housing and the NFHS Secretary reported that 'our postwar preparations are proceeding apace'(NFHS, *Official Bulletin* October 1943). In 1944 the CHAC issued a report on private enterprise housing, in which was included a warm endorsement of housing associations and a recommendation that local authorities should be encouraged to co-operate with them (Ministry of Health, 1944).

The January 1945 issue of the NFHS Bulletin contained the last fore-word written by Sir Reginald Rowe. He recognised that the output of societies in the past had been trifling by comparison with the local authorities, but he looked forward to a period of much higher levels of new building, and in this he was encouraged by the decision of the Co-operative Permanent Building Society (CPBS) to put aside £3 million to be lent to housing societies. He also sensed that the Ministry of Health now placed a higher value on the potential of housing societies, and that it really did want local authorities to work with them. During the prolonged final phases of the war the NFHS ran a campaign to promote awareness of housing societies and the role that they might play in future. One result was that several dozen new societies were formed: probably about fifty societies were formed during the war, although the long term impact of these organisations seems to have been very limited. The CPBS initiative led to a number of new soci-eties, including the South Western Co-operative Housing Society, the Bon-Accord HS in Aberdeen and in Merthyr the borough council decided to set up a new society to take responsibility for the whole of the town's housing and redevelopment needs (NFHS, *Official Bulletin*, January–March 1945). By the end of the war the Federation had 180 members, out of a total of around 350 housing societies registered as I and P Societies (Beveridge, 1948: 88).

However, although the Federation and other supporters of voluntary housing were doing their best to talk-up their potential (for example, in a House of Lords speech Lord Balfour referred the new societies alone having plans for 100,000 dwellings (NFHS, *Official Bulletin*, December 1945)), the attitude within the Ministry of Health was not very encour-aging. Whatever was said in public by NFHS representatives about the welcome they received from the Ministry, in fact the old scepticism remained. The wartime coalition government planned to have 300,000 permanent houses built or under construction within two years of the end of hostilities, and it was accepted even then that the great majority would be built by local authorities. Moreover, it was explicitly recog-nised that setting up housing associations in areas where the local authorities were under-performing might lead to resentment among authorities generally (PRO, HLG 101/790).

A spirit of frustration and hope deferred

The general election of July 1945 brought in a Labour government, the first since 1931, and the first to have an overall majority in the House of Commons. This was also the first election to feature public opinion polling: housing was easily the most important issue identified by the voters, well ahead of full employment and social security (Hennessy, 1992: 85). The new Minister of Health, who retained responsibility for housing as well as the creation of the National Health Service, was Aneurin Bevan, a leading left winger in the cabinet appointed by the prime minister, Clement Attlee. The situation inherited by the new government was desperate, for although Britain had emerged on the winning side, the war effort had left the country virtually bankrupt. The economy had been heavily geared to the demands of wartime production, requiring painful restructuring to accommodate the return to peace, and there was a powerful case, articulated by the Chancellor, Stafford Cripps, for saying that the priority should be given to reviving export industries. Domestic consumption, including housing, would have to wait (Holmans, 1987: 94). However, the politics of the transition from war to peace made it impossible to ignore the demands of the public for social as well as economic reconstruction.

The housing situation in 1945 was very bad indeed, and any incoming government would have had to tackle it in some way. As mentioned earlier, there had been very little new building since 1940, a period in which, in normal circumstances, a million houses might have been built. In addition there had been the loss of over 450,000 houses due to bombing; some of the 3 million houses damaged by enemy action had received patching repairs, but in general the condition of the housing stock had deteriorated because of lack of investment throughout the war. Meanwhile the population had actually increased by about one million. Labour's approach to the problem was to place the emphasis on new building by local authorities, and to facilitate their work by retaining the stringent wartime controls on the supply of materials, and by introducing a new, more generous subsidy regime, in which the Exchequer contribution was raised to three times the value of the prewar subsidies (Malpass, 1990: 75–6).

Where did the housing associations fit in? The NFHS lobbied the Ministry of Health, and used its spokesmen in both the Lords and Commons to make the case for subsidy on equal terms with local authorities. Mention has been made above of Lord Balfour of Burleigh speaking in the Lords, and he was joined by Lord Gage, another Conservative, who became the NFHS president in the autumn of 1945. In the Commons the NFHS was represented by its former Secretary, Ron Chamberlain (Labour). The power of the local authorities and the long established stance of the Labour Party towards housing societies meant that despite the activities of the Federation, housing societies received very little attention. Nevertheless, campaigning by the Federation brought sufficient pressure to bear on the Ministry for it be necessary for a decision to be made about future policy. A memorandum written by Sir John Wrigley (the civil servant in charge of housing) in November 1945 set out the position:

> For the most part the housing associations which have been formed locally are comparatively small affairs which make the same kind of contribution as the local authorities – often inducing people of good will to lend them money free or at low rates of interest, thus enabling them to let at low rents, but with the normal Exchequer contribution paid to them through the local authority. These, I think, do good work, within their limits, which it is right for us to approve when our approval is sought by the local authority.

> While a local authority may make a rate contribution to the work of a housing association it would seem to me wrong to allow an authority to contract out of its responsibilities by handing over the execution to another body.

> I think, therefore, that the line should be that we should look favourably on proposals submitted by local authorities for assisting housing associations which are ready to build at once and which will, in the opinion of the local authority (and ourselves) make a useful supplement to local housing provision but that we should look askance at proposals which look like an attempt of local authorities to unload their responsibilities. (PRO, HLG 101/790)

A hand written note in the margin says that this memorandum has been seen and approved by the Minister. Bevan then told the Commons:

> I am prepared to approve arrangements made by a local authority with a housing association under Section 94 of the Housing Act 1936, where I am satisfied that the houses which the association propose to provide will be houses of the kind which are most needed, and will effectively supplement the local authority's own housing programme. This will apply in rural areas as elsewhere. Approval under the Section means that the same financial assistance can be given to the associa-

tion as to the local authority; and the same priorities for materials and labour will also be made available.

I am prepared to consider sympathetically upon their specific merits all applications, but I am not prepared to encourage housing authorities to farm out their housing powers. (*House of Commons Debates*, 22 November 1945, Vol. 416, col. 584)

This statement by Bevan was quoted extensively by Ministry civil servants in the late 1940s in response to enquiries from individuals and associations about the possibility of support for new building (PRO, HLG 101/263). Among the organisations to be sent the standard reply, telling them to get in touch with the local authorities in the areas in which they planned to build, was the East End Dwellings Company, whose Secretary wrote in October 1946 seeking information about assistance that might be available to his organisation, which was contemplating building on sites in its ownership in London.

Meanwhile, the directors of the North Eastern Housing Association had been engaged in their own campaign to secure the future of the organisation. Many of the local authorities in the area where the Association operated remained opposed to it on principle, and demanded that after the war it should be wound up, with the houses already built reverting to municipal ownership. The directors, on the other hand, fought hard for a continued role, and for the continuation of special financial assistance. The Distribution of Industry Act 1945, wound up the Commission for Special Areas, along with the powers to assist the NEHA. But the government sheltered behind the argument that there were no legal powers enabling them to wind up the Association itself. The situation thus was that the NEHA was left in being, able to operate much like any other housing association under the terms of the 1936 Act (PRO, HLG 101/798). Its postwar building activities were concentrated in a number of districts in Cumberland, but the local authority campaign to take over the dwellings carried on right up to 1979 (Malpass and Jones, 1995).

The first postwar decade was the only prolonged period in the twentieth century when local authority production was predominant, overshadowing the contribution of the speculative builders and eclipsing the housing associations, as Table 6.1 shows.

Table 6.1 Completions of permanent dwellings, 1945–61

England and Wales	Local Authorities	Private Builders	Housing Assocs
1945–46	741	2,570	n.a.
1946–47	27,159	31,899	145
1947–48	112,183	29,111	1,185
1948–49	117,406	15,958	1,836
1949–50	134,552	22,299	1,229
1950	139,158	24,108	1,540
1951	141,554	20,056	1,658
1952	165,506	31,364	1,868
1953	202,835	59,747	7,707
1954	199,604	87,755	14,761
1955	162,525	109,934	4,444
1956	139,977	119,585	2,518
1957	137,584	122,942	1,913
1958	113,146	124,087	1,133
1959	99,456	146,476	1,113
1960	103,235	162,100	1,650
1961	92,880	170,366	1,585

Source: 1945–46 to 1949–50: MoH Annual Reports; 1950–61: MoHLG Annual Reports. MoH Reports based on years to 31 March, MoHLG Reports based on calendar years.

Established accounts of housing policy in the late 1940s (Merrett, 1979: 235–46; Morgan, 1984: 163–70; Hennessy, 1992: 163–74; Harloe, 1995) tend to reflect the emphasis on building by local authorities, and pay virtually no attention to the activities of housing associations. They concentrate on the difficulties experienced by the government in achieving and maintaining a high level of output in the face of shortages of labour and materials, and later of capital. Some lessons were learned from the experience of 1918–20, and the maintenance of controls and building licensing meant that the local authorities did not have to compete in the same way for the materials with which to build. The incoming government in 1945 declined to commit itself to precise output targets, but it did operate on the basis that local authorities should license only one private house for every four new council houses, and this ratio was broadly maintained throughout the six years of the Labour administration. However, local authorities were known to vary in commitment and efficiency. Drawing on her prewar research

Bowley (1945: 258) argued that local authorities needed to be closely supervised and controlled, and that there was no evidence that the Ministry of Health was competent to do this. In taking this line she revived the debate about some sort of dedicated body with overall responsibility for delivering housing policy objectives. At the end of 1945 Douglas Jay (then an adviser to the prime minister) proposed the creation of a Housing Corporation, but Bevan was 'very doctrinal' in his opposition (Morgan, 1984: 165).

In most accounts the Housing (Financial and Miscellaneous Provisions) Act 1946, does not rank alongside the great reforming statutes of the 1940s dealing with education, health and social security, but it was nonetheless important, for under its provisions a million council houses were built in just seven years. As in prewar legislation, the Act provided for housing associations to be eligible for Exchequer subsidy on the same terms as local authorities. This can be regarded as something of a success for the NFHS, because it was by no means taken for granted that associations would be eligible for subsidy. The Labour government's position was that it was not prepared to subsidise private enterprise, and so the first task for the Federation was to ensure that associations were not classified alongside the speculative private builders. This may well mark the emergence of the idea of housing associations as non-profit-making organisations, in order to distance them from the commercial private sector. There is a certain amount of evidence that the Ministry had to be persuaded to include housing associations within the scope of the subsidy legislation. For instance, in a submission on the issue of classification from the NFHS to the Ministry of Health in November 1945 the point was made that associations were non-profit making, but a hand-written comment in the margin says 'untrue' (PRO, HLG 101/790). It should also be noted that subsidy for housing associations was not included in early drafts of the Bill that became the Housing Act 1946 (PRO, HLG 29/286).

However, eligibility for subsidy was only the first hurdle, and throughout the next few years housing association development was severely curtailed by financial factors. First, while local authorities were free to increase rents to take account of inflation and higher costs, housing associations remained subject to rent control for a decade after the war. Moreover, associations building in the immediate aftermath of the war had to agree not raise rents on new houses until at least the end of 1949 (Jones, 1985: 28). Second, associations were entitled to receive the full Exchequer subsidy on new houses, but the rate fund contribution which was mandatory on new council houses was discretionary for housing associations; it seems that in 'most cases' the local authorities declined to make a rate fund contribution (PRO, HLG 101/263). Third, despite this reduced level of subsidy, housing associations were expected to set rents of new houses at levels close to those charged by the local authority in the same area. Fourth, in terms of the capital for new building, housing associations in the late 1940s were eligible for 90 per cent loans from the PWLB, but they were not allowed to pay more than 2.75 per cent on private loans raised in respect of the remaining 10 per cent, on the grounds that philanthropic bodies should be able to attract cheap money, and employer based associations should be able to borrow cheaply from the parent company (PRO, HLG 101/263).

Another problem, from the point of view of the housing associations, was that they were heavily dependent on the goodwill of the local authorities; there was no specific allocation of building licences for housing associations, and so in effect associations could build only when and where local authorities agreed to forego part of their own allocations. Some local authorities were willing to co-operate (for example, there is a record of Westminster Housing Trust 'collaborating very closely' with Westminster City Council on the redevelopment of Pimlico (PRO, HLG 101/263)), but most, it seems, continued to display the same kind of reluctance that had been in evidence before the war. Among London boroughs, for instance, the Guinness Trust found that only Kensington and Chelsea (which were then separate authorities) were supportive. The Trust had a frustrating period at the end of the war and beyond, during which it pursued several possible development opportunities without success. This seems to have been a common enough experience, for Lord Gage referred to housing societies 'living in a spirit of frustration and hope deferred' (NFHS, *Quarterly Bulletin*, July 1947).

It is important to see the frustrations of housing associations in the wider context of the new welfare state, in which the voluntary organisations 'lost ground to new custodians of social welfare in Whitehall offices' (Hardy, 1991: 3). As central and local government took on greater responsibility for organising essential services, 'Voluntary agencies ...were driven to the margins of social policy, tarnished with a Victorian authoritarianism and a lady bountiful image that took decades to wear off' (Glennerster, 1995: 7). The report of the Wolfenden Committee (1978: 20) also described the voluntary sector as marking time during the first fifteen years after the war. This was something that was seen by Beveridge and others as undesirable, and in a book devoted to explaining the virtues and strengths of voluntary organisations Beveridge (1948: 10) wrote that,

> It is clear that the State must in future do more things than it has attempted in the past. But it is equally clear, or should be equally clear, that room, opportunity and encouragement must be kept for Voluntary Action in seeking ways of social advance.

Developing a distinctive role

Beveridge shared the view previously set out by Sidney and Beatrice Webb, that the role of the voluntary sector was to extend rather than duplicate public services. The government's position was quite clearly that housing associations should supplement rather than substitute the work of local authorities, and since the latter were concentrating on building family-sized houses to meet the general shortage, associations were encouraged to focus on other types of need, especially housing for elderly people. This was reinforced by a report published by the Nuffield Foundation, based on the work of a committee chaired by Seebohm Rowntree (1947). The report highlighted the deplorable conditions endured by many elderly people living alone, and criticised the lack of priority given to the housing needs of elderly people. However, in practice it continued to be very difficult for housing associations to secure the resources and approvals necessary for new building. Beveridge (1948: 292) joined in the debate and wrote, 'The government should make up its mind whether it wants voluntary housing societies or not. If it does, it must make their work possible'.

Among the first new build schemes for elderly people after the war was one undertaken by the Howard Cottage Society in Letchworth. Consisting of just 16 bungalows and completed in 1948, the scheme was overshadowed by the construction of nearly 700 houses by the local council in the five years after the war, but nevertheless it was sufficiently novel for the first conference of old people's housing societies to be held at Letchworth in October 1947. It was said that there were 68 specialist old people's societies, out a total NFHS membership of 334; most of these specialist societies had been formed within the previous two years, and most of them concentrated on converting existing properties. At that time there was no still subsidy for converted houses, but there were some examples of county councils providing assistance, (for example Hampshire invested in the Hampshire Old People's Housing Society, and East Sussex agreed to underwrite annual deficits incurred by East Sussex County Housing Association). Under the National Assistance Act 1948, county and county borough councils were given new responsibilities for providing residential accommodation for elderly people, and the level of demand was such that voluntary organisations were seen as providing a valuable addition to the public sector. In this context there is an interesting comparison to be drawn between Bevan's lukewarm attitude to housing associations and his endorsement of the notion of a voluntary-statutory partnership in relation to care for elderly people (Owen, 1965: 547). The 1948 Act empowered authorities to make grants or loans to societies providing for elderly people, in addition to the powers under the Housing Act 1936. Financial assistance was also available from the National Corporation for the Care of Old People, which was set up in July 1947 to disburse £0.5 million provided by the Nuffield Foundation, plus other money from the Lord Mayor of London's Air Raid Distress Fund.

In addition to the growth of specialist societies for elderly people in the late 1940s, existing organisations with no previous track record began to diversify. Mention has already been made of the Howard Cottage Society's scheme, which simply consisted of grouped bungalows, with no additional services. A different sort of development from the same period took place in Notting Hill, where the Improved Tenements Association developed its first schemes for elderly people; in a conscious move away from its historic focus on the very poor, the Association developed a scheme for elderly people retiring after a lifetime working in domestic service, and then another for elderly professional people. In Hampstead the Guinness Trust also undertook its first ever scheme specifically for elderly people. In its Avenue Road scheme (opened in 1949) the Trust converted a large house into a 'residential club' for ageing women. The Trustees proceeded cautiously, specifying that they were aiming to accommodate women over fifty, and seeking guarantees from relatives that they would be responsible for residents who became too frail. Another indicator of the changing situation was that for the first time in sixty years the Trust entered into a management agreement with another organisation; the management at Avenue Road was provided by the Women's Royal Voluntary Service.

During the 1940s there was the beginning of marked growth in the numbers of two other kinds of specialist society. First, there were associations promoted by employers or groups of employers in particular industries. These were referred to as industrial societies, and their main purpose was to provide for workers who required to be housed within reach of their place of employment, but who would not necessarily qualify for a council house. Mobile workers moving into an area to take up work in a growth industry, for example, would often find it difficult to obtain a council house. There were said to be three main reasons for industrial concerns setting up housing associations in the years after the war; first, an association could obtain an allocation out of the local authority's quota (and thereby it might secure more houses than were allocated to the whole of the private sector); second, housing associations were eligible for Exchequer subsidy (and sometimes also received a local rate fund contribution), and third, 90 per cent of the capital could be raised in a loan from the PWLB (Ashmore, 1957: 5–6).

A good example of the circumstances which encouraged the formation of industrial housing associations occurred soon after the end of the war when the British Overseas Airways Corporation (forerunner of British Airways), decided to consolidate its activities on the then recently established London airport at Heathrow. This required many staff to move to west London, where there was a shortage of housing and where council housing was reserved for people with a local residence qualification. A group of airline employees set up the British Airways Staff Housing Society in January 1947, with support from BOAC, which set up Airways Housing Trust Ltd as a subsidiary for the purpose of acquiring suitable sites to be leased to the Housing Society, and then making loans to help with house building. By 1956 the Society had built 1,000 houses (Airways Housing Society, 1997). Airways is unusual in that it has made the transition into a successful modern housing association, but it is not alone: another example would be Westfield HA, which was also set up after the war, to accommodate workers employed by United Steels Ltd in Workington.

Numerous industrial housing societies were set up over the next few years, but the evidence of new registrations suggests that such activity had virtually ceased by 1960 when the total stood at 84 (NFHS, *Annual Report 1961*: 10). And what happened to them in the long run has not been researched, but it seems likely that in most cases societies set up by employers were later sold off, either to sitting tenants or as going concerns (as in the case of the three associations set up by S. Smith and Sons (Smiths Industries), which were merged into Ceewood HA in 1979 and disposed of in 1995). A rather different initiative was the Eastern Counties Housing Association, which was set up by the NFHS itself in 1951, in order to assist industrial expansion in the region. Some industrial societies became quite large undertakings; for example, the three Smiths' associations owned over 1,000 dwellings by 1961, and Kingsway Housing Association (which was set up by the

English Electric Company) had 1,700 houses at that time (NFHS, *Annual Report 1961*: 9). However, the largest of all was the Coal Industry Housing Association, which absorbed numerous existing colliery associations when it was formed in 1952. In 1953–55 it built 17,000 houses, dwarfing the output of all other associations put together (Ministry of Housing and Local Government, 1955: 8). The Coal Industry Housing Association became a gargantuan organisation, with 111,000 houses by 1971 (Cohen Committee, 1971: 31).

Lack of research on industrial housing societies makes generalisation risky, but it is clear that their character and purpose was very different from the societies formed between the wars and which based themselves on the Octavia Hill system of outreach to the poor. An example of rents charged helps to make the point: Kelvin and Hughes Ltd, manufacturers of aircraft instruments in Basingstoke, set up Kelvin and Hughes Housing Association, which built 30 houses for its workers at rents of 32s-6d (£1.62) per week for a three-bedroomed house in 1954, and 30s (£1.50) for two bedrooms (NFHS, *Quarterly Bulletin*, January 1955: 11–13). The average rent for a three-bedroomed postwar council house in 1954 was just 16s-10d (£0.84), and the councils with the highest rents charged considerably less than Kelvin and Hughes HA (Malpass, 1990: 96). The objective of industrial societies was to house people who were in work, and mainly people who were in well paid skilled jobs. They were essentially artefacts of shortages in the housing and labour markets – they were about the recruitment and retention of scarce skilled labour, and as such they differed from the established ethos of the NFHS.

Another very different group of societies formed a significant minority of NFHS members; these were self-build societies, established by people banding together to build houses for themselves to live in. By 1952 there were 54 self-build societies out of a total Federation membership of over 500 (NFHS, *Quarterly Bulletin*, July 1952: 27). Most of the activity at that time seems to have been in and around London, but there were also examples elsewhere, including some in Scotland and Wales. Like industrial societies at that time, interest in self-building can be explained as a response to the severity of the housing shortage and the conditions attached to building licences, rather than as an expression of commitment to values shared with the majority of members of the NFHS. Self-builders joined the Federation for the technical and legal advice that they needed during the development phase, and because it helped to open up access to loans, but it seems that in the longer term the majority of schemes were converted into owner occupation and societies were dissolved. According to the Cohen Committee (1971: 33), 'as soon as it was possible for them to build for owner occupation the self-build associations did so, because most of their members were would-be home owners even more than they were frustrated tenants'. In 1961 there were 121 self-build societies in membership, and it seems to have been usual for them to disaffiliate on completion of building work.

Reshaping housing policy

Overall membership of the NFHS rose steadily during the years after the war, from 180 in 1944 to 679 in 1961 (NFHS, *Annual Report 1964*), but, as has been stressed above, the production of new and improved houses proceeded at a slow pace. NFHS member societies built just 45,000 new dwellings between 1945 and 1961, and at that date the total stock was only 106,831 (NFHS, *Annual Report 1961*: 16). Reference has been made to the Labour government's decision to concentrate on new building by local authorities, but there were other factors holding back the associations and it is now necessary to return to wider developments in housing policy. In October 1951 the Conservatives won the general election, partly by attacking Labour's performance on housing, and partly on their own commitment to build 300,000 houses per year (Morgan, 1984: 485). Harold Macmillan became the first Minister of Housing and Local Government, and set out to redeem the pledge on housing production by increasing completions by local authorities, so that 1953 and 1954 became the peak years ever for council house building. Thereafter, however, housing policy took on a more familiar Conservative appearance; private builders were encouraged and production of council houses was cut back, by 50 per cent by 1961. In 1954 slum clearance was re-launched after being in abeyance since 1939; in 1956 subsidies for new building were removed, apart from one bedroomed dwellings (that is, housing for elderly people) and houses built to replace cleared slums. As Merrett (1979: 246) says, this reshaping of housing policy was a reversion to the strategy of the 1930s, removing the local authority competition in the field on general needs housing, and directing them into areas that private builders found unprofitable. The final piece in the new strategy was the deregulation of rents in the private rented sector, under the terms of the Rent Act 1957, further evidence of the commitment to market forces as the framework for housing provision.

This restructuring of housing policy was mainly about cutting back and narrowing local authority activity and reviving the profit-seeking private sector. As such it largely passed by the housing associations, despite the return of a nominally more sympathetic Conservative government; as instruments of housing policy, housing associations remained on the outer edge of official concerns throughout the 1950s. In this respect, policy towards housing associations continued much the same under the Conservatives as it had been under Labour. However, it should not be inferred from this that nothing was happening to housing associations, nor that the decade was unimportant for them. Emsley (1986: 105) argues that the continued decline of private renting during the 1950s boosted the housing associations in two ways, first by highlighting the position of people who had relied on private renting and who were unlikely to secure local authority housing: these groups, including many elderly people, came to be classified as having 'special needs', and housing associations were encouraged to move into this area of work (Ministry of Housing and Local Government, 1951). An early example of the sort of innovative schemes developed by associations at this time was at West Ham, where on a single site the Guinness Trust built dwellings for elderly people (including hostel accommodation for those needing care), a hostel for single young people and some homes for families. The second boost to associations came through concern about the declining quality of private rented housing, much of it concentrated in urban areas where the local authorities had their hands full with slum clearance; this led to a revival and reinforcement of their established interest in reconditioning.

The Housing Act 1949, had given associations something that they had been campaigning for since the 1930s, namely financial assistance with reconditioning (Gibson and Langstaff, 1982: 52–4). The Act introduced grants for improvement and conversion, but they were awarded only at the discretion of the local authorities, only on works costing no more than £800 and only where the property was judged to have a useful life of at least thirty years. There was much criticism of these restrictions, and in practice only 6,000 grants were awarded across the entire private sector in the whole country in the first five years (Gibson and Langstaff, 1982: 54). The NFHS had also been campaigning since 1945 for associations to be released from rent control. Despite impassioned pleas on behalf of associations that were suffering badly from higher costs the Federation made no headway on this issue. However, the Girdwood Committee (Ministry of Housing and Local Government, 1953) showed that the cost of repairs had risen by a factor of three since 1939, evidence which contributed to the passing of the Housing Repairs and Rents Act 1954. The main provisions of the Act were the re-launch of slum clearance, a relaxation of the restrictions on improve ment grants, the removal of rent control on properties owned by housing associations, and relaxation of rent control on private landlords who carried out repairs to their houses.

From the point of view of housing associations, the 1954 Act was seen as a distinct boost to their prospects, for it enabled them to ease their financial difficulties, to raise rents in line with increased expenditure on the existing stock and to contemplate greater involve ment in grant aided improvement work. However, by 1956 optimism had given way to pessimism. One important factor here was that by the end of that year the government had withdrawn Exchequer subsidy for new building for general needs, ostensibly to concentrate local authority energy on slum clearance, but this had only a negative effect on housing associations. Writing in the summer of 1956 James Macnabb (long-established Secretary of the Peabody Donation Fund) concluded that:

At the present time the prospects for the Housing Associations and their future development look very dark indeed. With loan charges at their present high level, subsidies on new buildings already reduced and probably to be reduced still further, and but little sign of a halt in the increase in building costs, the difficulties in erecting new buildings are overwhelming. In fact, new building by the Associ- ations is regarded by many as at an end for the time being. (Macnabb, 1956: 153)

Macnabb was also pessimistic about two other factors: the working of the improvement grant legislation, despite the changes in the 1954 Act, and the apparent reluctance of younger people to come forward to replace the ageing activists in the movement. On the latter point, the explanation was probably partly related to the tarnished, old fashioned image of voluntary organisations in general in the early years of the postwar welfare state, as mentioned above.

However, there was still a good deal of energy within individual associations, even if some of the longer established ones were begin- ning to lose their earlier vitality. One option for associations that were running out of steam was merger or takeover. In west London, for example, organisations closely associated with the Octavia Hill tradi- tion, such as the Aubrey Trust and the Wilsham Trust, sought to offload their responsibilities. The Aubrey Trust had long been close to the Improved Tenements Association (known as Rowe Housing Trust from 1950), with which it merged in 1957, and at the same time the

Wilsham Trust offered to sell its entire stock to the Horace Street Trust (which had been set up by Octavia Hill herself in 1886); these two trusts finally merged in 1961, forming the Octavia Hill Housing Association, which itself later merged with the Rowe Housing Trust (Malpass, 1999a).

Organisations that were unable to do much new building were at least free to invest in their existing stock. In the case of the great London housing trusts there was an urgent need for such investment, and during the 1950s the Guinness Trust carried out a programme of modernisation work on its pre-1914 buildings. The whole of this programme was paid for from the Trust's own revenue, without resort to long term borrowing, and without grant aid under the 1949 Act. This was because the limited nature of the improvements meant that they did not qualify for grants; although tenants were given a water supply within their flats, WCs remained on the landings, and the communal bathhouses continued in use; in some cases whole estates were still without electric power sockets, although they had electric light.

Meanwhile, the diversity within the housing association 'movement' was increasing as new organisations were formed to meet newly identified needs. Of particular interest here is the way that associations responded to the needs of people arriving in Britain from the West Indies and other Commonwealth countries during the 1950s. Whereas some of the older trusts and societies were slow to provide for new arrivals there were people who recognised the difficulties they faced, and set out to help. A good example of an association set up specifically to provide for new arrivals was Birmingham Friendship HA (Malpass and Jones, 1996b), which was founded in 1956 to house and befriend immigrants, who were otherwise mostly reliant on the least satisfactory parts of the private rented sector and were prey to the most unscrupulous landlords (Banting, 1979; Smith, 1989). The Association was formed by a group of people with a shared involvement in church and welfare work in inner Birmingham and began by converting one house into a hostel for 10–12 people in Handsworth.

Overall, new building by associations continued at a very low level up to the end of the 1950s, but reconditioning received a boost in the form of the House Purchase and Housing Act 1959, which introduced a new type of grant, known as the 'standard grant', which was not discretionary and provided for the provision of basic facilities in houses with at least a fifteen-year life, and which had not previously had hot water, internal WCs or bathrooms. The new legislation, coupled with better promotion of the availability of grants, led to a large increase in take-up, although the majority of beneficiaries were owner occupiers (Gibson and Langstaff, 1982: 55).

By the start of the new decade it was becoming clear that new investment in private renting was not forthcoming, and that the Rent Act 1957, had actually hastened the rate of decline in this sector. By comparison with the attitudes of Conservative governments of the 1980s and 90s the administration led by Harold Macmillan was very supportive of local government, but it remained committed to promoting private solutions to housing needs. In this context the government produced a White Paper (Ministry of Housing and Local Government, 1961) which outlined, among other things, a proposal to make available up to £25 million to be lent to housing societies in England and Wales (plus £3 million in Scotland), for the construction of unsubsidised rented housing. The sums of money on offer at that stage were not huge, but the principle was important: for the first time a government was proposing a scheme specifically aimed at the voluntary non-profit sector. The details of the scheme are discussed in the following chapter, but it will be apparent that the prospect of a government choosing to pursue policy objectives through the medium of housing societies was sufficient to raise a degree of excitement among the leaders of the NFHS and others involved in housing. For example, an editorial in *Housing Review* (May–June 1961: 71) suggested that the Housing Act 1961 might come to be seen in future as 'the Housing Association Act'. And addressing the AGM of the NFHS in 1962 the Minister of Housing, Dr Charles Hill, said of the 1961 Act scheme:

> If, as I believe it will be, it is successful, it could spark off something really big. It could open up a new and continuing activity for housing associations. I do not think I exaggerate when I say that it could give them a major place in the housing structure of this country. They could become large providers of rented accommodation on a self-supporting basis. (NFHS, *Quarterly Bulletin*, July 1962)

Even allowing for a degree of political rhetoric here, it is reasonable to see this as a sign of exciting prospects for the voluntary housing movement.

Conclusion

The objective of this chapter has been to show how in the post war period housing associations remained firmly on the margins of policy, tolerated rather than welcomed by successive governments. The attitude of local authorities was generally hostile, and their power at the time was such that governments deferred to their view. Housing associations suffered from being seen by local authorities as undemocratic and unaccountable, while from the central government point of view they were seen as incapable of operating on the scale that was required. The Labour Party was unsympathetic to housing associations because they appeared to be (as indeed they were) largely run by well off middle-class and titled people who were suspected of having Tory leanings (Jones, 1985). Emsley (1986: 106) describes the housing associations in the 1950s in these terms:

> The Movement at this time was conservative in tone, muted in its criticism and predominantly composed of middle-aged or elderly, respectable professional people – the sort of people a Tory government could regard as its own.

Irrespective of who had won the 1945 general election, the period of postwar reconstruction required that the housing problem be tackled very much as an extension of the war effort, and for this purpose the local authorities were the ideal agencies. And the creation of the welfare state in the late 1940s reflected widespread public support for state-run services, with voluntary organisations in general suffering from image problems. Nevertheless, the coolness of the Conservative governments towards housing associations throughout the 1950s is striking.

Despite the lack of official encouragement, the chapter has shown that there remained considerable vitality within the housing association movement, albeit much more evident in some parts than others. Although in quantitative terms housing associations produced very little, the postwar period in particular was characterised by growing diversity as new organisations sprang up to meet newly recognised needs or to take advantage of the opportunities provided by the flexibility of the association model. It is appropriate to reiterate that while the emergent focus on elderly people on low incomes was consistent with mainstream housing association values, the growth of both self-build and industrial associations reflects a more instrumental approach, and Emsley (1986: 108) has suggested that they were never fully embraced by the NFHS.

7

Housing's Third Arm, 1961–74

Introduction

The title of this chapter borrows a phrase that was quite widely used during the 1960s and 70s to describe the position and role envisaged for housing associations. It was a term which reflected concern (eventually shared by both main political parties) to counter the perceived development of the housing system into a duopoly of owner occupation and council housing, with little or no choice for those who did not fit, or did not want to fit, into either tenure. During the period from 1961 to 1974 housing associations underwent considerable growth, in terms of the number of organisations, the volume of funding available to them and the scale of their activities. After so many years of being tolerated rather than encouraged, in 1961 the government launched a pilot project involving housing associations in an attempt to stimulate unsubsidised private renting, and by the early 1970s associations were coming to be seen by government as having a significant part to play in meeting housing need and in tackling problems of inner city decay. 1961 was an important year for the NFHS, which took two important decisions: to accept the MoHLG's invitation to run the new cost-rent experiment, and to launch a campaign to increase the number and distribution of societies providing specifically for elderly people.

The major turning point was the Housing Act 1974 (see Chapter 8), but it was in the preceding decade that the modern housing association movement really began to take shape. In particular, this chapter sets out to highlight two key themes: first, the emergence of a definite and distinct policy role for housing associations, and, second, the extent to which associations were changing and expanding for reasons other than direct encouragement from the government. Indeed it can be argued that in the longer term it was activity in the 1960s *in reaction* to government policy, rather than in compliance with it, that had the greater impact.

The 1960s were years of great optimism about the possibilities for modernisation, change and improvement (Marwick, 1998). Economic growth, full employment and rising living standards appeared to be established as permanent features of postwar society, and the persistent inflation (modest compared with what came later) seemed to be a price worth paying. This period represented the high point of Keynesian economic policy and the Beveridge welfare state, before the collapse of the long postwar boom in the 1970s and the subsequent restructuring. However, there were also problems and fluctuations, such that, 'When the Conservatives were defeated in 1964, they left the country with the most dangerous sterling crisis since that which they had inherited from the previous Labour Government in 1951' (Bogdanor and Skidelsky, 1970: 57). The tail end of thirteen years of Conservative rule was mired in scandal and sleaze, but the Tories nearly won the general election of October 1964. Labour crept in with a tiny majority, which they managed to increase at the next election in March 1966.

During the period of Labour government there were recurrent economic crises, culminating in the devaluation of sterling in November 1967. In retrospect this can be seen as an indicator of the increasing stresses on the established Keynesian policy framework and as a precursor to the collapse of that approach in the 1970s (Harvey, 1989). Domestically the consequences of the devaluation crisis were manifested in a series of cuts in public expenditure, from which housing was apparently excluded, but nevertheless housing production peaked at more than 400,000 in that year and then began a steep decline. With the benefit of hindsight, 1968 can be seen as a major turning point in British housing policy. It was not apparent at the time, but 1968 marked the end of the high output policies pursued by governments of both main parties since the war.

Housing societies and the Housing Act 1961

In April 1960 the MoHLG set up a working party on building to let, to which were invited representatives of the Building Societies Association and the National Federation of Building Trades Employers, but not the NFHS (PRO, HLG 29/511). The composition of the working party is a clear sign that at that stage it was expected, or hoped, that some way could be found to stimulate a revival of investment in private renting, especially for the sorts of households who then had incomes of £12 to £18 per week, and who could be expected to pay rents of £1-10s (£1.50) to £4 per week (that is rents considerably above those charged by most local authorities at that time (Malpass, 1990: 96)). It was considered that some kind of 'housing trust' might be a suitable vehicle for the purpose; the model being considered was 'a responsible, non-profit making body formed with the object of providing houses to let or for occupation on a co-operative basis' (PRO, HLG 29/511). The reference to co-operative housing was explicitly linked to the model widely employed in Scandinavia. However, it appears that the building societies and builders were not convinced; they did not think there would be sufficient capital available, nor sufficient interest from builders in the on-going management of housing to make the idea a success.

It was soon agreed that the way forward would be to bring in the existing housing associations, and proposals were outlined in a White Paper, which also covered a number of other important matters, including a recasting of housing subsidies (Great Britain, 1961, Malpass, 1990). The White Paper explained the government's perception that there was a need to provide '...for people who do not wish or cannot afford to buy a house although they require no help from public funds' (Great Britain, 1961: 10). Accordingly,

> As an experiment the Government propose to make arrangements under which money will be advanced to approved non-profit making housing associations which are prepared to build houses to let at economic rents. They regard this as essentially a pump-priming operation and hope that it will serve to show the way to the investment of private capital once again in building houses to let. (Great Britain, 1961: 10)

The scheme was limited to a loan fund of £25 million, plus £3 million for Scotland, and with no element of subsidy. Loans were to be made to approved housing associations at the same rate that the PWLB lent to local authorities, on the condition that the houses be kept available for renting, and on the expectation that rents would be 'of the order of £4 a week exclusive of rates' (Great Britain, 1961: 10). To be approved to participate in the scheme associations had to be registered I and P societies, which meant that the old trusts were excluded, but it was expected that existing associations would take part. The White Paper also referred to the government's hope that housing associations would experiment in the field of 'co-operative ownership on lines already established in the Scandinavian countries and elsewhere' (Great Britain, 1961: 10).

This initiative by a Conservative government was conceived in terms of reviving private renting, and it may be seen as an attempt to move towards a modernised form of private renting. Addressing the NFHS in 1962 the Minister of Housing, Charles Hill, stressed this point:

> We do not regard housing associations as a temporary expedient, a stop-gap, to do their job only until private enterprise builds again and all landlords become angels. We see the movement as an increasingly new and important partner in balanced housing progress. (NFHS, *Quarterly Bulletin*, July 1962: xxi)

Implementation of the scheme was largely in the hands of the NFHS, on behalf of the MoHLG. This had a big impact on the NFHS, giving it a central role in the delivery of policy, thereby bringing into a closer working relationship with the Ministry. The extra work also added substantially to the Federation's income and enabled it to employ more staff (PRO, HLG 29/629).

While initially it had been assumed that existing associations would become directly involved in building for cost renting, in practice it proved to be necessary to form new societies (Milner Holland, 1965: 32). One explanation for this is that existing charitable associations were precluded from providing for people who could afford cost rents. Another view, expressed by one of the people most closely involved with the experiment, is that the existing associations were too set in their ways or not interested, and that therefore it was necessary to start afresh (Emsley, 1986: 121). However, some existing associations and trusts did form new bodies to take advantage of the scheme. For example, the Sutton, Peabody and Guinness Trusts all set up new bodies to work under the Act.

It was not until April 1963 that the first cost-rent dwellings were completed (NFHS, *Quarterly Bulletin,* January 1964), but altogether 5,540 dwellings were built in England and Wales by 39 cost-rent societies operating under the 1961 scheme (Cohen Committee, 1971: 36). The total included only five co-ownership projects, amounting to only 102 dwellings, reflecting slow progress on devising a form of society that would be acceptable to the Inland Revenue.

Co-ownership was, in effect, a re-launch of copartnership housing, although the parallel was scarcely referred to at the time, and the reason was probably that in the context of the 1960s housing market the objective was to emphasise the similarities with home ownership. The adoption of the term *co-ownership* was significant in itself, and it is clear that as early as February 1961 the objective was to secure owner occupier status for individual members of co-operative schemes (PRO, HLG 29/510). At that stage it seemed that the Inland Revenue would agree to this requirement for tax purposes, provided that a satisfactory form of agreement could be worked out making it clear that payments by members were not rent, and that their relationship with the society was not one of landlord and tenant. The Finance Act 1963 introduced tax relief for co-owners, putting them in the same position as conventionally mortgaged tax-paying home buyers.

The basic principles of co-ownership were that the members of a society were the people living in the dwellings provided, and that each member was required to pay a proportion of the cost of construction. The balance of capital cost was borrowed over forty years, and members benefited from mortgage interest tax relief – after 1967 this was normally through the option mortgage subsidy. Members took leases which were not tradeable on the open market, but members leaving were entitled to return of their downpayment together with a proportion of any increase in capital value during their occupancy.

The 1961 Act experiment has been described as 'hugely successful', leading the government to propose in 1963 a much expanded budget and the creation of a national Housing Corporation to take over administration (Morton, 1989: 7). However, up to April 1963 only £5 million of the initial pool had been committed (Great Britain, 1963: 7). Nevertheless, before the completion of the planned five-year experiment, the government was persuaded that sufficient demand had been demonstrated to go ahead on a larger scale.

The Housing Act 1964, and the creation of the Housing Corporation

In May 1963 the government published another White Paper on housing (Great Britain, 1963), dealing mainly with ways of increasing total output and the improvement of existing dwellings. In view of the importance that it has subsequently acquired it is interesting to note that the creation of the Housing Corporation was given very little space in the White Paper. All that was said at that stage was that the government intended to establish the Corporation to stimulate the development of housing societies, that the government would make available funds for the Corporation to lend to societies, and that the Corporation would be given powers to buy land for societies to develop, and if necessary it would lay out sites in readiness for development. Why was it decided to create an entirely new body and to terminate the role of the NFHS in relation to loans to societies? One view is that the Federation 'had singularly failed to impress those in the Ministry with its capabilities' (Emsley, 1986: 232).

In consultations on the White Paper, the NFHS was given an assurance that the Housing Corporation would be independent, not an offshoot of the Ministry, and it was envisaged within the MoHLG that in addition to providing technical advice to housing societies, the Corporation might even build and manage houses (PRO, HLG 29/629). The Corporation was to have a board of nine salaried members, appointed by the Minister, and it was seen as being similar in constitution to the Commission for New Towns. However, in the light of the discussion in Chapter 5 it is the similarities to the models being debated thirty years earlier that are most striking. The Corporation was to operate across the United Kingdom as a whole, but only in relation to promoting and lending to cost-rent and co-ownership societies: it had no brief covering the traditional housing associations or their work.

The Corporation was established before the general election of October 1964, but it was not actually operational nor so well established that an incoming government could not have prevented it from going forward. In fact the new Minister of Housing, Richard Crossman, expressed his support and the future of the Corporation was assured, at least in the short run. In addition to its head office in London the Corporation set up bases in Cardiff and Edinburgh, and a series of English regional offices. This organisational structure was a reflection of the much increased scale of planned activity compared with the limited pilot project under the 1961 Act. It was proposed to establish a government loans pool of £200 million, supplemented by £100 million from the building societies. The intention was that normally two-thirds of the cost of new schemes would be covered by building society loans over forty years, with the balance being in the form of a second mortgage from the Housing Corporation. The White Paper referred to dwellings being built to let at £4 to £7 per week, exclusive of rates; this was considerably more than had been envisaged three years earlier, and, as mentioned above, far higher than the rents charged by local authorities – in 1964 the average rent for a postwar council house was only £1-10s-6d (£1.52) (Malpass, 1990: 96). There was no doubt, then, that the policy was designed to provide for people on higher incomes, the sort of people who could afford the cost of home ownership.

Although the government was putting up much more loan capital, success ultimately rested on three key factors:

1. the willingness of building societies to lend into an unfamiliar market;
2. sufficient volunteers coming forward to form new housing societies; and
3. the economic viability of the cost-rent and co-ownership models of provision.

The 1963 White Paper was explicit in saying that the objective was 'to secure the formation of strongly organised societies operating (with paid staff) in the main centres of population, each capable of undertaking a series of building schemes and managing a substantial number of dwellings' (Great Britain, 1963: 8). The Ministry did not want to see a vast number of small societies building houses. The sorts of societies envisaged 'would consist of local people, active in the local authority field, on voluntary bodies, employed by building societies, and other professional men with the right know-how' (PRO, HLG 29/629). In practice the government supported the formation of societies by groups of property-based professionals, such as solicitors, architects, surveyors and estate agents, who were allowed to charge their normal fee for work awarded to them in connection with development and management of houses. It is important to emphasise that, although this sort of thing was later prohibited, at that time it was not only acceptable but positively encouraged. Part of the reason for this was that groups of potential co-owners did not form spontaneously, and so it was necessary to have sponsoring societies to undertake the development function. Once schemes were built and occupied their residents became the members of separate societies. In some cases the 'daughter' societies then contracted with the 'parent' society to purchase management services provided by the parent or by companies run by members of the parent committee.

A number of prominent housing associations today trace their origins back to the cost-rent and co-ownership initiative. Examples include North British HA, Northern Counties HA, Orbit HA and Sanctuary HA (Jones, 1985, Erdman, 1982: 186 7). Another is Knightstone HA, which dates from the early 1960s when, under the name HSM Housing Society Ltd, it promoted more than 30 co-ownership schemes across the south west of England. In this case the standard arrangement was that the daughter societies contracted with HSM to provide management services, and HSM then delegated this work to a private company run by one of its committee members.

It is very difficult to be precise about how many dwellings were actually built under the 1961 and 1964 Act schemes, but the broad outlines of what happened are clear. When the pilot scheme was set up it was expected that cost renting would predominate, with co-ownership being seen as an interesting and more experimental option with some potential. In the event, as mentioned above, cost renting did indeed produce more dwellings under the 1961 Act, but the available figures seem to refer to approvals rather than completions, and it is known that some approved cost rent schemes converted into co-ownership, and, later, some schemes approved as co-ownership went ahead as fair-rent housing. The Cohen Committee (1971: 37) reported that by 1970 new cost rent proposals had dried up completely, and that only 1,575 dwellings remained in cost rent projects.

Reasons for the failure of cost-renting included difficulty in raising loan finance from building societies, increasing interest rates pushing rents above affordable levels, and the increased attractiveness of co-ownership as a result of certain simplifications to the terms, and the introduction of the option mortgage subsidy (Cohen Committee, 1971: 47). Difficulties with raising capital have been referred to throughout this history of voluntary housing and it is worth emphasising the extent of the problem even when the government was prepared to advance a third of the cost. The original intention that the building societies would provide two-thirds of the capital had to be relaxed to a less-demanding minimum of at least half. Morton (1989: 11) describes what happened in these terms:

> The assumptions built into the Corporation's 1964 brief rapidly grew shaky from 1966 onwards. There was a growing problem of raising the expected first mortgage covering two thirds of the cost from the building societies. Four large building societies, led by the Co-operative Permanent [now the Nationwide], met at least three quarters of the total lent throughout this period. There were quibbles over what two thirds meant: by and large building societies took the view that it meant two thirds the value of the scheme, almost invariably below its cost. In the later 1960s, acute pressure on building society resources made it very difficult to fund schemes at all.

The cost-rent experiment was effectively over by 1970, and was finally terminated by the Housing Finance Act 1972, which converted cost rents to fair rents, and made cost-rent societies indistinguishable from conventional associations (DoE, 1973: para 13). However, co-ownership continued to grow for several more years, no doubt assisted in this by the availability of a degree of subsidy that was unavailable to cost-rent societies. The total number of dwellings completed in co-ownership schemes across Great Britain was 36,306 (Housing Corporation, 1980: 25), most of which were completed before 1973, when new schemes began to be converted to fair rent.

It is interesting to note the extent to which the Housing Corporation played a part in shaping and steering the development of housing societies at that time. In evidence to the Cohen Committee (1971: 65) the Corporation explained that it aimed to limit individual co-ownership societies of no more than about 40 dwellings, in order to preserve some sense of 'true co-ownership spirit', and (pp. 59–60) that it encouraged sponsoring societies with professional skills to be the main driving force behind co-ownership. It went on to say that,

> In recent years, the Corporation have encouraged promotional societies with comparatively small numbers of dwellings under their control, to merge with larger groupings so as to avoid dissipation of effort and to achieve economies of scale. In the result, although there are more than 1,200 registered Societies, there are now fewer than 200 main Societies which actively promote and manage estate development, and these cover the country.

The rejuvenation of housing associations

The promotion of cost-rent and co-ownership societies has to be seen as an attempt to develop a more diverse and modernised pattern of housing provision. As such it effectively bypassed existing housing associations and was distinct from new ones that were formed in the 1960s to carry on the work of providing for people on low incomes. However, important changes were taking place among what might be called the mainstream housing associations. These changes ran in parallel with, and independently of, government policy on tenure diversity. In contrast to the immediate postwar years, when high levels of local authority building crushed virtually all opportunities for housing associations, in the 1960s, when local authority programmes were again cranked up to high levels, housing associations prospered and grew. There were several different aspects to their growth, and corresponding reasons for it.

First, there was a continuing emphasis within government policy on increasing provision for elderly people, and housing associations responded to that. Second, as local authorities attempted to increase their slum clearance and redevelopment activities they actually intensified problems of dilapidation in areas awaiting clearance, and there were growing concerns in some circles about the social impact of comprehensive redevelopment. A number of the most dynamic new associations formed in the 1960s were brought into existence precisely to respond to problems of this kind, hence the argument that housing association growth in this period can be understood partly in terms of a reaction to the perceived failings of official policy. Third, there was a growing awareness of homelessness in cities, and of the plight of people (such as new arrivals from overseas and single parents) who could not easily gain access to council housing nor afford decent private rented accommodation.

Key factors facilitating the growth of housing association activity at that time were (a) promotional and fund raising efforts by various church based groups, (b) the formation of Shelter in 1966, specifically to raise funds for housing associations and (c) increased support from local authorities, notably the Greater London Council. The various fund raising activities led to a higher profile for housing associations, and this was bolstered by the promotion of new associations in different parts of the country.

During the 1960s there was an injection of new energy into the housing association movement. The old established associations and trusts were, on the whole, marking time, managing their existing stock in their traditional way (sometimes losing parts of it to slum clearance), but not moving forward. What then happened was that new people identified new needs and new funding opportunities, and they formed new associations, several of which have gone on to become major organisations in the present period. The old associations and trusts were ignored and outflanked by these new dynamic organisations. Trusts such as Guinness and Peabody were seen by the new activists as moribund, old fashioned and irrelevant. They were regarded as providing outmoded accommodation, overwhelmingly let to white families (even where the local population was increasingly mixed) and failing to respond to new needs and new opportunities. The old trusts were also criticised by the Milner Holland Committee (1965: 144) for their conservative attitude to borrowing for capital investment: 'If these housing associations are to play a significant role in the redevelopment of large areas of London, or to claim partnership with public authorities in opening up land newly allocated for housing, then these policies must clearly be changed'. In this context it is not inappropriate to talk about a new wave of associations, which set the pace for others to follow, thereby helping to energise and modernise the movement generally in advance of the great leap forward following the Housing Act 1974.

With respect to elderly people, it will be recalled from the previous chapter that ever since the war housing associations had been encouraged to expand their efforts for this group. The Housing Act 1961, introduced a two-tier system of housing subsidies for local authorities (Malpass, 1990: 94–5), but housing associations were entitled to the higher rate of assistance, £24 per dwelling per year. This represented a considerable improvement on the £10 subsidy that they had been receiving since 1956, albeit that there was the threat of a review after ten years. Another factor behind the increase in activity focused on elderly people was that in 1961 the NFHS was able to appoint a specialist development officer, funded by the National Corporation for the Care of Old People (NCCOP). In 1962, 40 new associations for elderly people were formed (more than the number of cost-rent societies set up in that year), bringing the total to 284 (NFHS, *Annual Report 1962*: 5). Notable formations from the early 1960s included Hanover HA (1963), which was also sponsored by the NCCOP, and which soon established itself as a rapidly growing organisation in many parts of the country (Stack, 1967). Anchor HA was set up a little later, in 1968, by a national charity, Help the Aged. Anchor (now Anchor Trust) has become established as one of the largest associations in the country, with over 31,000 dwellings in 1998. A different, more decentralised, model of provision for elderly people was developed by the Abbeyfields Society. By 1970 more than 8,250 dwellings for elderly people had been provided since 1961, compared with fewer than 3,500 in the previous twenty-five years, and at least 8 specialist associations were operating across the country (Jones, 1985: 53).

The next group of associations to consider is those that were set up in the 1960s to tackle problems in rundown inner-city areas. Among the most significant were:

- Notting Hill Housing Trust (NHHT), set up in 1963 by Revd Bruce Kenrick, who rapidly raised some £50,000 for work centred on the area of west London in which Rachman and other exploitative private landlords had been operating;

- Paddington Churches HA (PCHA) set up in 1965 by Revd Ken Bartlett who was then a young curate in Paddington (Mantle, 1995);

- Quadrant HA (now part of London and Quadrant HA) set up in 1965, emerging from a men's dining club.

These associations were among the first to promote a distinctive approach, advocating rehabilitation at a time when redevelopment was dominant, aiming at people who were not eligible for council housing, and favouring community based organisations. Rather than work through their local authorities, the individuals involved with these associations tended to see the local authorities as part of the problem to be tackled. These new activists saw themselves as a distinct, modernising force within the housing association movement, and it is interesting that several went on to senior positions in the Housing Corporation, either as managers or members of the board. It is also worth pausing here to remember that the term 'movement' implies a community of purpose and sentiment that was certainly not present at that time. Not only were there differences between the dynamic new associations and the old trusts, but there was an emerging cleavage between the rehabilitation associations and the new-build housing societies funded under the 1961 and 1964 Acts.

Contributing to the new dynamism among housing associations were initiatives taken by the main religious denominations. In 1964 the British Churches Housing Trust was established out of work conducted by the interdenominational London Churches Group (Jones, 1985: 69). The brief was to promote the formation of housing associations around the country, and altogether more than 60 associations were set up (Jones, 1985: 69). Among those organisations assisted into existence by the Trust were New Islington and Hackney HA, Richmond Churches HA and Coventry Churches HA. In parallel with this operation the Catholic Housing Aid Society (CHAS) and Father Eamon Casey were also actively promoting the formation of new associations, including: Family HA, South London Family HA and Birmingham Family HA. An important theme in this work was concern for the position of young single mothers, and until 1970 Family HA, for example, provided exclusively for this group (Harloe *et al.*, 1974: 67).

Meanwhile, however, there was growing public awareness of the problem of homelessness in London and other major cities (Greve, 1964; Greve *et al.*, 1971). In December 1966, Shelter was launched as a national campaigning organisation on behalf of homeless people. Shelter was formed by a group of five organisations already involved in housing aid work (Housing the Homeless Central Fund, British Churches Housing Trust, CHAS, Christian Action and the Housing Societies Charitable Trust (HSCT had been set up in 1960 as the charitable arm of the NFHS)). The success of Bruce Kenrick's fund-raising activities at NHHT had apparently frightened the other organisations into collaboration (Seyd, 1975: 419). Shelter's role was to continue to raise public awareness of the problem of homelessness and to raise funds for housing associations. The launch of Shelter happened to take place just a fortnight after the screening of the BBC television drama-documentary, *Cathy Come Home*, which portrayed the experiences of a young family sinking into homelessness. This play made a big impact on the public at the time, just before Christmas, and has retained its status as a seminal broadcasting event. *Cathy Come Home*, together with a stream of emotive publications, helped Shelter to raise about £5,250,000 in seven years, some £2,250,000 of which was channelled to housing associations (Seyd, 1975: 421).

Shelter distributed funds to housing associations in a fairly informal way, mainly to pay for revenue costs (such as staffing) rather than capital grants for house purchase. Associations that received support from Shelter included NHHT, PCHA, Family HA, Quadrant, and Circle 33 in London, together with a number of associations elsewhere: Liverpool Improved Houses, Nottingham Community HA, COPEC in Birmingham and South Yorkshire HA. The latter, for example, was set up by a Shelter group in Sheffield and was given a grant to cover the salary of its first director. The amounts given to each association were not large, but they were often very valuable in helping the associations with their cash flow. Interestingly some associations refused even to apply for Shelter money, apparently on the basis of its perceived political image (Harloe *et al.*, 1974: 66).

Much more important in terms of the numbers of houses actually acquired and renovated was the support provided by some local authorities, notably the Greater London Council, especially under Conservative control from 1967 to 1973. Before the formation of the GLC the Labour controlled LCC had established a policy of helping associations, but only as very minor players in comparison with direct provision by the council (Fiske, 1962: 82). In the last four years of the LCC, 1961–64, just over £4 million was lent to housing associations (Arden, 1983: 105).

The new GLC continued to be Labour-controlled and broadly followed the policy established by its predecessor, although it raised to 100 per cent the loans that were available for acquisition and improvement; this, of course, was immensely valuable to newly formed associations, for it enabled them to begin work immediately, without having to raise private finance in advance of owning any property to offer as security. Associations such as Quadrant were able to take advantage of this arrangement and to grow very rapidly. By June 1967 27 associations were providing accommodation with GLC assistance (Arden, 1983: 106). However, this should not be interpreted as enthusiasm among Labour councillors, who retained a strong preference for municipal house building, and were outraged by the policies subsequently adopted by the Conservatives (Young and Kramer, 1978: 78–81). During the period 1967–73 the Conservatives were in control and their policy, promoted by the right wing Chair of Housing, Horace Cutler, was to encourage housing associations, by means of much increased volumes of lending and by stock transfers from the Council. In January 1970 it was agreed to increase the housing associations budget to £25 million per annum (Arden, 1983: 107). Even allowing for inflation, £75 million over three years was a massive increase on the £4 million over four years in the early 1960s, and by 1973 GLC assistance was funding a programme of some 10,000 per annum, mostly in inner London Boroughs. This level of funding bore no apparent relationship to demand from housing associations, nor to their capacity to absorb the available money (Harloe *et al.*, 1974: 76).

In addition to the assistance from local authorities, after 1967 there was increased Exchequer funding available to housing associations for the improvement of existing houses. Rehabilitation was to become a much more important aspect of their work in the 1970s, but the foundations upon which growth was then to be built were laid in the previous decade. Housing associations had had access to improvement grants since their introduction in 1949, but in addition in the Housing Subsidies Act 1967, associations were given subsidy in relation to costs associated with the acquisition and conversion of existing property.

So far this discussion has concentrated on the impact made by newly formed associations, but it must not be forgotten that existing organisations continued to grow and change, to a greater or lesser extent. Some of the dynamism of the new associations rubbed off on the older ones, leading to conscious attempts to modernise themselves and their dwellings. The old charitable trusts were wrestling with the problems of what to do with their pre-1914 dwellings; in 1960, for example, the Peabody Donation Fund improved 277 of its older tenements (NFHS, *Annual Report 1961*). The Guinness Trust had carried out modest improvements to all of its older dwellings by 1960, but then spent several years trying to decide a proper long term strategy. Two estates were sold to local authorities for redevelopment, and two others were redeveloped by the Trust itself.

This section has concentrated on positive aspects of housing association activity during the 1960s, emphasising the new dynamism brought to the movement by new associations and trusts. However, there is another side to the story. The scale of investment remained insignificant compared with that achieved by local authorities: it was only in 1964 that housing associations passed 50,000 completions since 1945 (Milner Holland, 1965: 142). Annual output during the 1960s remained below 5,000 newly built dwellings until 1968 (Table 7.1 below). This low level of achievement was a reflection of the serious financial difficulties still facing associations. The Milner Holland Committee (1965: 31–7) exposed the rigidities in the system which meant that associations received the same level of subsidy as local authorities but unlike local authorities, associations were required to apply the subsidy to the dwelling to which it was nominally attached; they were unable to practice rent pooling, even though since 1955 the level of subsidy had been calculated on the assumption that pooling was in operation (Malpass, 1990: 91). All this made it very difficult for associations to operate sensible rent setting policies. Adding to the problems of non-charitable associations was the burden of taxation, a burden that charitable associations did not carry. The Milner Holland Report (1965: 42) showed how, at a given capital outlay, the weekly cost of a housing association letting exceeded that for both a local authority house and house purchase. The Committee commented that,

> We have been unable to find any justification for the unfavourable tax treatment of housing associations and we conclude that unless the tax burden is lifted, the contribution to the supply of rented accommodation by housing associations will be seriously hampered. (p. 37)

The tax burden on non-charitable associations was eased by the Finance Act 1965, which allowed the Minister to make a grant equal to an association's tax liability. The Milner Holland Committee also expressed a degree of exasperation at the way in which the exclusion of cost rent and co-ownership societies from any direct subsidy kept them out of, 'the very sector of the London housing market in which their energy and initiative is most urgently required' (p. 145). Meanwhile, the charitable associations that specialised in housing the most needy were denied access to the capital resources at the disposal of the Housing Corporation. This led the Committee to conclude:

> It seems to us that if non-profit making housing associations are to make an effective contribution to the most urgent needs – and it is widely accepted that they should – then a rationalisation of the fiscal and legal provisions governing their activity is urgently needed; at present these seem to have the effect of discour-

aging the very associations which are equipped to give effective help in the area in which it is most needed. (p. 146)

On top of all this, levels of awareness of housing associations and their purpose remained low among many local authorities, and among the public at large. Associations continued to experience hostility from local councillors, mainly Labour councillors, who regarded them as organisations run by Tories and capable of doing nothing that the council could not do better itself. Lending by local authorities remained at very low levels throughout the first half of the 1960s, passing £2 million for the first time only in 1964, although by 1968 the figure had climbed to £11.3 million – still a pitifully small sum from local authorities across the whole of England and Wales (Great Britain, 1966, 1969).

Mounting difficulties

The general election of June 1970 and the return of a Conservative government with Edward Heath as prime minister heralded a sharp change in some aspects of housing policy, and accentuated trends already in train. New building by local authorities, for instance, continued to fall, reaching a low point of just 88,000 dwellings by 1973, half the total achieved in 1967. Housing association output had been rising year by year, reaching a peak of over 15,000 newly built and renovated dwellings in 1971. However, rising interest rates on new and existing loans, at a time when associations were not free to increase income correspondingly, meant that some encountered real financial difficulties, and completions were sharply reduced in 1972 and 1973 (see Table 7.1 below). The new government was strongly supportive of home ownership (Great Britain, 1971: 4), and it was during its period in office that the British housing market experienced its first episode of runaway house price inflation, in 1971–73, when the average price increased by more than 50 per cent (Boleat, 1982: 94). This was also a time that the sale of council houses reached then unprecedented levels (Murie, 1975).

In July 1971 the government published an important White Paper, *Fair Deal for Housing* (Great Britain, 1971). This outlined the government's determination to press ahead with what it referred to as 'a radical change in housing policy' (para. 4), mainly in the form of a complete recasting of housing subsidies and a shift to 'fair rents' in both the local authority and housing association sectors. The concept of fair rent had been introduced in the private sector in 1965, where its impact to date had been quite minor, in terms of the number of registered fair rents, although it can be argued that its real significance lay in the reassurance given to tenants that they could have recourse to the independent rent officer service if necessary. A fair rent was effectively a moderated market rent, disregarding the effect of shortage. In the great majority of cases fair rents would be higher than existing reasonable rents, and so the government also proposed to introduce a mandatory rent rebate scheme in the local authority sector, with a similar scheme of rent allowances for housing association and private tenants.

The proposals in the White Paper were embodied in the Housing Finance Act 1972, one of the most controversial pieces of housing legislation since 1945 (Malpass, 1990: 114–26). Public debate concentrated on the effect of the fair rents regime on both the level of rents in the council sector and the removal of local councillors' freedom to set rents. The impact of the Act on housing associations was given much less attention in Parliament and outside, but for those involved in running associations it was a very difficult time. First, although the White Paper had indicated that housing associations would, like private landlords, move to fair rents only gradually and at a pace that they would control, in the event associations were required to complete the complicated procedures involved in registering fair rents for all their dwellings within three and a half months of the Act coming into force (Baker, 1975: 161). Second, the new subsidies introduced in the Act were difficult to understand and operate, and they had a strongly deterrent effect on new building. However, a more positive development for associations was that the Act broadened the powers of the Housing Corporation beyond just cost-rent and co-ownership societies, enabling it to lend on fair-rent schemes, and raising its borrowing limit from £100 million to £300 million.

It is not necessary to go into a lot of detail about how the new subsidy system was intended to work, but it is important to appreciate that the Act consolidated all existing subsidies, paid under successive Acts since 1919, and set out a timetable for their withdrawal; excluded from this consolidation and withdrawal procedure were payments due to associations for improvement and conversion under the 1967 Act. The loss of income was to be broadly made good from higher rents, but it was recognised that new building would continue to require subsidy. Thus there was provision for a new-building subsidy, which was designed to make good 100 per cent of approved revenue deficits in the year of completion and for the next two years. However, the subsidy was then to be phased out, disappearing completely after ten years.

From the housing associations' point of view there were two main drawbacks to this arrangement. First, the deficit that would provide the basis of subsidy over the ten years was the approved deficit in year one, not the actual deficits in subsequent years, and of course there was the possibility that actual deficits could be much larger. Second, the system exposed associations to considerable risk and uncertainty, in the sense that on the one hand they faced the prospect of phased subsidy withdrawal while on the other hand the fair rent system (with rents set externally by independent rent officers) meant that they no freedom to adjust rental income to match spending commitments. The new building subsidy was, therefore, in fact a mechanism which discouraged new building.

The Housing Finance Act 1972, was so flawed, both technically and politically, that it was in operation for only eighteen months. In February 1974 the incoming Labour government froze rents as part of its anti-inflation strategy, and at the same time set at zero the rate of subsidy withdrawal for 1974–75. Local authorities were given back their freedom to set reasonable rents, and a new, temporary subsidy system for that sector was introduced in the Housing Rents and Subsidies Act 1975. Housing associations were treated rather differently, in that the fair rent regime stayed in place and a new subsidy system, specific to associations, was introduced. Thus, although the 1972 Act had only a short and troubled life, it nevertheless stands as a major watershed in British housing policy. In terms of rents policy it marked the transition from historic cost pricing to current value pricing (in the case of housing associations this took the form of fair rents), but it also marked the end of a fifty-year period in which housing associations and local authorities had shared the same rent and subsidy framework.

Taking stock

Table 7.1 shows the number of completions each year by housing associations of all sorts during the period covered by this chapter, reinforcing the theme of low, but rising, levels of activity. Figures for acquisition and renovation of existing houses are not available for years before 1969. During the years covered by the table at least 90 per cent of all housing association activity in Great Britain was concentrated in

England, with very low levels in Scotland and Wales, and even less in Northern Ireland.

Table 7.1   New building and renovation by housing associations, 1961–74 (Great Britain)

	No. dwellings completed	No. renovations
1961	1,638	
1962	1,626	
1963	1,957	
1964	2,864	
1965	3,991	
1966	4,558	
1967	4,984	
1968	6,291	
1969	7,336	1,462
1970	8,493	2,747
1971	10,667	5,126
1972	7,665	4,365
1973	8,852	3,351
1974	9,920	4,132

Source: *Housing Statistics* and *Housing and Construction Statistics* (HMSO). Renovations refer to work approved, not completed.

By 1973, housing associations again stood on the brink of far-reaching changes in the basis and scale of funding available to them. The cost-rent scheme had manifestly failed to take off, and co-ownership was flagging in the face of the attractions of conventional home ownership in a period of rapidly rising property values. The economics of co ownership were strained to the point where the Housing Corporation was having to advance the cost of repayments to departing co-owners (Morton, 1989: 14). The Corporation's own finances were not healthy – it had a deficit of £1 million by 1972 (Morton, 1989: 13) – and its future was inevitably thrown into question by the decline of the initiatives that were its sole reason for existence. The conclusions to be drawn from the whole cost rent and co-ownership initiative are that it did not produce a significant number of dwellings, nor did it establish new forms of private housing tenure. It must therefore be seen as an experiment which failed to achieve its main objectives. However, it was not without a lasting impact on the housing system, but its impact was essentially organisational, in that it gave rise to a number of today's largest and most active associations, and it led to the establishment of the Housing Corporation, which of course has become a major and apparently permanent institution.

The NFHS was already established as a permanent part of the housing scene, having celebrated its twenty-fifth anniversary in 1960. Its role in administering the cost-rent and co-ownership scheme under the 1961 Act seems not to have been a great success, but the Federation was expanding in other ways at the same time: membership, which stood at 651 in 1960 leapt up to 1,141 by 1964 and 1,948 by 1969. Cost-rent and co-ownership societies accounted for only one-third of this growth, the rest being due to general family, elderly people's and self-build associations. Table 7.2 shows the composition of the Federation in 1969.

Table 7.2   Membership of the NFHS in 1969 (Great Britain)

	No. of associations
General family	269
General family (charitable)	399
Old people's associations	565
Industrial associations	81
Self-build associations	198
Cost rent and co-ownership societies	436
Total	1,948

Source: NFHS, *Annual Report 1969*, quoted in Cohen Committee (1971).

The total number of dwellings owned by member organisations grew relatively more slowly (Table 7.3). At the start of the decade member associations owned a total of 104,183 dwellings, with a further 2,300 in the pipeline (NFHS, *Annual Report 1961*).

Table 7.3   Housing association dwellings in 1960 and 1969

	No. of dwellings	
	1960	*1969*
Old people's associations	3,036	10,000
Industrial associations	30,453	121,000
Self-build associations	2,971	5,000
Cost rent and co-ownership		18,200
General family associations	67,723	83,000
Total	104,183	237,200

Sources: 1960: NFHS, *Annual Report 1961, 1969*: Cohen Committee (1971).

The figure of 237,200 for 1969 given by the Cohen Committee (1971: 121) is approximate, and includes cost-rent and co-ownership dwellings of societies that were not members of the NFHS. The 1969 total was much inflated by the 111,000 attributed to the Coal Industry HA, which must have acquired a very large number of dwellings in the second half of the decade, because in 1964 it was reported to own just under 23,000 dwellings. It was easily the largest industrial housing association, and continued to grow at a time when subsidies were no longer available for such associations. The second largest association in the 1960s was the North Eastern HA, which owned 16,884 dwellings in 1966. However, the NEHA was also atypical in its origins and contemporary role (since it was effectively carrying the entire house building programmes of a number of local authorities). The next largest association was probably the Sutton Dwellings Trust, which owned 8,148 in 1961. Then, as now, the great majority of associations owned very few dwellings; a survey conducted for the Cohen Committee (1971: 73) found that 51 per cent of associations owned fewer than 20 dwellings, and 75 per cent owned fewer than 100. Even well-established associations that subsequently grew very large, such as Liverpool Improved Houses (now Riverside HA), had under 1,200 dwellings at the start of the 1960s.

Several references have been made in this chapter to the Cohen Committee, which was set up in 1968 as a sub-committee of the Central Housing Advisory Committee with a brief to review the activities of housing associations and to make recommendations. By the time of the general election in June 1970 the Committee had carried out a considerable amount of work but was apparently some distance from a full written report. The incoming government decided, allegedly in the interests of hastening the process, to disband the Committee and to instruct officials in the MoHLG, to pull the evidence together in a report that went directly to the CHAC. Thus, technically the Cohen Committee never actually reported, and references to its work relate to the paper published by the DoE in 1971. Nevertheless, the Committee performed a valuable function in pulling together information and opinions on the situation that existed in 1970, after a period of heightened activity and before the acceleration injected by the Housing Act 1974. It is therefore appropriate to conclude this chapter by looking at the analysis and recommendations produced by the Committee.

Then, as now, the housing association movement was characterised by variety, but to an even greater degree (Best, 1997: 104). As has been mentioned above, there were some very large associations, and some very old ones, but the majority were very small and of very recent origin. Some were highly specialised while others catered for a wide range of needs. Some operated in just one locality and others adopted a national profile. The preponderance of small associations was seen by the Cohen Committee as a problem to be tackled, on the basis that it was important to be big enough to be able to employ professional staff and to establish financial credibility with lenders. The unregulated proliferation of associations was seen as an issue, because it led to unhealthy competition, and the Committee supported the idea of local authorities allocating assistance to associations on a zonal basis. The report stated quite bluntly, 'There are too many associations' (p. 75), and the Committee supported mergers between existing small associations to produce more viable large ones.

On the question of finance for development, local authorities were the main lenders to conventional associations, and it was clear that the building societies and other private financial institutions were at that stage completely uninterested. The reluctance of the building societies to lend to cost-rent and co-ownership societies has been note above, and pension funds and insurance companies were found to be even less willing to lend. Thus the report says,

> It would go far to meet the desire for independence of local authorities as a lending source… if the Housing Corporation were empowered to lend to housing associations of all types. (p. 101)

The report was produced before the passing of the Housing Finance Act 1972, as so it had nothing to say about the problems that arose from the new rents and subsidies regime, but it is clear that in certain other respects the work of the Cohen Committee did much to prepare the ground for the reforms implemented via the Housing Act 1974. Irrespective of the difficulties arising from the 1972 Act there had been so much growth and change since the early 1960s that there was a need to rationalise the movement, and it this process that is discussed in the following chapter.

8

Instruments of Housing Policy, 1974–88

Introduction

The choice of break points in historical narratives is often arbitrary and contestable, and there are arguments for choosing the economic crisis of 1976 (Glennerster, 1995), or the election of the first Thatcher government in 1979 (Malpass and Murie, 1999) as major turning points, but few people would argue with 1974 and 1988 as key dates in the development of housing associations in Britain. Both were associated with new financial arrangements, designed to increase the output of housing associations, bringing them into a more prominent position in housing policy, but also leading to significant changes in associations as organisations. These two dates also have a wider significance in the history of the welfare state. The years around 1974 have come to be seen as marking the beginning of the end of the dominance of the Keynesian welfare state (Pierson, 1994), while 1988 has been identified (for example by Le Grand, 1990; Le Grand and Bartlett, 1993: 3) as a point when a series of radical reforms were introduced across a range of services, including housing.

The 1970s was a turbulent decade, both domestically and internationally as the long postwar economic boom enjoyed by the industrialised capitalist countries stuttered to an end. In Britain the effects of wider economic change were felt in terms of higher inflation, higher interest rates, rising unemployment and industrial strife. The value of the pound fell against other currencies and the balance of payments was in deep deficit, until the arrival of growing quantities of oil from the North Sea at the end of the decade. The rate of inflation peaked in 1975 at an annual rate of 25 per cent, and with the pound falling in value and interest rates at record levels the economy reached a crisis point in

1976, when the Chancellor was forced to apply to the International Monetary Fund for assistance. The price to be paid was partly measured in terms of a squeeze on the expansion of credit and savage cuts in public expenditure (Pollard, 1983: 417). Total public expenditure rose very rapidly in 1974–75, but then fell in 1976 and 1977, creating the largest fall since the rundown after the peak during the Second World War (Hogwood, 1992: 41). The severity of the difficulties facing the economy was sufficient to bring about a retreat from the long-established commitment to full employment, macro-economic demand management and growth-funded expansion of the welfare state – in other words, it was the beginning of the end for Keynesianism and the start of the rise of monetarism (Bosanquet, 1980: 31).

The Labour government's hardening attitude to public expenditure foreshadowed the tight monetary policy which was to be enthusiastically embraced by the Thatcherite Conservatives from 1979. It also had serious implications for housing during the later 1970s. Useful accounts of housing and housing policy in the 1970s have been produced by Lansley (1979), Webster (1980) and Hills and Mullings (1991). The housing market began to display marked instability in the form of a series of boom and slump cycles. House prices rose very rapidly in 1971–73, and then fell in real terms. Another price spiral developed in 1978–79. These market events contributed towards the emergence of finance as the dominant housing policy issue.

Labour came into office in February 1974 committed to repealing those parts of the Housing Finance Act 1972, dealing with fair rents in the local authority sector (but not housing associations), but it had no clear idea of what to put in its place. It therefore set up a fundamental review of housing finance, which was later widened into a more general policy review (Great Britain, 1977). However, by the time it was published the government had lost its majority and the time for radical change had passed. The housing policy Green Paper has been widely interpreted as a pallid document, generally supporting the status quo and containing few real policy recommendations (Merrett, 1979; Harloe, 1978; Lansley, 1979; Malpass, 1990). The Green Paper did contain proposals for housing investment programmes (HIPs) and an outline of a new subsidy system for public sector housing. The HIP system was introduced in 1977–78 as a way of giving local authorities greater flexibility in planning their capital expenditure programmes, while at the same time giving central government a mechanism for controlling overall expenditure. The HIP system survives in modified form today, but the proposals on local authority rents and subsidies were not implemented before the 1979 general election, and the subsequent Housing Act 1980, bore the distinctive stamp of the new Tory government. The Green Paper had very little to say about housing associations, but what it did say will be picked up later in the chapter.

The making of the Housing Act 1974

There is a tendency in some quarters to see housing policy in Britain as a political football, implying that incoming governments begin to kick in a different direction, reversing the policies of their predecessors. The Labour government's immediate suspension and subsequent repeal of the contentious parts of the Housing Act 1972, would support such a view, but there are also examples of continuity, and the Housing Act 1974, is a case of legislation prepared under one government being passed into law by another virtually without amendment. The background to the Act was a growing consensus around two main strands of thinking: first, a shift of opinion away from large-scale comprehensive redevelopment of inner-city neighbourhoods towards a strategy of more gradual renewal based on rehabilitation and selective rebuilding, and second, a growing dissatisfaction with the performance of local housing authorities and a corresponding feeling that it was necessary to foster variety of ownership of rented housing, a sentiment that was strengthened by the apparently inexorable decline of the traditional private rented sector. In the face of the decline of private renting Tory thinkers were in favour of supporting housing associations as agents of tenure diversity in urban areas. Leading Labour politicians, such as Anthony Crosland (then shadow Environment minister), supported a 'third arm' in housing provision (Emsley, 1986. 212). This is not to suggest that the Labour Party as a whole had turned away from its long-established support for the leading role for local authorities in housing, nor even that Crosland had done so, but there was at the highest levels in the Party a new willingness to consider other approaches which complemented the work of the local authorities (Back and Hamnett, 1985: 403).

Looking back at the 1974 Act, its main significance lies in the introduction of a new regulatory and financial regime for housing associations, and so it is important to establish that at the time the focus of public and parliamentary debate was much more on aspects of urban renewal in the light of the switch of emphasis away from slum clearance. The government's thinking was set out in two White Papers, in

April and June 1973 (Great Britain, 1973a and 1973b), neither of which said anything about changes in the regulatory or financial regime beyond oblique references to strengthening the Housing Corporation. The first White Paper, *Widening the Choice: The Next Steps in Housing*, set out a number of policy objectives, first of which was rein- forcement of the momentum towards wider home ownership. The White Paper expressed the government's view that the trend towards a municipal monopoly of the supply of new rented housing was unhealthy, and set out a policy commitment to 'expand the role of the voluntary housing movement as a provider of rented housing, particu- larly where the decline of the private rented sector has created severe problems'. Under the Housing Finance Act 1972, the Housing Corpora- tion had been given power to lend to fair rent associations as well as to co-ownership societies, and the White Paper envisaged an expansion on both fronts, but the implication was that this would be within the framework of the 1972 Act subsidy system.

The second White Paper, *Better Homes: The Next Priorities*, was mainly concerned with developments in relation to area-based improvement, and in particular with the introduction of the concept of Housing Action Areas (HAAs), in which housing associations would be expected to play a part. Local authorities were to be given the power to declare HAAs in areas of housing stress. The intention was to focus resources on a programme of gradual renewal in areas with the worst conditions, although it was expected that normally HAAs would contain around 4–500 dwellings. The concept of gradual renewal meant some demolition, some minor improvement pending demolition in the medium term and some more thoroughgoing rehabilitation of houses that were fundamentally sound and which could be given a longer life. It was intended that HAAs would normally run for about five years, after which they might move on to general improvement area status, or in areas where initial conditions were really bad the HAA might be seen as a temporary holding operation pending complete redevelop- ment (Gibson and Langstaff, 1982).

The White Paper was explicit in saying that:

> The Government will look to housing associations increasingly to acquire and manage property in Housing Action Areas and so preserve a wide range of choice of rented accommodation. The Housing Corporation, together with the National Building Agency, will be ready to help housing associations to carry out this key social role, by supporting them both financially and with technical advice. The Government looks to local authorities to work closely with housing associations

and make full use of their expertise and enthusiasm in attacking the problems caused by the decline of the private rented sector. (Great Britain, 1973b: 7)

As soon as the 1972 Act was passed discussions began about the possibility of further legislation to facilitate the expansion of the movement towards an annual total of 30,000 dwellings, which ministers had mentioned as a target (Morton, 1989: 19). The collapse of cost-renting and the difficulties being experienced by the co-ownership societies had left a question mark over the future of the Housing Corporation, but the emerging policy was to rescue it and give it a much enhanced role, as both funder and regulator of housing associations in general. Expanding the role of the Corporation to embrace the funding of traditional associations, including rehabilitation work on existing dwellings, was not opposed within the Corporation, although it represented a real departure from its established role and area of competence.

A DoE Consultation Document of October 1973 set out the Conservative government's acceptance of the weaknesses of the existing financial arrangements for housing associations:

> It has been represented both by housing associations and local authorities that the present grant systems for housing associations are unsatisfactory. It seems that the voluntary housing movement lacks confidence in them and the inadequate levels of subsidy force associations increasingly to depend on substantial local authority subventions from the rates. For the most part housing associations have no effective sources of income other than subsidies and fair rent and rental income, following recent property price inflation, often meets only a small proportion of total costs. The viability of many associations is therefore doubtful and likely to be prejudicial to the continued expansion for which the Government is looking.

The two White Papers of 1973 gave no commitment to a new subsidy for associations, for the details were still subject to negotiation. During 1973–74 there was a considerable amount of consultation between the DoE, the Housing Corporation and the NFHS about the new framework for housing associations, and the whole legislative process was extended by the change of government in February 1974. However, the new Secretary of State for the Environment, Anthony Crosland, was supportive and the Bill that had had its second reading in the House of Commons in January 1973, and which had fallen at the dissolution of parliament, was revived intact.

It was accepted that associations were operating within a straitjacket consisting of fair rents (over which they had no control) and requirements to meet public sector design standards and cost limits. This left them with insufficient financial flexibility to undertake the long-term commitments implicit in property development. The solution that emerged was based on a capital grant towards development costs. This represented a real departure from established practice, for British housing policy had virtually no history of capital grants, and annual revenue subsidies continued to be the preferred mode of assistance for local authorities. The explanation probably lies in the small size of most associations, and their long track record of difficulties in raising capital. Revenue subsidies which left associations with responsibility for raising development capital could not be expected to produce sufficient activity, especially given the known reluctance of the principal lending institutions to lend into this part of the housing system (as discussed in Chapter 7). Two factors reinforcing this kind of conclusion were the emphasis on housing associations as agents of inner-city rehabilitation – a type of housing not obviously attractive as a sound investment – and the fair-rent system, which left associations with insufficient flexibility to provide potential lenders with the assurances that they craved.

A charter for housing associations

The DoE Circular (170/74) explaining the Act described it as a charter for housing associations, and it is necessary to ask why they were given such a boost at that particular time, for while it is true that there was a strong case for doing something about the funding for housing associations in the light of the demise of cost renting, the obvious decline of co-ownership and the problems with the 1972 Act subsidy system, it was not self-evident that associations should be given such a generous subsidy, nor that they should be given such a prominent role in urban renewal. The Cohen Committee had expressed reservations about the capabilities of housing associations in general, and the DoE's Consultation Document had admitted that, 'The need has long been felt to bring housing associations under tighter control and, in particular, to prevent any possible diversion of public funds to private benefit' (DoE, 1973: para 7). It seems reasonable, therefore, to interpret the decision to expand the sector as one which was more a reflection of the perceived failures of other tenures than a positive endorsement of housing associations. The deficiencies of the private rented market, especially in rundown inner city areas, and criticism of the performance of local authorities, allied to reluctance to see further progress towards a municipal monopoly of good quality, affordable rented housing, meant that the government turned to housing associations, but without investing great confidence in them. Acceptance of the need for a new, tailor-made and very generous subsidy was a sign of the inherent weakness of the voluntary sector model. And the introduction of registration as a condition of receipt of subsidy was a reflection of the long established, and well founded, suspicion within government circles that voluntary housing organisations could not always be trusted to act in a completely disinterested way. Scepticism about housing associations has been seen in previous chapters to have led to a series of proposals, since the early 1930s, for their activities to be overseen by some sort of central body, and at last the Housing Act 1974, brought all associations within the scope of the re-invigorated Housing Corporation.

The importance of the 1974 Act lies in both the step-change in housing association development activity resulting from the new grant system and the fact that the introduction of registration marked the start of the process through which successive governments have moulded the movement into its present shape. The changes introduced in 1974 were essentially top-down in character, for while it is true that housing associations had been expanding and modernising, and had begun to demonstrate a capacity to play a part in improving conditions in inner city areas (Figure 8.1), their activities remained at a small scale – their total stock of dwellings in the early 1970s was only around 200,000. Collectively the voluntary housing movement did not amount to a powerful lobby, especially in comparison to local government, and so the decision to divert resources to associations, to introduce a very generous subsidy system and to give associations a key role in inner-city renewal has to be seen as a central government initiative. Rather than government responding to pressure from below, it was the government consciously adopting associations as instruments of housing policy, despite doubts about their competence and capacity to expand into a significant force.

The Housing Act received Royal Assent on 31 July 1974, having had a rapid passage through all its parliamentary stages during which little attention was paid to the provisions affecting housing associations. Debate around the Bill tended to concentrate on issues of urban renewal rather than the potential for growth among voluntary housing organisations, and it is probably true to say that very few people were then aware of the significance of the provisions affecting associations and the Housing Corporation. After all, on all the available evidence,

Figure 8.1   Grosvenor Road, St Paul's, Bristol, typical of
many inner city areas that have been extensively
refurbished by housing associations since the 1970s

housing associations had shown themselves to be very minor players compared with the local authorities.

Part I of the Act referred to the Housing Corporation, Section 1 defining its objectives as:

1. to promote and assist housing associations;
2. to facilitate the proper exercise and performance of the functions of associations;
3. to establish and maintain a register, and to exercise supervision and control over housing associations;
4. to undertake the provision of dwellings.

Thus the Corporation was to be both promoter and regulator of associations, and its position as provider of development funds gave strength to its regulatory role. In relation to the funding role, the Act referred to the Corporation acting as agent for the Secretary of State for the consideration of applications for Housing Association Grant (HAG) and for the payment of grant to registered associations. Part I of the Act extended the powers of the Corporation to include control of disposals of land by housing associations, and the development and management of property by the Corporation itself. It gave the Corporation powers to acquire, develop and dispose of land for housing and related purposes. Thus the Corporation was seen to have an active development role of its own.

Part II of the Act provided for the registration of associations; hitherto the Corporation had operated a system known as listing, but registration was to be a more formal process, and the basic criterion of eligibility for entitlement to grant aid. A Housing Associations Registration Advisory Committee was to be set up to work with the Corporation during the initial process of getting existing associations onto the new register. The Corporation was given powers to deregister associations in certain circumstances, but associations which had received grant aid were not permitted to deregister.

Part III gave the Secretary of State (not the Housing Corporation) power to pay HAG to registered housing associations for approved projects, and to pay grants to cover certain revenue deficits (revenue deficit grant). HAG replaced provisions under existing legislation, and covered both new building, renovation and conversion. The principle was that grants would cover net deficits arising on projects designed to meet the needs of people whose needs and circumstances justified the provision of subsidised accommodation. Associations were expected to liaise with local authorities about the need for grant-aided investment, and to make available at least half of first lettings to tenants nominated by the local authority (this was effectively a continuation of the nomination arrangements which had been in existence since the 1930s). HAG was calculated by reference to three key factors: the total allowable capital cost, the schedule of management and maintenance allowances issued by the Corporation and the income from fair rents set by the independent rent officer service.

HAG was a one-off capital grant, typically covering 80–90 per cent of allowable costs, which left associations with a small residual loan capable of being paid from net rental income. Whereas associations had complained about the risk and uncertainty attached to the 1972 Act subsidies, the 1974 Act effectively gave them a risk-free environment. Once an association had approval for a scheme it was lent the money to meet the construction and other approved capital costs, and when the work was complete the fair rent was set and the grant calculated. Another comforting aspect of the HAG regime was that approved schemes were 100 per cent public funded – which meant that loans (both the initial working capital and long-term residual loan) were provided by the Housing Corporation and local authorities. This relieved associations from the need to raise private finance. Moreover, the introduction of the rent allowance scheme in 1972 meant that associations could be confident that people on very low incomes could afford their rents, thereby removing the need for the sort of charitable fund raising that had sometimes been necessary in order to keep rents affordable.

Finally, turning to the role of housing associations in housing action areas, the Act did not make it a statutory duty of local authorities to involve associations, but as the subsequent DoE Circular (14/75) explained, Ministers expected them to 'play an important role in supporting local authorities, particularly in tackling areas of housing stress and meeting the housing needs of special groups of people'. It was recognised that in some areas there were no appropriate associations, and, in an echo of proposals discussed forty years before, in such cases the Housing Corporation would offer advice on their formation. It was also stated in the Circular that where there were several active associations their participation should be zoned, so that only one was involved in each HAA. In view of the emphasis on competition that emerged in the 1990s, it is important to note two things, first, that in the 1970s zoning was an officially approved policy designed to reduce the undesirable side effects of competition, and, second, that housing associations operated a system of site registration, which meant that the only association that would be considered for HAG funding on a particular site was the one that had registered with the Corporation its interest in that site (irrespective of ownership). However, the real significance of the HAA policy is that for the first time local authorities were told quite explicitly that they were to co-operate with housing associations, and even councils with ingrained resistance to such collaboration were left with little alternative but to comply.

Implementing the charter

Responsibility for implementing the new powers and duties of the Corporation was in the hands of the recently appointed chairman, Lord Goodman, and a new senior management team. Goodman later described the mood in the Corporation on his arrival in 1973 as 'deep bleak gloom'. 'It was', he said, 'an organisation which had become conscious in a relatively short space of time of its own futility and it plainly did not believe that ordinary human exertions could correct this situation' (Housing Corporation, 1977: 1). One of the first tasks of the Corporation after the passing of the Act was to recruit additional staff to discharge its new responsibilities, and the numbers employed doubled in two years (Housing Corporation, 1976: 14). Two senior executives were recruited from the DoE, where they had been responsible for designing the HAG system.

A major part of the workload in these early years was the processing of applications for registration from more than 2,000 associations. In view of the Cohen Committee's conclusion that there were too many associations (Cohen Committee, 1971: 75), it is interesting that the introduction of registration was not used as a device to reduce numbers. Part of the explanation may be that the NFHA had insisted on all its members being regarded as eligible for registration as a condition of co-operation (Emsley, 1986: 251–2). The approach adopted was to use what was seen as a 'coarse sieve', which essentially meant registering almost all applicants in the first instance, with the intention of dealing with problems later, through the monitoring process. It was later claimed that, 'only the "obvious crooks" had been caught by the registration net and many "rogues" had slipped through' (Noble, 1979: 122).

Despite the initial coarse sieve approach there is some evidence that Corporation officials did exercise some degree of influence over events. For example, in Leeds where a multiplicity of small associations were seeking registration they were steered by the Corporation's regional office into an amalgamation that gave rise to Leeds Federated HA. At the other end of the country the Exeter regional office insisted that the organisation then known as HSM Housing Society should split into two quite separate associations, which became Knightstone HA and Devon and Cornwall HA. Other associations, such as North British, WPHT (now Sanctuary), the Guinness Trust and Anchor, were able to establish themselves as national players.

The 1974 Act had an impact on housing associations in a number of ways. Several hundred associations received regular allocations of HAG, enabling them to grow into substantial organisations, and growth itself had organisational consequences. But in addition, the Housing Corporation helped to mould the shape of associations by, *inter alia*, leaning on them to bring housing management activity in-house. The new policy emphasis on rehabilitation also drew some suburban new-build associations into a new area of work in the inner city, and involved them in closer partnerships with local authorities.

A key aspect of the registration regime was the stance that was to be taken in relation to committee members who had a financial interest in their associations. Representatives of the housing associations on the Housing Associations Registration Advisory Committee supported a move to exclude associations that were seen as run by 'fee grabbers'. This had been a divisive issue within the movement, with the more traditional and philanthropic activists tending to deplore what they saw as the cynical and self-serving involvement of property professionals. In 1973 the Greater London Council (the largest funder of housing associations at that time) had taken a decision to ban further support for associations tainted with accusations of fee grabbing (Arden, 1983: 196), and the introduction of substantial amounts of public subsidy under the 1974 Act, together with the change of government, was sufficient to bring about a significant shift in national policy. The Act did not specifically prohibit committee members from undertaking paid work for their associations, but Corporation registration staff tried (not always successfully) to minimise the extent of the practice. The Corporation was in a somewhat difficult position, partly because of the lack of statutory powers, but also because it was charged with meeting the government's output targets for the sector as a whole, and the fee grabbers were among the most effective developers. Many small tradi-tional associations, on the other hand, were not geared to high levels of development activity. In the years immediately after 1974:

The evidence points to the fact that the HC [Housing Corporation] was disproportionately funding the 'professionally based' associations. While not being the sort of organisations that the government had in mind and usually operating in the wrong locations, they were, in the most part, the associations best geared to spending money on a large scale. However, many of them were the same people as those which the HC had worked with before 1974. (Emsley, 1986: 242)

Similarly, the emphasis on output led to allocations of HAG funding being channelled predominantly to larger associations (Emsley, 1986: 235). Thus, in the days before the emergence of a more formalised and rational distribution system, this created a positive feedback loop in which successful development attracted further large allocations in subsequent years, thereby promoting a process of concentration within the movement. This, of course, was consistent with the policy implications of the Cohen Committee's view that there were too many associations. In 1976–77 the Corporation funded 312 associations, and 408 in 1977–78 (Housing Corporation, 1977, 1978). In 1978–79 the pattern of loans approved is shown in Table 8.1.

Table 8.1   Numbers of HAs with HC loans approved in 1978–79 and 1979–80

Size of programme	New Build		Rehabilitation	
	1978–79	1979–80	1978–79	1979–80
1–24 units	111	108	165	171
25–49	55	59	52	48
50–99	55	48	44	53
100–249	42	29	55	53
250+	13	15	13	15
Total	276	259	329	340

Source: Housing Corporation *Annual Reports 1978–79* and *1979–80.*

It should be noted that there is a good deal of overlap between the new build and rehabilitation columns in Table 8.1. It is clear that today's big associations were already established as major players in terms of the Housing Corporation funded development programme. Having said that, it must be acknowledged that the lists of associations receiving funding in the 1970s contained some very small organisations including self-build associations and almshouse charities.

On the question of housing associations' participation in HAAs, it must be remembered that the initiation of such areas lay with the local authorities, which inevitably varied in their commitment and performance. And the associations that were appointed as local authority partners in HAAs also varied in their experience and competence to undertake challenging rehabilitation work. Sometimes enthusiasm for expansion outran ability to ensure a satisfactory standard of work, subsequently leading to problems of premature dilapidation and expensive re-improvement (Malpass and Jones, 1996b: 29). By 1978, housing associations were working with local authorities in 195 HAAs in England (out of a total of 276 declared areas) (Housing Corporation, 1978: 9).

The implementation of the 1974 Act took place against the background of very difficult economic circumstance, not the best setting in which to conduct an orderly expansion of housing association development activity, using new and untried organisational and financial mechanisms. In the three years to 1976 public expenditure grew by 20 per cent while output grew by only 2 per cent (Great Britain, 1976: 1), and economic policy therefore turned to the containment of public expenditure as a priority. The 1974 Act had increased to £500 million the Housing Corporation's borrowing limit, and initially associations were able to expand their development activity almost at will, producing a doubling of completions between 1974 and 1976. Subsequently, however, associations were, inevitably, affected by the squeeze on public expenditure. The Corporation's Annual Report for 1976–77 commented that:

> the cuts imposed on us in 1976 were of a very serious nature and threatened to cast into disarray the planning and programming processes that we have built up, and to undermine the confidence and efficiency of housing associations. (p. 4)

The Corporation's programme for 1977–78 was cut by a quarter and, as Table 8.2 shows, completions never exceeded 46,000, reaching a peak of 44,700 in 1977. In the remaining years of the decade housing association capital expenditure held up well in comparison with the deep cuts then beginning to bite in the local authority sector. A feature of housing association capital spending at this time was the rising share coming from the Housing Corporation as it took over from local authorities as the main funder. In 1975–76 the Corporation and local authorities each provided half of the total lending to associations, but by 1978–79 two-thirds came from the Corporation (Arden, 1983: 77).

Table 8.2   New building and renovations by housing associations in
Great Britain, 1974–79

	New Building	*Renovation*	*Total*
1974	9,920	4,132	14,052
1975	14,693	5,078	19,771
1976	15,770	13,544	29,314
1977	25,091	19,630	44,721
1978	22,676	16,079	38,755
1979	17,835	20,097	37,932
Total	105,985	78,560	184,545

Source: *Housing and Construction Statistics* (HMSO).

Although it is clear that in terms of numbers of dwellings built and improved, the five years after the relaunching of housing associations as instruments of housing policy amounted to a success story, there was nevertheless mounting criticism from a number of directions. First, the Housing Corporation came under scrutiny for an accumulated deficit of £7.5 million in its revenue accounts for 1977–78. This attracted the attention of the House of Commons Public Accounts Committee, which criticised the Corporation and the wider movement on three counts: the thoroughness of the Corporation's vetting of associations before registration, the high proportion of associations that were late in submitting their annual accounts, and the quality of housing association management (House of Commons, 1979: viii). Elsewhere there was criticism of the problems arising from the Corporation's approach to registration during 1975–76. Holmes (1978: 111), for example, argued that too many 'shark' associations had been registered, and that 'The critical failure was the Corporation's reluctance to impose very rigid standards when associations were initially registered'. It was only during 1977, as the weight of registration work reduced, that the Corporation was able to move on to address the question of monitoring. However, this work was slow to gather momentum, and the Corporation was held up to ridicule for the very limited amount of monitoring carried out: by the end of 1978 only 71 associations had been visited (Noble, 1979: 122–5).

Less criticism might have been aimed at the Corporation had it not been for a spate of exposures of scandals and corruption in housing associations during 1978. In a number of cases the Corporation had to exercise its powers to carry out what were known as Section 19 investigations, leading in some instances to Corporation nominees taking committee places from people who were removed or forced to resign

(Housing Corporation, 1978: 14–15). Further criticism of the housing association movement took the form of unfavourable comparisons between their rents and those of local authorities. In 1976 there were reports of fair rents being set at levels twice as high as council rents for equivalent dwellings in the same locality (Weir, 1976: 130). Associations were also criticised for being remote from their tenants, in terms of both housing management practices and the conduct of committee business. Committees were accused of being 'self-perpetuating oligarchies', reluctant to admit tenants to membership. A final aspect of voluntary sector performance that attracted unfavourable comment was the slow process of turning proposed schemes into lettable homes, a problem that was exacerbated by the phenomenon of 'double scrutiny' whereby before a scheme could proceed it was checked in detail by both the Corporation and the DoE. There were good accountancy reasons for this – the DoE had responsibility for paying HAG on schemes approved by the Corporation (House of Commons, 1979: 2) – but it was extremely frustrating for associations to find that the DoE was checking schemes at the level of querying whether larders should contain two shelves or three!

By the late 1970s, then, the widespread political support enjoyed by housing associations in 1974 was beginning to erode:

> The Conservative Party has now apparently realised that housing associations consume roughly as much subsidy as local councils, and there are signs that official enthusiasm for 'voluntary' housing is on the wane. The Labour Party is experiencing growing pressures to restore resources to local authorities at the expense of housing associations. In the long run the movement will be unable to resist attack unless it can show a more convincing rationale and a more satisfactory performance. (Holmes, 1978: 112)

At a more technical level questions were being raised about the future of the HAG system, without which housing associations would have made only a fraction of their post-1974 growth. The government recognised that HAG had some serious defects, and acknowledged that there was a case for bringing housing associations within the scope of its proposed new subsidy system for council housing (Great Britain, 1977: 88). The drawbacks of HAG were said to be:

1. the large amount of work involved in its calculation;
2. the implied assumptions about future rent levels and running costs about which there was great uncertainty;
3. the absence of a means of recovering excess grant if inflation reduced the real burden of debt charges.

The suggestion was that associations could transfer to an annual revenue deficit subsidy, as proposed for local authorities, and that they would also be taken out of the fair-rent system. This was then the subject of discussion with associations and the Corporation, and in February 1979 the DoE issued a consultation paper in which it announced the retention of HAG, although it intended to proceed to the restoration of associations' freedom to set their own rents and the introduction of a grant redemption fund designed to mop up revenue surpluses (House of Commons, 1979: 62–6). A Housing Bill was published in March 1979, but almost immediately the government was defeated in the House of Commons and a general election was called.

The arrival of 'Thatcherism'

The general election of 9 May 1979 proved to be an epoch-making event, ushering in what became eighteen years of Conservative government. The 1980s was a decade politically dominated by the prime minister, Margaret Thatcher. The term Thatcherism summed up not only the distinctiveness of her brand of right-wing Conservatism but also her dominance of the party and the cabinet (Gilmour, 1992: 4). A great deal has now been written about the meaning and impact of Thatcherism (Hall and Jacques, 1983; Kavanagh, 1987; Gamble, 1988; Marsh and Rhodes, 1992), and it is not appropriate to go into a lot of detail here, but it is necessary to say a little about the changing political and economic context in the years following the 1979 election.

Thatcherism has been described as nineteenth-century liberalism dressed up in twentieth-century clothes (Gilmour, 1992: 11), meaning that it was a doctrine which exalted the power of market forces and deplored the interventionism of postwar governments, particularly in terms of their attempts to manage the economy to ensure full employment, and their commitment to expanding tax-funded public expenditure on a range of welfare services. Thatcherism was characterised by a commitment to 'rolling back the state', which took the form of attempts to cut public expenditure as a proportion of gross domestic product, and the privatisation of state-run industries and services. Public expenditure was seen as being at the heart of Britain's economic difficulties, and local authority services, especially housing, were targeted for cuts. Margaret Thatcher's governments became deeply hostile to local government in general, partly because it was responsible for delivering a large proportion of public services and partly because it provided a platform for the articulation of different political perspectives (Boddy and Fudge, 1984). This hostility ranged from measures to limit councils' revenue raising powers to the abolition of the whole class of metropolitan councils, together with the Greater London Council.

A number of accounts of housing and housing policy since 1979 are now available (Hills, 1998; Malpass, 1993; Malpass and Murie, 1999). In general they refer to the extent to which the new government increased the emphasis given to growth in home ownership and broke with past assumptions about the role of council housing. The Thatcher governments were scornful of the housing lobby's preoccupation with homelessness and housing need, concentrating instead 'what the country can afford'. Apparently the country could not afford as much housing investment as it had in the past, and housing was singled out to bear the brunt of the cuts in public expenditure during the government's first period. Although the main aim was promote the growth of home ownership, the prime target of policy was council housing, which was subject to a three pronged attack:

1. the Housing Act 1980, introduced the right for council tenants to buy their homes at substantial discounts (initially between 33 and 50 per cent, depending on length of tenancy (Forrest and Murie, 1988: 56–61)); more than 200,000 homes were sold in 1982 alone;

2. the 1980 Act also introduced a new subsidy system (based on the one contained in Labour's 1979 Bill), enabling the Secretary of State to exert considerable upwards pressure on rents, by reductions in subsidy – in April 1981 council rents rose by an average of 48 per cent (Malpass, 1990: 141);

3. there were deep cuts in capital resources available to local authorities for new building: HIP allocations to English local authorities fell by more than half between 1979–80 and 1987–88, and new building fell from 77,000 in 1980 to just 19,000 in 1988.

The cuts perspective must be seen alongside areas of growth. First, reductions in general housing subsidy were substantially offset by the increased expenditure on means-tested assistance to low-income tenants. In 1982–83 the government introduced the housing benefit system, to replace existing rent rebate and allowance schemes. Although this was designed to be implemented at no addition to public expenditure, it was inevitable that if rents rose then so too would aggregate housing benefit expenditure (Malpass, 1984). Second, the Conservatives' support for the growth of home ownership led them to tolerate a huge increase in the cost of tax relief on mortgage interest (although this was not actually counted as public expenditure), from £1.4 billion in 1978–79 to £4.8 billion in 1987–88 (Wilcox, 1993: 165).

The arrival of the Thatcherite Conservatives in office represented a step change in support for home ownership, which grew from 55 per cent of the total stock in 1979 to 65 per cent by 1988; and it was a watershed for council housing, which had grown to 32 per cent in 1979, only to fall back to less than 25 per cent by 1988. But what did it mean for housing associations?

Housing associations under Thatcherism

When the Conservatives came into office they had a well-worked-out housing strategy, which they proceeded to implement through the Housing Act 1980 (Scotland had a separate Housing (Tenants' Rights and so on) Act 1980). As mentioned above, the target of their attention was council housing, which provided a major reservoir of potential home owners, and insofar as housing associations featured in government thinking it was in much the same terms. The effect of five years of Labour government after the 1974 Act had been to draw associations within the boundaries of the public sector. Depicting them in this way helped to make them acceptable to the Labour Party, especially local councillors, but at the same time it made them less attractive to the Conservatives, who now saw them as absorbing unacceptably large amounts of public expenditure. In one sense Tory housing policy after 1979 was drawn on a scale that rendered housing associations virtually invisible, a mere adjunct of an overgrown council sector. It has even been argued that in the early and mid-1980s housing associations were subject to 'benign neglect' (Langstaff, 1992: 32).

Although housing associations were not at the centre of the government's housing policy they were nonetheless affected in a number of ways. First, under the Housing Act 1980, there were legislative changes, the most significant of which was the inclusion of English and Welsh associations in proposals for the right to buy. This was resisted by the NFHA, using its contacts in the House of Lords, where the government eventually conceded that the right to buy would only apply to tenants of non-charitable associations, which meant that the majority (including the big old charitable trusts) were unaffected, although all were given the power to sell to tenants at prices discounted on the same terms as proposed for council tenants. However, the government did not abandon its intention to give tenants of all associations the right to buy, and in 1982 it returned to the issue in the Housing and Building Control Bill. Again the Lords were effectively mobilised in defence of the charitable associations and the proposal was defeated. Nevertheless, the Act (eventually passed in 1984) introduced a form of cash incentive, equivalent in value to right to buy discounts, to enable tenants of charitable associations to buy houses on the open market.

Included within the 1980 Act was provision for members of co-ownership societies to buy their homes, under terms that in some cases were extremely attractive. All that was required of a group of co-owners wishing to buy was that collectively they cleared the outstanding debt and the costs of sales transactions, the amount to be paid by each individual being calculated by a formula approved by the Housing Corporation. In the longer established societies the burden of mortgage debt had been substantially reduced by inflation, and so some people were able to buy their homes for less than £1,000. In these circumstances it is not at all surprising that the majority of co-owners quickly took advantage of the opportunity to become conventional home owners.

Other legislative changes included the inclusion of housing associations within the terms of the 'tenants' charter', which conferred certain rights, including secure tenancies. Also in the 1980 Act were, as mentioned earlier, measures to prohibit housing association committee members from receiving any fee or other remuneration for services rendered to the association; the terms of the ban were drawn very widely, so as to include any member of the family of a committee member. This was part of a general tightening of the disciplinary powers of the Corporation over registered associations. There was also progress on the question of double scrutiny of housing association development schemes – the Act removed the obstacles to HAG being paid by the DoE on schemes checked and approved by the Housing Corporation (House of Commons, 1981). A final point about the 1980 Act is that it gave the government power to assist associations undertaking improvement for sale. This was consistent with the wider policy of encouraging home ownership, and in particular the series of initiatives collectively referred to as low-cost home ownership. Under the improvement-for-sale scheme associations (and local authorities) were reimbursed for losses arising when houses were sold at market prices less than the costs incurred in their purchase and improvement.

Table 8.3 shows that a total of over 90,000 housing association dwellings were sold during the period 1980–88, only a fifth of which were right-to-buy sales. The right to buy did not apply to tenants of Scottish housing associations until 1987. In the same period local authorities in Great Britain sold a total of more than 1.1 million dwellings.

Table 8.3   Sales of housing association dwellings, 1980–88 (Great Britain)

	Right to buy	*All sales*
1980	–	–
1981	574	7,263
1982	2,003	17,431
1983	2,140	16,464
1984	1,965	12,565
1985	1,522	9,520
1986	2,876	10,500
1987	2,448	7,947
1988	3,766	8,570
Total	17,294	90,260

Source: *Housing and Construction Statistics* (HMSO).

Although right-to-buy sales ran at modest levels, total sales over the period significantly slowed the growth of the housing association sector. Sales of 90,000 dwellings represented nearly a third of new building and rehabilitation by associations during 1980–88 (Table 8.4).

Table 8.4   New-build and rehabilitation completions by housing associations, 1980–88 (Great Britain)

	New Build	*Rehabilitation*	*Total*
1980	21,097	17,715	38,812
1981	19,306	13,770	33,076
1982	13,118	21,795	34,913
1983	16,092	18,036	34,128
1984	16,642	20,701	37,343
1985	13,073	13,419	26,492
1986	12,624	15,035	27,659
1987	12,571	13,267	25,838
1988	12,781	13,636	26,417
Total	137,304	147,374	284,678

Source: Housing and Construction Statistics (HMSO).

In 1979 housing associations managed nearly 400,000 dwellings, double the number at the start of the decade. However, under the influence of Conservative housing policy after May 1979 they did not prosper to the same extent that had seemed likely in the late 1970s. There were several dimensions of change. First, in terms of the overall size of the investment programme, severe cuts were imposed by the government during 1980, with a complete moratorium on new approvals during the second half of the year. Whereas the Corporation had been able to approve loans for 41,369 dwellings in 1979–80, in the following year the total was a mere 15,256 – a cut of almost two-thirds – with new-build approvals slashed to just 5,000 dwellings (Housing Corporation, 1981: 5). Although the total number of completions recovered during 1982–84, the record set in 1977 was not threatened, and then there was a sharp step down to a new low-level plateau in 1985–88, when the average number of completions was 26,600, or more than a third less than the average for the late 1970s.

In terms of investment expenditure on housing associations during this period the following table highlights the shifting balance in favour of the contributions of the Housing Corporation. The Corporation accounted for 68 per cent in 1979–80, but 84–87 per cent after 1982–83.

Table 8.5 Public expenditure on housing association investment, 1979–80 to 1987–88 (£million cash)

	Housing Corporation	Local Authorities	Total
1979–80	401	189	590
1980–81	508	170	678
1981–82	522	142	664
1982–83	755	134	889
1983–84	734	134	868
1984–85	697	134	831
1985–86	711	110	821
1986–87	715	120	835
1987–88	752	122	874

Sources: Public Expenditure White Papers, 1984 and 1989 (Cmnd 9143 and Cm 609).

The next point to draw out is that during the 1980s the Housing Corporation began to exert greater influence on housing associations and their activities, in ways that directly reflected government priorities. First, there was renewed emphasis on rehabilitation; during the 1970s new building generally exceeded rehabilitation completions, but after 1981 rehabilitation exceeded new building in every year up to 1988.

Second, there was increased concentration of funding on schemes for elderly people and people with physical disabilities and learning difficulties (Housing Corporation, 1981: 5). These priorities went with the grain of the movement as a whole, but the third aspect was very much a reflection of government priorities, and at odds with the traditional emphasis of voluntary housing on providing rented accommodation. This was the encouragement of various home-ownership initiatives, which have been mentioned above. There had been Corporation-backed experiments with shared ownership in the late 1970s, but the Conservative government's obsession with home ownership as the solution to all housing problems led to associations being firmly steered in this direction. In 1981–82 home ownership initiatives accounted for 6 per cent of total housing association investment in England, but by 1985–86 they absorbed 28 per cent (Great Britain, 1984, 1989). Included under this heading were improvement for sale, leasehold schemes for the elderly, shared ownership and portable discounts for tenants of charitable associations.

There was also evidence of the Corporation seeking to steer associations in other ways. For instance, in a development from the exclusion of management committee members with financial interests in associations the Corporation leaned on associations to acquire competent in-house development staff, and to rely less on outside consultants. Pressure was brought to bear both through monitoring reports and the Corporation's power to determine which associations received allocations of HAG. Another way in which the Corporation influenced the evolving shape and composition of the movement was through the registration process. New associations seeking registration were not necessarily accepted:

> Applications from new associations were... examined to see if there was a role for them given the need and the work of existing associations in the area where they proposed to operate. Eight associations which reached the stage of making a formal application were rejected for registration. Other groups of people who wanted to help in housing were encouraged and helped to lend their support to existing associations. (Housing Corporation, 1980: 17)

However, associations retained a degree of freedom to innovate, and in what turned out later to have been an experiment of the greatest significance for the development of the movement as a whole, in the mid-1980s a number of associations began to discuss the possibility of raising private finance to augment the perceived shortfall in public funding. The idea of using private finance was increasingly popular among housing practitioners and academics at the time (Langstaff (1992: 33), and it was already under discussion within the Corporation, all of which no doubt helped the associations' initiative to succeed. The lead was taken by North HA (now Home HA), which, by virtue of its large size, strong asset base and non-charitable status, was well-placed to pioneer private finance (Malpass and Jones, 1995: 47–54). The post-1974 growth of associations had been entirely funded by public expenditure and so the financial institutions had no recent experience of approaches from this direction, nor did they properly understand what housing associations were.

The North HA initiative began in the early part of 1986, with the development of a financial model showing the viability of private finance for housing associations. In order to make the project attractive to potential lenders the model incorporated four key points:

1. North HA would seek to develop in the south of England (where property values were higher),
2. the Association would contribute £12.2 million from its reserves,
3. houses would be let on assured tenancies, that is 25 per cent above equivalent fair rents, and
4. local authorities would provide land at nil cost, and they would collectively guarantee the loan.

With support from the Corporation and the Minister of Housing, John Patten, the project was eventually launched in May 1987, when £65 million was raised by the successful sale of loan stock to city institutions. Meanwhile, in 1987–88 the Corporation launched its own private finance initiative using 30 per cent HAG (rather than the usual 75–80 per cent), with the balance of scheme costs being raised privately, and, crucially, not counting as public expenditure. One of the first schemes to be funded in this way was at St Mellons, Cardiff, where 600 dwellings were built by two associations (Wales and the West and Secondary Housing Association for Wales) on land donated by the city council, and with private finance provided by the Halifax (Brookes, 1987). A key feature of this initiative, like the North HA scheme, was the use of assured tenancies, allowing rents to be set outside the fair-rent system. Assured tenancies had been introduced in 1980 as an inducement to approved landlords to invest in new private rented housing, but virtually nothing had been made of them until private finance for housing associations.

Conclusion

The period 1974–88 was a time of rapid growth and change for associations, when some were transformed in terms of both the scale of their operations and their organisational character. In some cases organisations which had led a rather precarious financial existence for decades were suddenly given the opportunity to grow at a pace that they had never previously been able to contemplate. Moreover, this opportunity was very largely risk-free. The fair-rent and HAG systems effectively removed associations from the effects of market forces, creating a rather closed environment. The price attached to this privileged situation was that associations became instruments of government housing policy, incorporated into the public sector. Faced with a choice between continuing freedom on the margins of housing provision and giving up much of that freedom in return for a significant role in meeting housing need most associations rapidly opted for the latter. However, in practice only a small proportion of registered associations managed to establish themselves as active developers. In any one year only 5–600 associations received HAG allocations for new building or rehabilitation, and only a subset of them received regular allocations each year. To some extent this was a product of differences among associations – the initiative lay with them to apply for grant. But not all those that asked for HAG were successful, and it is important to keep in mind the extent to which the Corporation was able to shape the growth of the movement through its control of the distribution of grant to associations. The Corporation, on behalf of the government, also influenced the type of housing provided and the terms on which it was offered, that is for rent, shared ownership or sale, and it is safe to say that, left to themselves, associations would not have developed home ownership schemes in the way or to the extent that they did in the 1980s. This leads to the conclusion that whereas associations have always seen themselves, and been seen by governments, as organisations whose independence enabled them to experiment and innovate, in the 1980s they were used as agents of government experiments. It was their incorporation into the apparatus of the state that rendered them suggestible to Ministerial whim.

A final point to note here is that although the generous public funding and risk-free framework in the period 1974–88 now looks somewhat unreal, it is probably true that without it associations would not have been able to make the transition to private finance after 1988. During 1974–88 some associations were able to grow into organisations of sufficient size and maturity, with large enough asset bases, to be taken seriously by the lending institutions.

PART III

9

Housing and Housing Policy Since 1988

The boundary between the past and the present is never easy to draw, but for the purpose of constructing an account of the growth of housing associations as key players in the British housing system it is reasonable to treat the Housing Act 1988 as marking the beginning of the contemporary period. It was this Act and associated changes which substantially changed the existing legislative and policy framework, establishing a new regime for the 1990s. Although there have been subsequent refinements and changes of emphasis, the reforms of the late 1980s remain in place as the basis for housing association activity into the new century. The Housing Act of 1974 has been presented above as launching housing associations onto a new plane, with a distinct role in housing policy, but it is arguable that the reforms following the 1988 Act are of even greater long-term significance. Whereas after 1974 associations continued to be very much junior partners to local authorities, since 1988 they have become the dominant providers of new rented housing and the main vehicle for the break up of the local authority sector. For a decade after the election of Margaret Thatcher's first government housing associations carried on much as before, but the effect of the 1988 reforms was to move them firmly in the direction of a closer engagement with private financial institutions, requiring them to come to terms with the rigours of competition and the risks associated with greater exposure to market forces.

Dealing with the recent past and with current developments requires a more thematic approach, and so Chapters 10 to 12 examine in some detail aspects of housing association finance, development and governance since 1988. The purpose of this chapter, therefore, is to provide an overview of the wider context. In order to do so it is necessary to refer back to policies which had their origins in the run up to the general election of 1987, at which Margaret Thatcher was returned to office as prime minister for a third consecutive term.

The political and economic context

At the time of the 1987 election Thatcher was at the peak of her power: the economy was recovering from the recession of the early part of the decade and the prospects for Britain seemed to be generally good (notwithstanding concerns in some, non-governmental, quarters about the growth of poverty and widening inequalities in society). Following their third successive victory the Thatcherite Conservatives pressed ahead with their programme of privatisation of nationalised industries, and set about implementing radical changes in the way that welfare state services were organised. However, within a short time the economic boom turned to the deepest slump for many years, Thatcher's flagship policy, the poll tax or community charge, proved to be deeply unpopular and at the end of 1990 the prime minister was persuaded by her senior cabinet colleagues to resign after eleven years in Downing Street. John Major took over as prime minister, but things soon became even worse, epitomised by Britain's ignominious withdrawal from the European exchange rate mechanism. Nevertheless, Major managed to secure, almost single handedly, an unexpected fourth election victory for the Tories in May 1992. Over the next five years the divisions within the Conservative Party over Europe, coupled with a series of rather sordid scandals involving the private lives of ministers and MPs, brought the Party into such disrepute that at the election of 1 May 1997 the revitalised Labour Party was elected with a huge majority over all other parties and the Conservatives suffered their worst election defeat since before the First World War.

Margaret Thatcher's legacy to British politics was thus finally revealed: she had pledged to see off socialism, and she succeeded in the sense that New Labour ministers now scrupulously avoid the term, purporting instead to be engaged in developing something known as the 'third way'. Eighteen years of Conservative government brought about a sea change in political discourse in Britain. Thatcher's dominance of British politics in the 1980s meant that the Labour Party had to change in order to be elected, and such a long period in opposition gave the Party time to distance itself from its predecessors in the 1970s. The lasting achievement of the Thatcherites is that, despite always being a minority in their own party, and never winning over a majority of voters in the country at large, they managed to shift the terms of debate onto their own ground. Indeed it is arguable that the general election of 1997 brought in new people to carry on the Thatcherite revolution: what had made Labour electable was not just the ditching of socialism but the acceptance of much of the Thatcherite analysis and policy. The other side of the Thatcher legacy, of course, is that she so divided her own party that it is currently very difficult to envisage a Conservative election victory until well into the twenty-first century.

The development of policy towards housing associations during the years since 1988 has to be seen in the context of events in the housing market, changes in the labour market and attempts by successive governments to contain and restructure public expenditure. The best account of recent housing policy is probably that provided by John Hills (1998), but see also Malpass (1996), and Malpass and Murie (1999). The late 1980s economic boom, and subsequent slump, was closely linked to the rise and fall of the housing market. At the time of the 1987 election the market was rising strongly, fuelling an expansion in consumption spending, much of it apparently underpinned by rising property values, although at the same time there were concerns that house prices were rising to such a level that home ownership was becoming unaffordable for a growing proportion of the population (Bramley, 1994). The housing market went through a bout of frenzied activity during the first half of 1988, but then transactions rapidly declined and prices fell away. The wider economy was tipped into recession, which deepened through to the early 1990s, with rising unemployment, very high interest rates and the worst housing market slump for decades. As house prices fell and unemployment rose so people who had taken out large mortgages at the peak of the market now found themselves in 'negative equity', where the value of their property was less than the size of the outstanding loan (Dorling and Cornford, 1995). Where this coincided with unemployment and/or a need to sell then there was a high probability of real hardship. Mortgage arrears reached record levels, as did the numbers of houses taken into possession by lenders. In the peak year, 1991, some 75,500 homes were taken into possession by lenders, representing a massive increase from under 6,000 in 1989; overall several hundred thousand households lost their homes during the recession in the housing market. The crisis in the housing market led to pressure on the government to intervene, which it was reluctant to do, but in 1992–93 it launched the 'housing market package', which was a scheme to soak up excess supply by enabling selected housing associations to spend £570 million on purchasing houses on the open market (this is discussed further in Chapter 11). Despite this the housing market continued in a rather depressed condition, with prices remaining below their late 1980s peak until well into the second half of the decade.

The economic recession of the early 1990s differed from earlier downturns in the extent to which it affected highly-paid home owners employed in modern high-tech sectors such as financial services, most spectacularly in the City of London, which had been the epicentre of the late 1980s boom. This served to highlight the changed circumstances and the transition to a more flexible labour market, a term which means, first, that people can no longer expect to remain in one occupation or with one employer throughout their working lives, and second, that employers increasingly seek to recruit staff on short-term contracts. In one sense the term flexible labour market is a euphemism for an insecure labour market, and one in which employers are able to drive down wage rates for low-skilled workers. This all has implications for housing, in that lack of security, with episodes of unemployment interspersed with periods in work, makes long-term mortgaged house purchase more difficult to contemplate. In relation to the rental housing market, low wages and episodic unemployment represent a challenge to the policy trend towards higher rents, underpinned by means-tested housing benefit. This, too, is an issue that will be discussed again later (Chapter 10), but it is important to acknowledge here that so strong has been the challenge posed by the conflict between high rents and low wages that since 1995 rents policy has been put into reverse.

The growth of housing associations since 1988 has taken place against a background of continuing government rhetoric about the need to contain public expenditure. The White Paper of 1995 (Great Britain, 1995: 8) claimed that in real terms public expenditure on housing was broadly the same as it had been in 1979–80, but within this there were some very important changes of emphasis, with capital expenditure by local authorities on new building having been virtually eliminated by the mid-1990s, while expenditure on renovating existing council houses had increased several fold. The other really significant change in the pattern of expenditure was the shift away from general subsidies to local authorities and capital grants to housing associations into means-tested housing benefit, which had grown to £11 billion in 1995–96 in England alone. If housing benefit is excluded from the calculation (on the grounds that it is properly seen as part of social security spending), then housing expenditure has fallen while social security, health and education have all increased (Wilcox, 1997: 41). This picture is strengthened if two other factors are taken into account, namely the major cuts in mortgage interest tax relief since 1990, and the extent to which the net level of local authority capital expenditure has been reduced over the years by receipts from the sale of assets.

Local authorities enjoyed an increase in capital expenditure in 1989–90, as they sought to use up accumulated receipts before the rules were tightened in April 1990, and then in the early 1990s housing associations also experienced a rapid increase in investment expenditure (detailed in Chapter 10). However, the subsequent course set by the Conservative government was firmly downwards:

> The priorities of the last government were made abundantly plain in the 1996 Budget. In England, Scotland and Wales social housing investment was put at the end of the queue compared to other services, as overall public spending was squeezed to make way for a reduction in income tax rates. Provision for housing investment has been reduced progressively for some years; the cut-backs announced in the 1996 Budget were, however, far more severe than in previous years. (Wilcox, 1997: 51)

A new strategy for rented housing

Commentaries on housing policy in the 1980s typically note the way in which the wave of activity initiated by the first Thatcher government was followed by a quieter period, during which the government carried out what one of Mrs Thatcher's succession of housing ministers described as a 'fundamental and much needed review of housing policy' (Young, 1991: 8). This then led to a renewed round of reforms introduced in 1988–90. Why did a government entering its third term feel the need for fundamental reform in this area? Part of the answer lies in the need to move on from the successes and failures of earlier policies. From the government's point of view its emphasis on expanding home ownership had been a resounding success (despite the recession in the housing market in the early 1980s, and the very limited impact of the package of low cost home ownership initiatives (Forrest, Lansley and Murie, 1984)). The right to buy had surpassed its supporters' expectations, with receipts exceeding those from all other privatisations put together (Forrest and Murie, 1988: 10). But the question arose as to how to keep up the momentum while accommodating the continuing need for rented housing, for it was becoming clear to Ministers that the economic circumstances of a considerable proportion of tenants in the council sector meant that they could not be expected to buy, and, more widely, there remained large numbers of households requiring rented housing.

Among the failures of early 1980s housing policy had been the reform of local authority rents and subsidies; the system introduced in 1981 had been losing its effectiveness for several years and government had lost control of council rent levels across a large part of the country (Malpass, 1990: 155–6). Local authority capital spending was also proving to be nothing like as controllable as had been intended under legislation passed in 1980 (Malpass and Murie, 1994: 111–12). The government's policy of supporting private renting was another example of unsuccessful legislation by the first Thatcher government, and the sector continued to decline (Kemp, 1993). The reform of means tested assistance with housing costs in 1982–83 had been widely criticised at the time and the whole housing benefit system was clearly in need of further attention. Indeed the problems arising from the housing benefits scheme served to highlight the continuing need to address the reform of housing finance, and in 1985 the NFHA sponsored an inquiry on the subject, chaired by the Duke of Edinburgh (NFHA, 1985). A final point is the failure to address the deficiencies in the HAG system, which had been acknowledged in the Green Paper of 1977.

It was in these circumstances, then, that the government began to put together a set of proposals amounting to a new strategy for rented housing. The approach, consistent with wider Thatcherite values, was based on deregulation, privatisation, marketisation and competition. The new thinking on housing took place alongside a wider restructuring of welfare state services, designed to create markets or quasi-markets (Le Grand and Bartlett, 1993) in health and education as well as housing. In the case of housing the existence of a large number of independent providers, housing associations, already used to bidding for funds on an annual basis from a central purchaser, meant that a quasi-market was effectively already operating. The new concern for rented housing represented an addition to the continuing emphasis on home ownership rather than a change of direction. Rejecting calls for reforms based on tenure neutrality (which involved removing home owners' entitlement to mortgage interest tax relief), the government opted for a package of measures aimed at simultaneously reviving investment in private renting and further undermining the local authority sector, while bolstering housing associations. Thus renewed policy interest in rented housing did not imply returning local authorities to their former pre-eminence as house builders. On the contrary, by the mid-1980s Ministers saw local authority housing as part of the problem to be tackled.

The new rented housing strategy was developed during 1987, with new elements revealed in the course of the general election campaign in the spring, and the whole plan being set out in a White Paper in the autumn (Great Britain, 1987). The White Paper explained that local authorities would be expected to play a different role in the housing system:

> The future role of local authorities will essentially be a strategic one identifying housing needs and demands, encouraging innovative methods of provision by other bodies to meet such needs, maximising the use of private finance, and encouraging the new interest in the revival of the independent rented sector. In order to fulfil this strategic role they will have to work closely with housing associations; private landlords; developers; and building societies and other providers of finance. (Great Britain, 1987: 14)

The strategic role was subsequently generally referred to as enabling, emphasising that councils should move away from acting as providers and concentrate on enabling provision to be made by others (Bramley, 1993; Goodlad, 1993). This was obviously important for housing associations as potential partners with local authorities in meeting housing needs at local level.

The new strategy for rented housing had three main components:

1. a continued attack on local authority housing,
2. an attempt to revive investment in private renting, and
3. a reform of the financial and legislative framework for housing associations.

The assault on public housing took the form of measures designed to promote further break-up of council owned stocks, and the introduction of a new financial regime covering both capital and revenue. The government announced plans to introduce Housing Action Trusts (HATs), which were to be bodies similar to Urban Development Corporations, appointed by the Secretary of State, with powers to take over designated areas of poor quality council housing for the purpose of improvement and subsequent disposal to new owners, 'including housing associations, tenants' co-operatives and approved private landlords' (Great Britain, 1987: 16; Karn, 1993; Woodward, 1991). In other areas tenants would have the right to opt out of the local authority sector and to transfer to new landlords – a scheme referred to as tenants' choice, although in fact the legislation was written in a way which gave the initiative to private landlords. The idea was that landlords would be able to acquire selected parts of a council's stock, subject to the agreement of the tenants. These two measures were included in the Housing Act 1988, but the new financial regime for local authority housing was delayed until the Local Government and Housing Act 1989.

It is not necessary to go into the details of the new financial regime for local authorities (Malpass *et al.*, 1993). On the capital side the 1989 Act represented a significant tightening of the rules covering capital receipts and borrowing. It required local authorities to set aside for debt redemption purposes three-quarters of all capital receipts accumulated since 1980, together with the same proportion of receipts in future years. Additionally there was a closing of the various loopholes that inventive councils had used to evade controls during the 1980s. On the revenue side, too, the Act was designed to tighten the control exercised by the centre over the decisions made by local authorities. It introduced a single housing revenue account subsidy, enabling the government to exert renewed leverage on rents. In relation to rents the government's stated policy was that,

> Rents generally should not exceed levels within the reach of people in low paid employment, and in practice they will frequently be below market levels. They should, however, be set by reference to these two parameters: what people can pay, and what the property is worth, rather than by reference to historic cost accounting figures. (DoE, 1988: 5–6)

This is quoted here because, as will become clear in Chapter 10, there were significant differences between this approach and the one adopted for housing associations.

In relation to private renting, which the government now bracketed together with the housing associations in the so-called 'independent' sector, the strategy was quite subtle, for although it contained measures designed to stimulate new investment in traditional landlordism it also sought to promote new-style landlord organisations, with existing housing associations in the background as a kind of fail-safe mechanism. The Minister of Housing in 1987, John Patten, spoke of his vision of a multiplicity of new model landlords which would be governed by a new version of the three Rs: they would be respectable, responsible and registered (Platt, 1987: 24). The plan was to move all new private sector lettings onto an assured, or assured shorthold, tenancy basis, which effectively meant less security of tenure for tenants, and the phasing out of the fair-rent system, since new lettings would have rents set at market levels (Kemp, 1993). A further boost to investment in private renting was given by the extension of the Business Expansion Scheme (BES) to cover housing in the budget of 1988. This was conceived as a way of kick-starting investment by giving investors generous tax breaks (Crook and Kemp, 1996).

The third component of the rented housing strategy, covering housing associations, is examined in detail in Chapter 10, and it is sufficient to say here that it was designed to:

- increase total output for a given amount of public expenditure, by bringing in private finance;
- expose associations to the business risks of new development; and
- allow rents to rise towards market levels (while remaining affordable), with housing benefit 'taking the strain'.

It should be noted here that at the same time the government established new bodies, Scottish Homes and Tai Cymru (Housing for Wales) to take over the Housing Corporation's responsibilities in Scotland and Wales respectively. Henceforth distinct policies and practices developed in the three parts of Great Britain, although unfortunately the full richness of these differences cannot be reflected in this book.

Implementing the strategy

The deregulation of private renting began to take effect for new lettings in January 1989, and, given the high rates of turnover in this sector, it soon spread quite widely. Rents increased, as was intended, and there was an expansion in the total supply of private lettings, amounting to more than 200,000 dwellings in four years, including 81,000 dwellings built with BES support. However, Crook and Kemp (1996) have shown that net yields remained uncompetitive and that a significant proportion of the increased supply was due to the slump in the property market, which led owners into temporarily letting houses that they could not sell. Higher rents inflated the aggregate cost of rent allowances (covering both private and housing association tenants), which nearly trebled in five years – from under £1.4 billion in 1989–90 to over £5.4 billion in 1995–96 (Wilcox, 1997: 187). This was clearly a huge price to pay for a relatively small number of new dwellings.

In relation to local authority housing, there was intense opposition from tenants to the first wave of HATs, and none of them went ahead, although to save face the government increased the level of funding and ultimately established six projects. Tenants' choice was even less successful, and by the time that the scheme was abandoned in 1995 fewer than 1,000 homes had been transferred to new landlords using this route. However, the threat of HATs and tenants' choice had a galvanising effect on other routes out of council ownership, contributing to a temporary rise in right-to-buy sales in 1988–90, although the rate subsequently fell away again. Of more lasting impact was the effect on large-scale voluntary transfers (LSVT) of council housing to new housing associations established for the purpose. It is important to remember that the growth of LSVT was the outcome of local initiatives in reaction to the perceived implications of the Housing Act 1988 – it was not provided for in the Act and was not initially a component of government policy. Advocates of LSVT justified it as a way of ensuring retention of a supply of social rented housing in areas which already had very high levels of home ownership and where private landlords were expected to take advantage of the opportunity presented by tenants' choice. In the event, of course, private landlords showed no interest in acquiring parts of the council sector, but LSVT developed a momentum of its own, driven forward by the financial advantages of housing associations able to raise capital unconstrained by Treasury rules on public expenditure.

Another factor which helped the appeal and spread of LSVT was the impact of the new financial regime for local authority housing. The 1989 Act made it much more difficult for local authorities to raise capital for new building and for the increasingly urgent renovation of their ageing houses. On the one hand, expenditure on capitalised repairs fell dramatically (Malpass *et al.*, 1993: 45–6), while on the other hand rents rose much faster than inflation. The increase in council rents was partly a direct and intended outcome of government policy, which during the period 1990–91 to 1995–96 was based on guideline rent increases above the rate of inflation; in fact, many councils found that it was necessary to increase rents even faster, and some chose to impose very high increases as a way of encouraging tenants to vote for LSVT. The upshot was that council rents in England rose by 40 per cent in real terms by 1995–96 (AMA/ADC, 1995: 3). Meanwhile, real-terms capital expenditure by local authorities fell from the artificial peak in 1989–90 to less than half as much by 1996–97 (Hills, 1998: 182), and new building had been effectively eliminated by the middle of the decade.

In the context of cuts in expenditure by local authorities, the slump in the housing market and the modest growth in private renting, the performance of housing associations in the early 1990s was outstanding. Faced with the challenges of private finance, responsibility for rent setting and the new burden of development risk, associations demonstrated a collectively enthusiastic response. Their output of new building trebled, from 12,781 in 1988 to a peak of 38,441 in 1995 (Wilcox, 1997: 91).

Turning the screw

During the 1990s local authorities came under increasing pressure to demonstrate through their annual housing strategy statements that they were working in effective partnerships with associations and other providers (Lambert and Malpass, 1998). The distribution of resources to local authorities was moved away from a needs basis, towards more Ministerial discretion. Authorities were encouraged, indeed required, to compete with each other for credit approvals on the basis of bids submitted in the light of published criteria. Liaison with the Housing Corporation, housing associations and other private sector organisations became an explicit requirement. After 1992, 60 per cent of allocations to local authorities were based on discretionary criteria, the primary one being the relative efficiency and effectiveness of authorities in capital investment, including the extent to which they were likely to use their allocations to develop their enabling role in co-operation with housing associations and other parts of the private sector. From April 1997 the distribution of credit approvals to local authorities became entirely discretionary. Meanwhile, in 1994 the Conservatives had introduced the Single Regeneration Budget (SRB) as a way of bringing together resources from a number of different government departments in order to focus them on particular projects, again to be decided on a competitive basis.

> We have therefore moved from a situation where housing resources were distributed primarily on the basis of evidence about the condition of the local authority and private stock and indicators of housing stress to one where discretionary judgements of relative performance are the key factor. This has been accompanied by a shift from control of the volume of expenditure, to control of what money is spent on, and the way in which it is spent. As with other competitive bidding systems government [was] seeking both a shift in the content of policy, emphasising an expanded private and voluntary sector role and a diminishing local authority role, and a shift in the process of making and implementing policy, emphasising the involvement of the private and voluntary sectors. (Lambert and Malpass, 1998: 100)

Another aspect of the Conservative government's obsession with competition was the introduction of compulsory competitive tendering for local authority housing management. This was a manifesto commitment in 1992, but five years later, after an enormous amount of disruption to the routines of council housing services, not all authorities had gone through the tendering process, and very little interest had been shown by private sector competitors. Housing associations, on the whole, showed great reluctance to bid against in-house teams from their partner local authorities unless explicitly asked to do so.

After the general election of 1992 the government found itself with a huge budget deficit, which it set out to reduce by cuts in public expenditure, including, as always, housing. Net capital expenditure on housing fell by 50 per cent between 1992–93 and 1996–97 (Hills, 1998: 134). Housing benefit, on the other hand, continued to rise, prompting measures to restrict entitlement. Thus in 1996 new limits were introduced in the form of local reference rents, above which claimants would not be entitled to full benefit. There were also restrictions on benefit to young single people, limiting them to the equivalent of the rent of a room in a shared flat. It was proposed to extend this to all single people below retirement age, but the incoming Labour government withdrew the order.

A different approach to stemming the rising tide of housing benefit expenditure was to put rents policy into reverse, and the White Paper of 1995 admitted that,

> The most cost-effective way of ensuring that people with permanently low incomes have a decent home is to give a direct subsidy to landlords to provide social housing at rents below market levels. (Great Britain, 1995: 26)

Instead of putting pressure on authorities to raise rents, the government announced that from April 1996 guideline rent increases would be pegged to no more than the rate of inflation. Moreover, authorities that sought to impose higher increases would face subsidy penalties. In the case of housing associations the government moved towards a competition for grant based not only on the total amount of capital subsidy required but also the implications for housing benefit. The emphasis on keeping rents down has been one of the most important policy changes of the last few years, reflecting both the volume of housing benefit expenditure and the difficulties faced by successive governments in finding a workable reform package. It is also a sign of official awareness of the poverty trap and work incentive problems generated by a combination of high rents and low wages.

Other aspects of the 1995 White Paper included plans to increase competitiveness in social rented housing, by widening access to grant aid to bring in profit-seeking private developers, and new forms of not-for-profit organisations, specifically local housing companies. The Housing Act 1996, made some small changes opening the way for organisations other than housing associations to receive grant, introducing the new generic term 'registered social landlords'. However, the Act did not go so far as to entitle private developers to receive grant aid. The government had plans for a separate Bill on this matter, but nothing was published before the general election. Similarly the Major government was increasingly vocal in its exhortations to local authorities to consider stock transfers to housing associations and local housing companies, and in the last few weeks before the election it published proposals which would have required all councils to include plans for stock transfer in their housing strategies.

On homelessness, however, the government did succeed in making important legislative changes, despite solid opposition from the housing lobby. The Housing Act 1996, introduced the requirement that the only way into a local authority or housing association letting would be via the official local housing register, thereby cutting off homeless households from direct access to a secure tenancy. The Act established that in future people accepted as homeless and in priority need would have an entitlement to temporary accommodation for up to two years, during which time the onus was on them to secure suitable housing for themselves.

New Labour, new policies?

In May 1997 a Labour government took office for the first time for a generation, inheriting a situation that was very different from that which faced the last incoming Labour government in 1974. Social and economic change over the intervening period had had an impact and four successive election victories had given the Conservatives the opportunity to stamp their own ideological footprint on housing. In opposition the Labour Party had made a number of clear statements about aspects of its housing policy: there was a pre-election pledge that compulsory competitive tendering of local authority housing management had no future, a commitment to release local authorities' accumulated capital receipts and a promise to restore the rights of homeless people to the position obtaining before the Housing Act 1996. However, one important issue on which Labour's Treasury team had refused to give ground was the reform of the public spending conventions.

Once in office Labour introduced a series of comprehensive spending reviews across the board, including housing. In the meantime, the new government rapidly back-pedalled on compulsory competitive tendering, allowing existing tendering schedules to go ahead as planned, but proposing in future to introduce a new regime based on the notion of 'best value' (DETR, 1998a). On capital receipts, within months of taking office the government introduced a 'capital receipts initiative' which amounted to the first tranche of released resources, adding £800 million to local authority capital programmes over two years. And on homelessness the government gave local authorities discretion in the way they interpreted the Act, but there was no sign of primary legislation on homelessness or any other housing policy measures.

The results of the comprehensive spending review (CSR) were revealed in July 1998, in a carefully staged series of Ministerial announcements. Although most public attention focused on the large sums of additional spending allocated to health and education, the announcement of much smaller amounts for housing was generally well received by commentators and providers alike. The headline figure was the provision of £3.6 billion to be spent by local authorities over three years on the renovation of their housing stock. Taken together with the capital receipts initiative announced in 1997 this effectively fulfilled the election pledge to release the £5 billion of accumulated receipts. Coming after years of significant cuts in resources this was obviously very welcome, but there are a number of caveats that must be entered. First, the aggregate cost of outstanding repairs needed by local authority dwellings (officially acknowledged to be £10 billion in England alone) is far greater than the resources being released; second, after five years of Labour government overall annual capital spending on housing will remain below the levels achieved by the Conservatives in the early 1990s; and third, the Housing Corporation's capital programme is to remain static in real terms, at a quarter of the level of 1992–93.

The CSR was essentially a spending review, rather than a policy review, although some clear lines of thinking did emerge, such as the emphasis on renovation rather than new building in the social rented sectors. On the issue of stock transfers, where the Tories had published proposals requiring that councils transferred their houses to other landlords, Labour continued to support transfers without insisting on them.

In a pamphlet on the future of local government Tony Blair (1998) made it clear that in his view there could be no return to the model of local authorities as comprehensive service providers. The future, as he saw it, lay in local authorities developing stronger and more effective partnerships with a range of non-municipal providers, which suggests that in relation to housing provision policy will continue along the route started under the Conservatives. It is less clear what will happen in relation to the really big issue of housing benefit reform. So far this has proved to be just as puzzling to Labour as it had been to the Conservatives. It is not just that there has been no sign of action – there has been no indication that the government knows what to do. The same is true of rents in the social rented sectors, and the CSR appears to have made no progress towards the sort of robust, durable reform that is so urgently needed.

Housing associations and housing policy

Having sketched in an outline of the wider context it is now possible to return to the focus on housing associations. The significantly enhanced role planned for associations was a proposal that was certain to be well-received in most quarters of the movement. There were, nonetheless, a number of concerns expressed at the time, about the potential for, and mechanics of, growth and its implications for the traditional values of voluntary housing organisations. The sorts of questions being raised referred to doubts about whether sufficient private finance would be forthcoming on terms that enabled associations to carry on building at rents that were affordable to low income households. Would small associations be able to raise private loans, or would investment be increasingly concentrated among a small number of ever-larger associations? Would private finance and higher rents lead associations to prioritise applicants with rather higher and more secure incomes, thereby diluting their established commitment to low-income households? In due course it emerged that there was to be no drift up-market, but a rather different issue was raised concerning the implications of associations building relatively large estates occupied mainly by tenants who relied on state benefits for their income. In addition, attention within the movement came to focus on questions of corporate governance and accountability. As associations grew in size and as they took over from local authorities as the main providers of new rented housing, question were raised about how they managed their affairs, and how they could be held to account for the large amounts of public money underpinning their activities. There were also some more theoretical questions about how to locate housing associations within the wider fragmentation and privatisation of services historically provided by elected local authorities. These are some of the issues and themes explored in the following chapters.

Chapter 8 developed the notion of housing associations as instruments of housing policy, arguing that in the period after 1974 the price paid for generous state funding was that associations were used to pursue government policy objectives. This theme is continued in the remainder of the book, where it is argued that the process of incorporation has intensified, although at the same time the picture has become more complicated. On the surface housing associations have been freed from the constraints of the previous system, in the sense that they can raise private finance at will in order to top up grant aid, and they are responsible for setting their own rents. In one sense they have been 'reprivatised' (Randolph, 1993). But, on the other hand, they remain heavily constrained by a combination of factors, including:

● Treasury attempts to manage the economy, control public expenditure and balance the budget (affecting the volume of grant available and the price that has to be paid for private finance);

● government housing policies (affecting what sorts of housing are to be developed – this refers to both the specification of the dwellings and their tenure arrangements);

● local authority priorities (affecting what gets built, where and by which associations).

In terms of macro-economic management, housing associations have seen the amounts of capital flowing their way rise and fall steeply during the 1990s, partly reflecting their involvement in counter cyclical expenditure to support the building industry during the recession, followed by cuts as government sought scope for reductions in income tax. Although the amount of grant per dwelling is now much reduced, associations remain heavily dependent on grant aid for new building and rehabilitation, and on housing benefit to underpin their income streams. Very little housing is built by associations without some level of grant, which clearly means that the Housing Corporation and the local authorities, as the sources of grant, have control over what gets built. The stock of housing association dwellings grew by more than two thirds between 1988 and 1995, but it was growth whose composition and geographical distribution was influenced more by government priorities than by associations themselves. Similarly, although associations gained responsibility for rent setting, the rents they found themselves having to charge reflected government policy, and they became a source of much concern as to their affordability.

In the late 1980s the government seized upon housing associations because of the acknowledged need for more rented housing, in circumstances where Ministers would not rely on local authorities and could not rely on the private sector to deliver that housing. Ministers were highly critical of local authorities for their alleged failings in terms of housing management and their large-scale bureaucratic structures which distanced them from their tenants. Housing associations, by contrast, were seen as smaller in scale, less bureaucratic and with a generally better track record on housing management (DoE, 1987). That this was not entirely borne out by the research evidence was not allowed to interfere with the decision to favour associations over municipal provision (Centre for Housing Research, 1989; Clinton *et al.*, 1989). However, the more they grew, and the more they expanded the geographical areas across which they operated, the more difficult it became for associations to retain the very characteristics which made them attractive in the first place. At the same time government and the Housing Corporation have developed an increasingly tight framework of controls over association activity.

10

Finance

Introduction

This chapter and the next look at finance and development, aspects of housing association activity which are so closely interconnected that it is a matter of choice as to whether some issues are discussed in one chapter or the other. Provision of a significant proportion of housing association development finance, through the grant system, gives government powerful levers of control over the total amount, type and location of development undertaken by RSLs. For government the grant system is the main mechanism by which it steers housing associations towards particular policy goals, and so it is appropriate to see finance as driving development. But governments are not in complete control, for private lenders also exercise influence over what gets built, by whom and for whom, and where it is located. Motivated by security and rates of return, rather than by concerns about social policy, lenders do not necessarily make decisions that are compatible with government objectives. Their power lies in the conditions that they can attach to loans, and their freedom to lend elsewhere; in this sense they have a degree of independence not available to RSLs whose whole *raison d'etre* is to provide decent housing at affordable rents. As a result individual RSLs can find themselves subject to tensions pulling them in different directions. Thus, although on the face of it the new financial regime introduced in 1989 was about giving housing associations greater control over their own affairs, it will be shown that freedom has been accompanied by a growth of controls.

The new financial regime of 1989

The government set out its proposals for changes affecting housing associations in the White Paper of 1987 and an accompanying consultation paper (DoE, 1987), which explained that the intention was to increase the amount of rented housing produced for a given volume of public expenditure, and to create new incentives for associations to be more cost effective by 'bringing to bear the disciplines of the private sector and strengthening the machinery of public support'. The first of these objectives was to be pursued through greater use of private finance, building on the experiment with 30 per cent HAG during 1987–88; the crucial breakthrough here was the agreement by the Treasury that private borrowing would not count as public expenditure, even if the majority of scheme costs were covered by HAG (for it was admitted that 30 per cent HAG would not work on most places). If only 25 per cent of capital was raised from private sources, then for every £100 of public subsidy £133 of investment could be procured. This idea became known as 'HAG-stretch'. The second objective meant exposing associations and their lenders to the business risks of development. This required, first, the removal of mixed funded schemes from entitlement to revenue deficit grant, which was seen as sufficiently insulating private lenders from risk to make loans count as public expenditure. Second, HAG was to be calculated *before* rather than after completion of development schemes, increasing the pressure on associations to bear down on costs and making them responsible for any cost overruns.

Additionally, schemes developed after April 1989 would not be entitled to major repairs grant (a form of assistance which had hitherto largely insulated associations from the long-term cost implications of expensive capital works). This important change gave associations a greater incentive to consider long-term maintenance costs at the initial design stage, but it also threw onto them responsibility for accumulating the necessary reserves to cover future costs; it was estimated that this requirement alone implied a 30 per cent increase on fair rents in 1988–89 (Hills, 1991: 123). At the same time, however, new schemes were removed from the strictures of the rent surplus fund (the successor to the grant redemption fund), leaving associations with greater flexibility to meet future costs from rental income.

It was implicit in the move towards private finance that rents would rise, due to three main factors:

1. the need to accumulate reserves in order to fund major repairs;
2. lower proportion of scheme costs covered by grant, and therefore a higher proportion to funded from rental income;
3. associations borrowing on their own account would inevitably have to pay higher interest rates than would be available to government.

Mitigating the impact of these factors was the expectation that associations would borrow private money on index-linked, low-start terms, and they were to set assured tenancy rents at below market levels. Nevertheless, the impending rise in rents in the housing associations sector was not only foreseen but intentional. The government's position on rents reflected its wider strategy across all sectors of moving from general, indiscriminate, price subsidy to reliance on personal, income related assistance through the housing benefit system. Ministers spoke of housing benefit 'taking the strain' of higher rents.

Deregulation of rents on new lettings was a key aspect of the new system. Whereas changes in the HAG system could be made under existing powers, the introduction of new tenancies outside the fair-rent regime required primary legislation, in the form of Part II of the Housing Act 1988. Deregulation was consistent with the Conservatives' general philosophy and with simultaneous reforms in the commercial private rented sector (Part I of the 1988 Act); but it was also a necessary precondition of the successful introduction of private finance into the housing association sector. It is important to remember that at that time the financial institutions were largely ignorant of housing associations and their potential; there was no history of lending, apart from very recent and experimental schemes, and because housing associations were not profit-driven (and did not present their accounts in the same way as commercial businesses) there remained considerable uncertainty about whether the institutions would be forthcoming with sufficient money for private finance to provide the basis for the expansion of the sector. In this situation it was necessary to provide prospective lenders with the reassurances that they appeared to need concerning the security of loans. One of these was that associations had the flexibility to raise rental income, if this proved necessary to sustain loan repayments in the longer term. The fair-rent system denied associations that freedom, and therefore it had to go. It has already been noted, in Chapter 8, that the mid-1980s experiments with private finance had been based on assured tenancies, outside the constraints of fair rents, and the assured tenancy became the standard form of tenancy for new housing association lettings after 15 January

1989. An important difference between assured tenancies and existing tenancies for non-charitable housing association tenants was the removal of the right to buy, which was interesting in view of the government's determined struggle to introduce it in the first place.

The financial regime for housing associations introduced in 1989 differed from the old system in that it exposed associations to risk, while giving them the appearance of greater autonomy and providing potential private lenders with the reassurances that they sought. At the same time it gave government much more control over grant rates and rents. Under the old system the government had effectively no control over these key variables, since rents were set by independent rent officers and grant was calculated as a residual amount, the product of actual scheme costs and rents. The post-1989 system, by contrast, is based on an implicit financial model which allows grant rates to be derived from data and assumptions about factors such as:

- construction costs
- interest rates
- management and maintenance allowances
- provision for long term major repairs
- use of reserves
- rent levels.

Actual grant rates reflect the assumptions fed into the model, giving the government, via the Housing Corporation, considerable purchase on what gets built, by whom and at what rent.

Operating the new system

This section looks at the way in which the capital side of the new system was operated by the various stakeholders – the government, the Housing Corporation, local authorities and lenders, as well as the associations themselves. The sorts of issues to be examined here concern the volumes of public expenditure flowing to housing associations via the grant system, changes in the grant rate per dwelling, and the growth of private finance. The questions of rents and affordability are dealt with subsequently.

Fuelling the system is the ADP, which sets the limit to grant aided capital expenditure, since little investment by RSLs takes place without some element of grant aid (apart from major repairs). The appropriate starting point, therefore, is to look at the aggregate flows of capital finance since 1989. The outturn expenditure figures (Table 10.1) show that ADP rose steeply during the first four years of the new system, almost trebling the 1988–89 figure, and then fell away. However, the overall impact of cuts in Housing Corporation spending after 1992–93 was cushioned by the recovery of local authority support and the growth of private lending. An interesting point to note here is that in its 1987 consultation paper on housing association finance the government had floated the idea of ending the arrangement whereby local authority lending to associations was eligible for HAG. This would have made the Corporation the only source of public sector subsidy and produced a simpler but more centralised system. In the event, local authorities have retained the freedom to lend as much as they like to RSLs, within the constraints of the capital control system, and the Housing Corporation pays grant on approved schemes.

Table 10.1   Housing associations' outturn capital expenditure, 1988–89 to 1999–2000 (England)

	ADP	LA HAG	Private finance	Total
	£m	£m	£m	£m
1988–89	881	128	100	1,009
1989–90	1,034	308	150	1,492
1990–91	1,063	193	175	1,430
1991–92	1,732	179	240	2,151
1992–93	2,368	286	950	3,604
1993–94	1,795	388	1,000	3,183
1994–95	1,487	331	1,100	2,918
1995–96	1,153	354	1,100	2,607
1996–97	1,030	327	1,100	2,457
1997–98	729	320	800	1,849
1998–99 est	735	350	800	1,885
1999–2000 plans	790	500	900	2,190

Sources: Column 1, 1988–89 to 1990–91, Wilcox (1997), 1991–92 onwards, DoE Annual Reports; column 2 (except 1998–99 and 1999–00) Wilcox (1998); column 2 1998–99 and 1999–00, and column 3, Williams and Wilcox (1999).

The outcome of the government's comprehensive spending review implied that Corporation spending for the next three years would remain flat in real terms (DETR, 1998c: 8).

These overall figures conceal a short-term funding crisis in 1990–91, and the extent to which actual expenditure after 1992–93 represented a retreat from plans announced in 1990. The transition to the new system in 1989–90 led to an unforeseen acceleration in grant claims by associations (Randolph, 1993: 43). This was a one-off episode, but it caught the Corporation unprepared and caused it to run out of cash at the start of 1990. The solution was to bring forward expenditure scheduled for 1990–91, and to cut back on approvals for that year. Thus, instead of producing a smooth and sustained increase in output, in 1990–91 the new system actually saw the lowest level of approvals since the earlier crisis year of 1980–81. As for expenditure planned for later years, the Conservatives' 1992 election manifesto referred to £6 billion for housing associations over the next three years, and a target of 153,000 dwellings. The Housing Corporation's policy statement for 1992–93, published in 1991, forecast ADP expenditure of £2.7 billion in 1992–93, and £2.8 billion in 1993–94. In fact expenditure peaked in 1992–93, at almost three times the 1988–89 level, but then cuts of £300 million were announced in the November budgets of 1993 and 1994, followed by a further £118 million in 1995, leaving the ADP for 1995–96 at less than half the level of 1992–93.

The government's aim was to increase production of dwellings with less than corresponding increases in public expenditure. Substituting private finance for public sector loans was one means of achieving this goal, followed by a gradual increase the proportion of scheme costs covered in this way. This was achieved by lowering the average grant rate, and encouraging associations to compete for it at lower and lower levels. At first only modest reductions in grant were introduced, but in 1992 the government announced plans to reduce the rate to 55 per cent by 1995–96. Table 10.2 shows how the headline grant rate has been reduced from over 75 per cent to 54 per cent by 1998–99.

Interpreting the significance of the falling grant rate is complicated by a number of factors, including changes in policy over time, but it is clear that falling rates were identified as a problem by associations concerned about three things: affordability of rents, poverty trap effects of higher rents and the availability of private finance. These concerns were shared by the House of Commons Environment Committee, which recommended that the government should 'consider very carefully the consequences of allowing rates of HAG to fall below 67 per cent' (Environment Committee, 1993: xxxiv).

Table 10.2   Headline grant rates, 1988–89 to
1999–2000

	Percentage
1988–89	75–80
1989–90	75–80
1990–91	75–80
1991–92	75
1992–93	72
1993–94	67
1994–95	62
1995–96	58
1996–97	58
1997–98	56
1998–99	54
1999–00	54

Source; DoF Annual Reports.

Until 1994 official references were to an 'average' grant rate, and only after that date was the notion of a ceiling rate introduced. When the system was introduced it was clear that grant rates were to be lower than previously, but there was no explicit commitment to reduce them to the extent that later became apparent. At first sight a lower grant rate implies higher rents, as associations have to meet the costs of borrowing a higher proportion of costs, but the government argued that cuts reflected lower prices for new construction, and claimed that the cuts were calculated on the assumption of rents remaining at a constant proportion of tenants' average income (Environment Committee, 1993: xxxvii). Additionally, headline rates are national ceilings, behind which lie a series of local rates, reflecting variations in costs (for example, the average grant rate in the West region had fallen to 41 per cent as early as 1993–94 (Housing Corporation n.d: iv).

There have also been several changes in government policy towards the grant rate since 1989. At first the Corporation operated schemes (known as tariff funding and then cash programmes – see Chapter 11) which gave developing associations the opportunity to plan over a three-year period at a known rate of grant, but these were phased out in favour of greater emphasis on competitive bidding for grant. Attention returned to the annual round of HAG allocations, on a scheme-by-scheme basis. Tariff and cash-programme agreements were allowed to run their course, but new allocations were made on the basis of competitive bids, with the rewards going to those seeking the lowest amount of public subsidy per dwelling. This resulted in actual grant rates well below the official headline and local rates. In order to bid at competitive rates associations either had to cut costs (while still meeting required standards), or cover a greater proportion of costs from their own resources. This generally meant a choice between drawing on cash reserves or raising more through private borrowing – with implications for rents. Some associations, particularly those with tariff agreements, were able to accumulate large amounts of cash as a result of falling development costs in the early 1990s. However, actively developing associations soon used up such surpluses and so borrowing became the main means of subsidising HAG bids. Eventually the government responded to critics who pointed to the damaging consequences of this narrowly defined measure of value for money, in terms of higher rents (thereby intensifying the poverty trap for tenants on benefit), higher housing benefit costs falling on the Treasury, and the rapid mortgaging of the equity held by associations in their existing stock (implicitly bringing forward the point at which they would have to stop developing). From 1996–97 the Corporation began to scrutinise bids in terms of proposed rents as well as grant costs (following an initiative in Wales in 1995–96), and in 1998 it was announced that in future bids would be successful only if they implied rents no higher than specified local maxima.

Private finance

Private finance was the key to the success of the new system, but it remained to be seen whether housing associations could raise sufficient capital, on acceptable terms, to achieve a significant expansion of output, while maintaining rents at affordable levels. As has been mentioned above, the financial institutions were unfamiliar with lending to not-for-profit organisations like housing associations, and it was not clear whether associations could provide the security that lenders required. The two key indicators of financial risk used to assess housing associations as potential borrowers are gearing and interest cover. Gearing can be defined in different ways but in simple terms it refers to the extent to which an organisation is externally financed, and lenders normally look for a maximum of 50–60 per cent.

Associations that have been actively developing during the period since 1988 have become increasingly aware of their rising gearing ratios, but the lenders have begun to attach more importance than in the past to the security of the income stream and the issue of interest cover. Interest cover is a measure of the income remaining to meet debt charges after deductions for management and maintenance. In this case lenders normally look for 125–130 per cent, that is, surplus income, after management and maintenance, sufficient to pay all debt charges at least one and a quarter times. This gives them the reassurance that a sudden increase in costs (whether for unplanned major repairs or to meet higher interest charges) would not immediately threaten repayments. In the case of interest cover, then, the higher the percentage the better the situation is.

Gearing and interest cover are indicators of risk which are negotiated between borrower and lender, but what is not open to negotiation in the same way is a third key variable, the ratio of borrowing to security. This is the relationship between the value of the stock and the amount of outstanding debt secured against the property. Thus if an association has property valued at £100 million and loans amounting to £50 million then it has a security ratio of 50 per cent. A key issue in this context is the method used to value the stock, and the usual one adopted in the case of British housing associations is known as 'existing use value – social housing' (EUV-SH), ie not the conventional vacant possession value but a value reflecting the fact that if the stock had to be sold in order to meet liabilities it would, in all probability, be occupied by sitting tenants with security of tenure. EUV-SH is a method which leads to valuations of approximately 60–70 per cent of vacant possession values. Thus, from the point of view of lenders, and potential borrowers, the lower the security ratio the better it is.

Although housing associations approaching private financial institutions after the start of the new system did so as unfamiliar customers they had the advantage that they owned significant property assets on which they had very low levels of external financing, high rates of interest cover and low security ratios. This helped to ensure that the lenders were at least prepared to discuss the prospects for developing a new market. The questions that need to be addressed now, therefore, concern the way in which the private finance market has developed over the period since 1989: who has lent what to whom, and on what terms? Beyond these sorts of quantitative factors there are some rather more qualitative issues, to do with the ways in which housing associations have changed as a result of their growing engagement with private financial institutions.

A number of studies and surveys have been carried out to look at how the market has developed. One of the first was conducted by the NFHA, who found that by the summer of 1991 some £1.2 billion of private finance had been arranged, although only a little over half had actually been drawn down (Randolph, 1992: ix). At that stage only a limited range of lenders had become much involved in this market; leading lenders included the NatWest Bank, the Nationwide Building Society and the Housing Finance Corporation (the latter is registered as an Industrial and provident Society and was created in 1987 by the Housing Corporation, the NFHA and private sector partners, specifically to raise funds for housing associations). Low start loans of various sorts accounted for just over half (52 per cent), which was perhaps unexpected given that the government's grant model was based on the assumption of low start arrangements as the means of delivering affordable rents. Associations that chose to take out conventional loans incurred higher costs in the short term, and therefore needed to generate either additional income or cost savings in order to keep rents within reach of low-income households. The most obvious ways of achieving affordable rents were to adopt a rent pooling strategy (that is, using income surpluses from older, lower-cost dwellings to support the higher costs of new ones) and/or to delay the start of making provision for long-term major repairs.

Differences in the size and financial strength of associations, and in the age profile of their existing stock, meant that there was considerable variety in the strategies adopted. The NFHA report noted that the largest associations (with more than 2,500 dwellings) had accounted for three-quarters of the money borrowed so far, but small associations had not been unable to raise money. The report concluded that 'the early years of the mixed funding regime have certainly not proved disastrous to smaller associations, nor have they proved an unmitigated success for the larger and stronger' (Randolph, 1992: 21).

A later study, carried out in 1995 by a team from the University of Cambridge (Chaplin *et al.*, 1995), commented on the impact of the changing economic context on the overall financial health of developing associations. Associations entered the new financial regime at a time of relatively high inflation and very high interest rates, but by the middle of the decade the risks inherent in private borrowing were mitigated by downwards trends in inflation, interest rates and construction costs, yet associations retained the freedom to raise rents in real terms, and revenue surpluses were seen to be rising rapidly (Chaplin *et al.*, 1995: 11). An interesting change in terms of private borrowing arrangements was the declining popularity of low start loans, indicating that associations had been able to depart from the assumptions in the government's grant rate model, although the authors note that the majority of associations did not have active loan portfolio management strategies, and that, 'Raising finance still has more to do with what the market will provide than what might be most suitable for a balanced portfolio' (Chaplin *et al.*, 1995: 13). The lack of sophistication in associations' approach to treasury management was beginning to be evident in two key areas: strategies on reserves and future major repair liabilities. The new financial regime required associations to be able to demonstrate that they were making sufficient revenue surpluses to attract private finance and to pay for future refurbishment of the stock, but, and this is an example of where the regulatory framework could have been stronger, associations were free to designate reserves which were not backed by cash, and to skimp on current maintenance in order to subsidise new development; Chaplin *et al.* (1995: 15) report that over 60 per cent of associations appeared to be underspending on maintenance. The issue of reserves is potentially very complicated, but associations found themselves in a situation where they were being criticised for having high levels of reserves (which was seen as undermining their opposition to further cuts in grant rates), while in reality many of them had spent the cash on subsidising bids for grant (as they were strongly encouraged to do up to 1995).

More recent evidence (from the Housing Corporation's unpublished annual Private Finance Survey 1997, but see also Wilcox and Williams, 1997) suggests that by March 1997 nearly 600 associations had raised £11.4 billion since 1988, and by the end of 1998 the total had risen to nearly £14 billion, representing some 40 per cent of the capital base of the sector (including funding for large scale voluntary transfers of local authority housing). This is a very clear demonstration of the success of both RSLs in attracting private finance into a field of activity that had previously been unknown territory for the main financial institutions, and the Conservative government's strategy of privatising the burden of funding the growth of social rented housing. Of the total borrowing from private sources, about £1 billion has been raised by bond issues, while the bulk of the remainder has come from a very limited number of major providers; at least 80 per cent has been provided by just 10 per cent of lenders. The 1997 figures show that 48 lenders had each committed more than £20 million, and topping the list were the Halifax and the NatWest (both banks), the Nationwide Building Society and The Housing Finance Corporation. A growing proportion of lending tends to come from banks – 58 per cent in 1996–97 – but this reflects the transformation of some building societies (such as the Halifax) into banks. Low start and index-linked loans now account for under 10 per cent of borrowing. Most associations rely on bilateral arrangements with lenders, although there have been a number of consortium deals, and, because of the large sums (at least £50 million) that are required to make bond issues cost effective, only consortia or the very largest associations acting alone can raise funds in the capital markets.

Turning to more qualitative issues, private finance has had a significant impact on housing associations in a number of quite subtle ways, which are inevitably more apparent in those RSLs that have been most actively developing since 1988. Some aspects, such as the types of development undertaken and the geographical areas of operation, are dealt with in the following chapter. Here it is appropriate to refer to factors such as the changing centre of gravity within associations as finance directors and their departments have acquired a much higher profile, with much more influence over strategic decision making (Pryke, 1994). Under the old system the role of finance staff was essentially to claim HAG on new developments, to make sure that the income and expenditure accounts balanced and to prepare the annual statement of accounts. There was virtually no treasury function to perform, and they were not involved in development decisions, for it was safe to assume that if an association was awarded HAG on a scheme then it could afford to do it. The arrival of the new financial regime, however, meant that associations were required to devise techniques of setting their own rents, to exercise judgement about the viability of proposed developments, to make provision for major repairs and to model future income streams. All this transformed the demands on finance staff and gave them a leading role. It also led to a need to be more explicitly forward looking, and a growth activity among housing associations in the 1990s was the production of business plans looking forward four or five years, often incorporating financial projections over twenty-five or thirty years. Before the 1990s associations had no need for business plans of this sort, because their growth was shaped by annual allocations of HAG, and because of the way that new schemes were financially self-supporting from year one the future could be relied upon to take care of itself. The new financial regime replaced this comfortable framework and exposed associations to a degree of uncertainty which put them in need of some kind of map of the way forward.

Another way of depicting the influence of the new financial regime is to refer to the perceptibly changing organisational culture in some associations, notably the more actively developing ones. Chaplin *et al.* (1995: 11), for example, refer to interview evidence from their research indicating that respondents within associations were aware of a move towards a more commercial approach. This, of course, was bolstered by the introduction of competition among associations for available grant resources.

By raising an average of £1.4 billion per year for ten years, RSLs have demonstrated successfully that they have been able to adapt to the new framework, and that there is no shortage of money for social housing, at least at the levels of demand that have been seen so far. The market has matured over the decade as both borrowers and lenders have become more familiar with each other. Lenders have realised that housing associations are pretty secure organisations, for although there have been occasional worries about individual associations that have experienced financial difficulties, none has actually been allowed to collapse. In a highly regulated sector lenders know that the Housing Corporation will (in all probability) step in before the point of collapse and arrange some kind of rescue (usually in the form of a merger with a larger RSL), not only to preserve market confidence in associations as a whole but also because of the fact that private lenders have priority over the Corporation in the recovery of assets in the event of default. The DoE (1995: 25) noted that no public or private money had been lost due to default by housing associations. Nevertheless, lenders were quick to show alarm when the Conservatives proposed to limit RSLs' rent increases, and when the Housing Bill 1995 appeared to threaten lenders' first claim on the assets of defaulting RSLs. In both cases the government rapidly backed down, although control of rent increases seems to have been accepted by lenders subsequently.

Rents and affordability

The main objective of this section is to show how the Conservative government's strategy designed to raise housing association rent levels in real terms succeeded to such an extent that it was put into reverse. After several years of upwards pressure on rents, since 1995 successive Conservative and Labour governments have rediscovered the attractions of capital subsidies and low rents. Although the gap between the rent of decent accommodation and the price that can be paid by low-income households has long been recognised as a central feature of the housing problem, the term 'affordability' has only emerged into common usage since the late 1980s. At a general level this can be understood in terms of what Whitehead (1991) has described as an attempt to move from a needs-based to an affordability-based approach to housing, meaning a more market-oriented system in which aggregate supply and individual consumption reflect demand and ability to pay rather than official measures of need. A key development was the government's decision in 1987 to deregulate rents in the housing associations sector, and to do so in a way which required associations to set rents at affordable levels, but without clear guidance as to what such levels might be, nor how to define them (Randolph, 1993: 44). The government initially referred to associations setting rents that were 'significantly below the free market level' (DoE, 1987: para 14), and this was followed by Housing Corporation circulars with a rather different message, referring to the need to maximise rental income. The government was pressed to say what it meant by affordability, but Ministers consistently refused to give any clear definition or guidance, relying instead on the formula that rent levels were a matter for the Housing Corporation and associations themselves to decide in the context of prevailing grant rates and local circumstances.

Why was the government so reluctant to offer more explicit and helpful advice on the subject? Kearns (1992: 527) suggested that the government had to take a view on affordability in order to operate its grant-rate model, 'However, the government cannot admit this because it does not want to get involved in a difficult public debate about what level of housing cost payments are affordable to poor working households'. It seems more likely that the main reason behind the government's uncharacteristic reticence was that it did not want to fetter the freedom of associations to raise rents to whatever levels were necessary (subject to the implicit ceiling of the open-market level) in order to meet their loan obligations. In other words, it appears that the government was still concerned that implicit restrictions on associations' control of rental income could reduce the supply of private finance.

The government's stance sparked off a prolonged debate about how to define and measure affordability. The NFHA initially took the view that 20 per cent of net income was an affordable level, based on evidence from actual expenditure in other tenures, although it subsequently moved to a 22 per cent benchmark, and then in 1994 it adopted a new position:

Rents are affordable if the majority of working households taking up new tenancies are not caught in the poverty trap (because of dependency on housing
benefit) or paying more than 25 per cent of their net income on housing. (*Housing
Associations Weekly*, 21 January 1994)

Meanwhile, in 1993 it emerged that Ministers were working on the
assumption that 35 per cent of net income was affordable (Environment
Committee, 1993: xxviii). The question of what is affordable is a lot
more complicated than is implied by attempts to set arbitrary percentage
levels (Hulchanski, 1995), and it is reasonable to argue in favour of
different approaches, focusing instead on residual income (what people
have left to cover other essential expenditure, after rent has been paid),
or on more subjective considerations, such as perceived value for
money. However, it is not necessary to expand on this debate here;
instead it is more important to explain why rents rose much faster than
prices generally in the first half of the 1990s, and why governments
have subsequently deployed mechanisms to restrain the rate of increase.

The best source of evidence of movements in housing association
rents is provided by the regular monitoring system set up by the
NFHA in 1989 and known as CORE (Continuous Recording). This
monitors rents of new lettings of all general needs dwellings by associations in England, together with information about tenants' incomes
(by 1998 it was drawing on data from an estimated 120,000 lettings
per annum). Figure 10.1 summarises information gathered over ten
years of CORE.

In its report on the early impact of the changes affecting housing
associations since the 1988 Act, the NFHA (Randolph, 1992: 55) found
that in the first two and a half years average rents for new tenants rose
by 49 per cent, during a period when the retail price index (RPI) rose
by only 20 per cent. This rapid increase was mainly due to the impact
of assured tenancies, for rents here were rising much faster than fair
rents. By the end of 1994, six full years after the system started, rents
had risen by 80 per cent, compared with an RPI increase of just 30 per
cent. The trend for rents to rise faster than prices and incomes has been
maintained throughout the period since January 1989. As Figure 10.1
shows, by the middle of 1998 the index of assured rents had reached
212, while the RPI had risen to only 146 and the index of tenants'
incomes had moved up to 163. By 1998 there was some evidence that
the policy of rent restraint was beginning to have an effect, but a large
majority of cases still failed the NHF's affordability test.

As early as 1993 there was anecdotal evidence of some housing association rents 'tending towards' market rents in some areas (Chaplin *et*

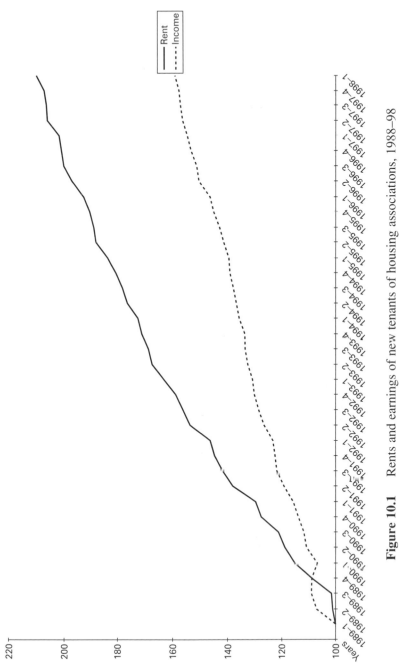

Figure 10.1 Rents and earnings of new tenants of housing associations, 1988–98

al., 1995: 21), and there have been subsequent reports of the same kind. The NFHA/NHF has consistently monitored the rising proportion of rents deemed to be unaffordable, with a peak of more than 75 per cent of cases in early 1996. To put the increase in housing association rents in context, local authorities were also under pressure to raise their rents from 1990 to 1995, and they too have been subject to restraint since that time. But local authority rents rose more slowly (by 114 per cent up to April 1997 (LGA, 1997: 6)) and on average they remain significantly lower than housing association rents. To explain why housing association rents increased so rapidly it is necessary to refer back to the point made earlier in this chapter: the new financial regime was designed to produce real-terms increases as part of a general pricing strategy for rented housing, and as a necessary condition of the introduction of private finance. What is not so clear cut is the extent to which rent increases were driven by the way that the system was operated from the centre and how much they were the result of decisions taken by housing associations themselves. It can be argued, for example, that in the early 1990s cuts in grant rates were more than offset by the falling costs of new construction, thereby considerably easing the pressure on associations to raise rents. Nevertheless, some associations accumulated large cash surpluses at that time, implying that there was a tendency for them to raise rents by more than was strictly necessary to balance their accounts.

From the government's point of view, as has been mentioned above, the assumption was that tenants could afford to spend at least a third of their income on rent, and therefore in terms of pricing policy rents were not generally considered to be unaffordable, and certainly not to the extent that was being argued by the NFHA. The government, having deregulated housing association rents, and having refused to define in public its view of affordability, was hardly in a strong position to criticise associations for the decisions that they made. However, government thinking on rents and subsidies was changed by two main factors that emerged with increasing force as the decade progressed. First, while it was arguable that in terms of housing policy there was not a problem with rising rents (which were still generally well below market rent levels), from the point of view of the Department of Social Security and the Treasury there was clearly a problem associated with the strongly rising, and open-ended, cost of housing benefit. Although it had been intended that housing benefit would take the strain of higher rents, the amount of strain was much more than had been anticipated. It is safe to conclude, therefore, that the pressure within Whitehall for a change of policy on rents came from this direction.

The second factor was the growth of concern about the work disincentives and poverty trap created for many tenants by the interaction of higher rents and the social security system. It was shown that for some households the move from benefit to work could produce reduced entitlement to housing benefit and other means tested benefits leading to a loss of 97 pence for every additional £ of income (Ford and Wilcox, 1994: 80). This was effectively a punitive rate of taxation on the transition from benefit to work, and was seen as a powerful disincentive. The problem was intensified by the extent to which the policy of higher rents had been implemented alongside encouragement of the so-called flexible labour market, which was producing an increasing number of low paid, part-time and insecure jobs. The blunt fact was that high rents and a low-wage economy do not fit comfortably together, hence the pressure for change.

It was in the Conservative government's White Paper on housing that the new approach was revealed:

> The most cost-effective way of ensuring that people with permanently low incomes have a decent home is to give direct subsidy to landlords to provide social housing at rents below market levels. (Great Britain, 1995: 26)

The White Paper (p. 41) also indicated that in future proposed rent levels for new schemes would be taken into account when deciding the distribution of grant aid. Thus, from 1996–97 the Housing Corporation began to scrutinise associations' bids for Social Housing Grant (SHG) for both the total public subsidy required and the implied rent levels. Since then the emphasis on rents has increased and developed to the point where associations are given explicit advice from the Housing Corporation that they should not consider bidding for SHG unless the rents on the new dwellings are below specified capped levels. The guidance given to associations in 1998 was in marked contrast with that of just three or four years previously. Whereas then associations were encouraged to bid at below the headline grant rate, now they are explicitly told not to do so. Now they are told that the Corporation is looking for rent increases substantially below the norm of RPI+1 per cent, especially among associations with relatively high rents. It has become clear that there is pressure on associations not only to bear down on the rents of new dwellings but also across the existing stock as a whole (Housing Corporation, 1998b).

Conclusion

The thesis being developed here is that the new financial regime introduced in 1989 enhanced the power of the centre to steer and control the
activities of housing associations. This chapter really needs to be read
in conjunction with the next, looking at development, but there are a
number of brief points to make by way of conclusion. It is important
not to underestimate the extent of the changes flowing from the new
financial regime. The much increased levels of investment activity are
only the most obvious indicators of change. Actively developing associations have been changed as organisations by growth since 1989, but
the impact of private finance and the risks associated with it have
changed the culture of even long-established associations, making them
much more businesslike in outlook.

On the theme of the growing influence of the centre, via the Corporation, it has been shown here that the new financial regime gave the
government the power to exert much more control, through both the
volume of grant and the assumptions fed into the grant model.
However, there are two caveats to be acknowledged. First, it is important to recognise that much of what the government has done since
1989 has been working with the grain of housing associations' own
objectives, and so it is just as relevant to refer to opportunities as to
control. Second, it has been shown that associations have retained the
ability to act independently. The retreat from low start and index-linked
private finance is one indicator of independent action. It should also be
recognised that it is the nature of the financial regime that it has most
impact on actively developing associations, and those that have built
few dwellings since 1989 have felt its effects the least, and in particular
they have been little affected by changing policies on rents.

Finally, a key point to emphasise is the extent to which government
policy towards housing associations has changed and developed over
the period since 1989, and how the main turning point was in 1995, not
after the election of the Labour government in 1997. It is also interesting that the introduction of measures to limit associations' rent
increases, which had to be abandoned in 1995 in the face of lender resistance, have subsequently been accepted without apparent difficulty.

11

Development

Introduction

Whereas Chapter 10 was devoted to an examination of how RSLs finance their activities, this chapter concentrates on how the money is spent, and how the pattern of expenditure since 1989 has been influenced by the financial regime, overlain by changes in government priorities. Between 1989 and 1998 the stock of dwellings owned by housing associations in England doubled, from 519,000 to 1,048,500 (not including bedspaces in hostels) (Housing Corporation, 1990a, 1999), and from 1991 associations overtook local authorities as providers of new homes. With the private housing market in recession for much of the decade housing associations were the most dynamic and fastest growing part of the housing system, albeit considerably boosted by stock transfers from the local authority sector. Key issues to be explored in this context include the geographical distribution of development activity, the allocation of grant aid to individual associations, the kinds of dwellings being produced and the categories of households intended to benefit from these dwellings.

The housing quasi-market

The notion of quasi-markets, which was developed as a way of comprehending changes in the British welfare state following a series of reforms in the late 1980s, can be applied to the mechanisms for the distribution of development resources among RSLs. In a conventional market, profit motivated suppliers compete for business from customers who are free to spend their money where they please. Demand, rather than need, is regarded as the main determinant of supply. In a quasi-market, although there is competition the participants are normally not-for-profit organisations seeking contracts awarded by public bodies, whose decisions are based on some official judgement of the level and type of consumer need in a given locality (Le Grand and Bartlett, 1993: 10). This is exactly what happens in the annual cycle of bids from and allocations to housing associations, where the Housing Corporation acts as a central purchasing authority, commissioning a needs-based quantity of housing investment from registered providers. The starting points are: (a) a macro-level Treasury decision about the total amount of grant aid to be made available in the coming year, as part of the overall public expenditure planning process, and (b) an assessment of need in each region. Housing Corporation regional offices then distribute their share around the local authority districts, again broadly on the basis of need. Assessments of need are based on the Housing Needs Index (HNI), which was originally developed in 1985 by the NFHA, the Housing Corporation and the DoE from a similar index used in the local authority sector. The HNI is a basket of weighted indices which attempt to measure the housing needs that are priorities for housing associations; the composition of the indices, and the weightings attached to them can be modified to reflect both changing circumstances and policy priorities. As such, the HNI provides a somewhat less than completely objective way of allocating resources down to local areas, and there is room for disagreement about the construction and operation of the Index. In fact, during the 1990s, the way that the HNI was used to distribute resources around the regions was actively contested, with northern associations complaining that the priority given to homelessness meant that too much money was being directed to the south. Nevertheless, the important point is that in terms of the determination of the total amount of grant aid and its geographical distribution the mechanisms are administrative rather than market-based.

The questions of how much new housing is needed in Britain in the foreseeable future, and how much of it should be provided by RSLs, have been widely debated, and it is not necessary to examine the complexities of the problem in great detail. A number of studies conducted during the 1990s concluded that there was a need for 60–150,000 new social rented dwellings per annum (Bramley, 1990; Whitehead and Kleinman, 1992; Environment Committee, 1995; Holmans, 1995; Holmans *et al.*, 1998; see also Environment, Transport and Regional Affairs Committee, 1998). In 1995 the DoE produced estimates suggesting a need to accommodate an additional 4.4 million households in the period 1991–2016, and even if a large proportion of these were to be provided by the private market there remained much work for the RSL sector to do. The important point here is that the expansion of housing association development activity after 1989 took place in circumstances where the available evidence all pointed towards continuing levels of overall need exceeding actual output. It was only in the mid 1990s that some people began to question whether there might be oversupply in certain parts of the north of England. By 1998, however, the idea of surplus affordable rented housing in some areas, while shortages continued in others, was widely accepted within housing circles, including the Minister (Blake, 1998: 20; see also Pawson and Kearns, 1998).

The distribution of ADP resources is the outcome of negotiations around three main factors. First, Ministers set priorities and objectives for the Corporation, in terms of the kinds of need to be met and the types of housing to be provided (for example, the balance between rented housing and various forms of home ownership). Second, within the scope of the ADP funds available at the local level, as determined by the HNI, priority needs are defined in consultation with the local authority; negotiations around the distribution of grant aid to different sorts of need and different parts of the district reflect the list of priorities drawn up by the local authority on the basis of its three-year housing strategy. It will be recalled that government housing policy after 1987 emphasised the idea of local authorities as strategic enablers of provision by others, including housing associations. Implicit in this approach was increased salience for local strategies, and a close relationship between them and the allocations made by the Corporation. In 1992 the DoE announced plans to bring the timetables and processes of the annual rounds of HIP and ADP bids and allocations closer together, in order to promote greater coherence in local strategic planning and implementation. At the same time greater emphasis was placed on local authorities demonstrating their commitment to, and performance in, the enabling role, ie the credit approvals given to them for their own expenditure needs would reflect their willingness to work with partner organisations. In return, it is now very unusual for the Corporation to provide grant aid for schemes that have not been prioritised by the appropriate local authority, and in 1998 the Corporation moved a step further by introducing pilot projects to examine the scope for 'joint commissioning', bringing it and the local authorities into closer collaboration.

Ministerial priorities (mediated via the Corporation) and local priorities together shape the pattern of funding available within the housing quasi-market on an annual basis. The final level of decision-making about the distribution of grant takes account of bids by individual associations, and here the third key factor comes into play, namely the extent to which bids reflect local priorities and the Corporation's current definition of cost effectiveness. It will be clear from this discussion that RSLs compete with each other within a highly structured quasi-market, in which the Treasury, the DETR, the Housing Corporation and the local authorities all have considerable influence over who builds what, where, and for whom. The unequivocal message given out to RSLs competing in the quasi-market for ADP funding is that in order to stand any chance of success they must take full account of the prevailing priorities of the Corporation and the particular local authorities in whose areas they wish to build. Each year the Corporation issues a series of Regional Policy Statements, which set out both the priorities of the government and the Corporation, and the needs in each local authority district. The existence of these documents and the nature of the language used to guide associations' grant bids provides the clearest possible evidence of the extent to which not-for-profit housing organisations have become incorporated into the state apparatus for the pursuit of housing and related policy objectives.

Having said that, it is now necessary to acknowledge that although the ADP remains the main source of grant aid, and therefore has a very considerable influence on the volume and composition of development activity, there are other sources of subsidy and support. In addition to grant from the Corporation RSLs can be supported by finance from local authorities (LASHG), who may provide free or discounted land. Local authorities can also help to provide sites for RSLs by means of negotiated agreements (Section 106 agreements) with private developers, who, in return for planning permission to build houses for open market sale, agree to make part of the site available for affordable rented housing (Barlow *et al.*, 1994; Farthing *et al.*, 1996). The ability to deploy resources which would stretch the number of dwellings produced for a given amount of public expenditure came to be seen as giving an association a competitive advantage in terms of bidding for grant. In the increasingly competitive environment of the 1990s, associations also found themselves having to put together more complex financial packages (for capital and revenue support) than they had been accustomed to having to do in the past. This was partly a reflection of the growing diversity of their activities.

Figure 11.1 Foundry Square, Hayle, Cornwall. An example of Guinness Trust general needs housing developed in the 1990s

The dynamics of the post-1988 system

Needs and priorities

Although housing associations are essentially organisations whose purpose is to provide for people in need, the detailed pattern of their development activity strongly reflects Ministers' definitions of needs and their relative priority at any given time. Table 11.1 shows the total output from the ADP over the period since 1989–90, broken down by various rent and home-ownership initiatives. The total output figures reflect the rise and fall in the money available for the ADP, although of course the decline in output is less than the fall in the ADP because of the effect of lower grant rates and rising amounts of private finance.

The first point to be made concerns the changing balance between the rented and home-ownership lines in the table. In the history of voluntary housing in Britain the strongest thread of continuity concerns shared commitment to the provision of decent accommodation that is affordable for people on the lowest incomes. Almost by definition this has meant rented housing, which remains the core business of RSLs in general. It is very difficult for people on low incomes successfully to enter the home-ownership market, and even schemes specifically conceived in terms of low-cost home ownership are unaffordable for the least well-off. Survey evidence shows that people buying into shared ownership schemes are much more likely to be in full-time employment, and to have much higher incomes, than the majority of new RSL tenants (Cousins, *et al.*, 1993; Bramley and Dunmore, 1995). Nevertheless, housing associations have become active providers of various opportunities for people to become home owners, or part-owners, and it was noted in Chapter 8 that such activity could be explained largely in terms of external pressures, from governments, rather than internal, association-driven diversification. During the 1990s the Conservatives introduced schemes such as Do-It-Yourself Shared Ownership (DIYSO) (this involved the prospective purchaser identifying a suitable house on the open market; the participating association would then buy it and enter into a shared ownership arrangement with the purchaser. Guidance was given to associations requiring them to target existing housing association and local authority tenants). In this and other ways the Conservatives racheted up the proportion of ADP allocated to home-ownership initiatives, from around 20 per cent in the early 1990s to 40 per cent by the middle of the decade, when the Corporation told associations:

Ministers consider that putting an increased share of resources into the Corporation's home-ownership initiatives is an important part of the government strategy for making the most effective use of the housing stock. (*Housing Corporation News*, December 1994)

Table 11.1 shows that in fact home-ownership totals never exceeded 31 per cent of actual output. It remains reasonable to conclude that even these levels of provision were much higher than associations would have achieved in the absence of the very clear messages coming from the centre, and not only for reasons to do with traditional preferences for rented housing: shared ownership has proved to be difficult to market successfully and it only works well in certain circumstances and market conditions (Bramley and Dunmore, 1996). Since Labour came into office less pressure has been placed on RSLs to meet home-ownership targets.

In other ways, too, successive Ministers have steered the ADP so that it reflects government policy priorities. For example, as associations took over as the main providers of new social rented housing so Ministers indicated that they should devote more of their effort to general family accommodation. This meant, first, a relative reduction in the emphasis given to special needs housing, and in particular to provision for elderly people (in 1989 some 28 per cent of the stock comprised dwellings designed for elderly people, whereas by 1997 the proportion had fallen to 16 per cent, albeit on a rather tighter definition (Housing Corporation, 1990a, 1998a)). After several decades of being encouraged to develop for elderly people associations are now actively discouraged from proposing new sheltered housing schemes. This is partly a reflection of growing problems in finding tenants for some existing sheltered schemes, and should be seen in the context of new policy towards meeting the needs of elderly people (Housing Corporation, 1996a).

Second, from 1990–91 to 1995–96 associations were expected to allocate half of new completions to homeless households, and this represented a major change from previous general practice; in 1990–91 only 11.5 per cent of association lettings went to statutorily homeless households (K. Miller, 1993: 20). Given that local authorities had a legal duty towards certain categories of homeless people it was perhaps not surprising that housing associations had not previously played a significant role in this respect, despite their orientation towards people in need. This pressure on associations to accommodate increasing numbers of homeless households inevitably had a big impact on the

Table 11.1 Output from the Housing Corporation Approved Development Programme, 1989–90 to 1999–2000

Dwelling completions	1989–90	1990–91	1991–92	1992–93	1993–94	1994–95	1995–96	1996–97	1997–98 est. outturn	1998–99 plans	1999–2000 plans
Rent:											
– transitional		11,350	6,562	{5,943							
– new public funded	{17,728	{6,260	1,425		{40,136	{40,309	{38,589	{29,051	{22,593	{22,100	{22,700
– mixed funded			13,198	26,221							
Short-life	500	990	1,607	1,381	1,924	1,260	1,482	2,000	2,777	1,500	1,500
HMP				18,430							
Total rent	18,228	18,600	22,792	51,975	42,060	41,569	40,071	31,051	25,370	23,600	24,200
HOTCHA/TIS	1,550	2,270	2,691	4,783	6,450	6,525	6,400	7,029	4,262	2,900	100
DIYSO/Lease/Homebuy					5,259	5,479	4,588	2,435	1,986	1,600	200
Purchase grant											1,500
LCHO/SO	1,611	780	1,279	5,379	2,731	5,569	5,845	4,531	4,350	4,500	4,200
Total HO	3,161	3,050	3,970	10,162	14,440	17,573	16,833	13,995	10,598	9,000	6,000
City Challenge						880	866	1,133	423	–	
RSI						175	1,166	335	250	230	430
Total	21,389	21,650	26,762	62,137	56,500	59,142	58,936	45,381	36,218	32,830	30,330

Sources: DoE/DETR Annual Reports.

Key:
HMP — Housing Market Package;
HOTCHA — Home Ownership for Tenants of Charitable Housing Associations;
TIS — Tenants' Incentive Scheme;
DIYSO — Do-It-Yourself Shared Ownership;
LCHO/SO — Low Cost Home Ownership/Shared Ownership;
Total HO — Total Home Ownership;
RSI — Rough Sleepers Initiative.

socio-economic profile of new tenants, an issue that will be picked up later in the chapter.

Alongside home ownership and provision for homeless people the Corporation identified other investment priorities, including, for example, a five-year programme of support for associations run by people from black and minority ethnic communities, a rural housing programme, and promotion of housing co-operatives. Associations have also been invited to take part in various initiatives, such as the promotion of homes above shops, the management of dwellings owned by private landlords (HAMA – housing associations as managing agents) and the development of foyer schemes, providing homes and training for young people. Noticeably absent from Housing Corporation policy statements in the early 1990s were references to rehabilitation, which, of course, had been a major activity of many associations in the past. The lack of emphasis on rehabilitation in the early years of the new regime reflects two main factors. First, from the point of view of associations themselves, now that they had to carry the risk of development, rehabilitation was less attractive than new building on greenfield sites. Final costs were much more difficult to predict at the point when the grant was settled, and therefore risk-averse associations, coming to terms with the new regime, tended to withdraw from rehabilitation; by 1991 rehabilitation and re-improvement accounted for a mere 17 per cent of the Housing Corporation funded programme, although it has to be admitted that the decline began before 1989 (DoE, 1993: 17). Second, in the early 1990s the emphasis on maximising output from ADP resources tended to favour new building over rehabilitation, simply because unit costs of rehabilitated properties were often higher than new-build costs.

In more recent years housing associations have been drawn into the growing concentration within government policy on regeneration and the creation of sustainable communities. This is partly about the economic revival of areas affected by industrial decline, and partly about tackling the complex social and economic problems of rundown residential areas, especially large council estates. Until 1994–95 records were not kept of how much housing associations were investing on council estates, although Crook and Darke (1996) have shown that there was a not inconsiderable amount of activity. Since 1994–95, Housing Corporation policy statements have discussed the issue of the renewal of council estates, stressing that ADP resources are not normally available to fund intensive renewal/refurbishment of such estates, but acknowledging that associations have a role to play in

promoting tenure-diversification (for example through shared ownership) and in terms of new building on cleared sites.

In addition to the increased prominence of council estates as locations of investment activity by housing associations there has been a
wider development of interest in the capacity of associations to deliver
more than simply new or improved houses. In 1995 the Corporation
launched the notion of 'housing plus' in recognition of the need to think
in terms broader than the straightforward provision and management of
houses. Housing plus can be understood in different ways, but three
main features can be identified:

● the need for sustainability to be at the heart of all the policies and
  processes for managing and developing social housing;

● the fundamental importance of establishing effective partnerships
  between service providers, tenants and residents in the drive to make
  communities sustainable;

● the overriding necessity of relating the management and
  development of social housing to the broader context of the needs of
  the communities where it is located (Housing Corporation, 1997b).

The housing-plus agenda has suffused the Corporation's approach to
evaluating bids for ADP resources and RSLs have become thoroughly
incorporated into the Labour government's regeneration strategy. The
advantages of housing-plus lie in the potential gains from taking a
wider view and from working with a range of partner organisations in
pursuit of genuinely sustainable communities. However, there are two
reservations that deserve to be set out: first, the emphasis on partnership and on delivering benefits beyond housing contrasts with the sorts
of arguments that were deployed in the late 1980s, when it was held
that the advantage of housing associations over local authorities was
precisely that they were dedicated, single-purpose organisations; and,
second, the objective of securing more from RSLs than simply good,
well-managed houses has emerged during the same period that they
have been under intense pressure to increase efficiency and to produce
more from less. Housing-plus is an illustration of how associations
have had to cope with greater demands and increased complexity,
issues that will be picked up again in the next sub-section.

Diversity and complexity

Partly as a result of channelling housing association development activity in accordance with the shifting priorities mentioned above, governments have fostered a situation in which RSLs have found themselves drawn into a more diverse range of activities, supported by more complex funding arrangements. For example, in 1990 the Corporation's Policy Statement observed that:

> We face much pressure to devote a substantial proportion of our ADP to care in the community projects, housing people whose accommodation costs have until now been met from Social Services or NHS budgets. The Corporation will increasingly look for capital and revenue costs of such schemes to be funded by a transfer of funds from the relevant authorities and Departments. (Housing Corporation, 1990b: 17)

For their part, associations wishing to expand their supported housing (previously referred to as special needs housing) and/or care-homes provision, or to diversify into this type of work, have faced the challenge of putting together appropriate capital and revenue funding arrangements, often involving tough negotiations with local authorities and health authorities about top-up payments. In some RSLs the provision of housing with a care element has become their main activity, while others have established specialist care operations within a group structure. On a similar scale to community care are the complexities of regeneration, which involve associations in bidding for funds controlled by different arms of government, under headings such as the Single Regeneration Budget (SRB), the Estates Renewal Challenge Fund and the Rough Sleepers Initiative (RSI). Involvement in regeneration schemes seems set to become an important source of funding for RSLs as their conventional programmes decline.

Another example of diversification in the 1990s has been the growth on interest in the development of foyers (Figure 11.2), which, in addition to requiring associations to link up with partner organisations to provide the training services that are an integral part of the package, also require considerable amounts of fund-raising to bridge gaps in terms of both initial capital costs and ongoing revenue expenditure.

Figure 11.2 The Bristol foyer under construction in 1999. An example of partnership working, with the site provided by the City Council, funding from the Housing Corporation, the National Lottery and others. The building is being developed by Knightstone but will be run by a separate non-profit company

The grant competition

There have been three distinct phases in policy towards the distribution of grant, beginning with the years 1989 to 1993. The first four years of the new regime were characterised by:

- the attempt to implement flexible medium term planning arrangements, as described above;
- growth in terms of planned expenditure and output;
- encouragement from the Housing Corporation for geographical expansion and greater competition among associations.

The Corporation's cash crisis of 1990 notwithstanding, the main problems facing housing associations at that time were how to spend the significantly increased amounts of capital being made available to them, and how to achieve the output targets expected of them. In November 1991, for instance, the government announced expenditure plans for 1992–92 that were double the outturn expenditure of 1988–89, and then in the run-up to the general election of April 1992 the Conservatives promised that housing associations would provide 153,000 additional dwellings in three years, (that is an annual rate of production equal to two and a half times the achievement of 1988–89). Then, at the end of 1992, with the private housing market continuing in deep recession, the chancellor, Norman Lamont, announced the housing market package (HMP), which brought forward expenditure from future years and required associations to spend £577 million of grant, plus a further £400 million of private finance, on the purchase of 18,000 existing empty homes in under 100 days. This was a Treasury initiative designed to revive the housing market by mopping up excess supply, and housing associations were merely convenient agencies for the task, which was dumped on the Housing Corporation without consultation and with virtually no lead-in time, just a month before Christmas. The Corporation initially identified 27 associations to carry out the work in designated areas, and although many of those involved were privately appalled at what they were being asked to do, not one association turned down the opportunity to take part, even though some were given areas in which they had little or no previous involvement.

Until 1989, as Chapter 8 has pointed out, associations were discouraged (by zoning for rehabilitation and site registration for new building) from actively competing one with another, but the Conservatives' faith in market mechanisms was leading towards greater use of competitive structures in pursuit of policy goals across a range of programme areas (Oatley, 1998). Along with rent deregulation, therefore, came competition, and although at first associations were not expected to compete by bidding for HAG at below the guideline rate, they were quite explicitly advised by Corporation officials that they should expand their operations by bidding for grant in new areas. Some associations, no doubt, needed no further encouragement to expand into new areas, and it would be wrong to give the impression that expansion and growth were simply the result of the Corporation leaning on unwilling associations. To some extent the Corporation's strategy was motivated by the wish to stiffen the competition faced by leading regional associations by encouraging other, bigger, players to move in, but even relatively small associations with a clear inner-city community orientation were advised that continued HAG allocations would depend on their expansion into new areas. Underlying this strategy was probably a desire to improve efficiency by injecting competition into situations where relationships among established associations, and between them and their local authorities, had become rather too cosy. Whatever the reasons for it, the period 1989–93 witnessed a remarkable episode of increased competition through geographical expansion (see Malpass, 1997, for evidence of expansionism among associations in the west region).

An additional point that needs to be made here is that at precisely the same time as the Corporation was encouraging associations to expand and compete in new areas, the government was raising the profile of local housing strategies. One way in which local authorities could demonstrate that they were good strategic enablers was to set up formal social housing agreements with partner housing associations, an idea that was supported by the NFHA and the local government associations. But the suggestion that a local authority would identify a small group of favoured developing partners opened up the possibility of charges of anti-competitive practices. Nevertheless, the practical necessity of limiting the numbers of associations actively seeking to compete for development opportunities within a given district meant that some sort of list of designated partner organisations came to be widely adopted.

The first period was brought to an end by the announcement in November 1992 of increased pressure on associations. First, the chancellor unveiled severe cutbacks in funding for housing associations after April 1993 as the government struggled to reduce the huge budget deficit which appeared after the 1992 general election. Second, it was announced that grant rates were to be cut year by year, with the intention of reaching 55 per cent by 1995–96. Third, despite the reduced level of ADP input associations were still expected to meet the pre-election output pledges. And, of course, overshadowing this squeeze on associations in the short term there were the intense pressures generated by the HMP.

The combined effect of a smaller ADP, high output targets and lower grant rates was to raise the pressure on associations to increase efficiency. To this was added a new dimension: in the bidding round for 1994–95 associations were encouraged to bid at less than the (falling) grant rate, thereby ushering in an unseemly and unsustainable scramble for ADP resources. It is important to be clear that as late as the summer of 1992, in the bidding round in advance of allocations for 1993–94, associations were being advised to bid at the published grant rate, which was then 67 per cent nationally. When the grant rate then fell to 62 per cent in 1994–95 associations were therefore having to cope with the need to make additional savings in order to produce competitive bids. Whereas the justification offered for previous rate reductions had been falling procurement costs, the planned cuts in 1994 and 1995 were all about levering in more private finance in order to meet the output targets from smaller amounts of public expenditure within the ADP. This was described by the chief executive of the NFHA at the time as, 'an arbitrary decision and not one which flows from any reasonable forecast of continuing decline in procurement and financing costs. There is no evidence of any precise formula being used by government to determine grant levels' (Coulter, 1993: 10).

During the period 1994–95 to 1996–97 associations were openly encouraged to bid at below the headline grant rate, although the terms of the advice were changed year by year. Initially the primarily criterion was the level of HAG required from the Corporation, and then the Corporation took into account the aggregate amount of public subsidy, from all sources. It is important to recognise that the government's strategy consisted of two distinct elements: downward pressure on headline grant rates and encouragement to associations to undercut the published rates. The latter served as a device to ensure the achievement of the former; but it also drew the teeth of critics who argued against rate reductions, for Ministers could point to the conflict between the arguments of the NFHA against grant rate cuts and the apparent willingness of its members to bid at rates well below the ceiling.

The third phase of policy towards the grant competition began to be signalled in 1996–97, when the Corporation started, on a trial basis, to look at rent levels as well as grant-rate bids. However, in the following year the guidance given to associations was explicit in saying that, 'For 1997/98, rents will be at the forefront of the bidding process; and bidders will be required to set actual rents for completed dwellings in line with those put forward at bid stage as a condition of receiving SHG' (Housing Corporation, 1996b: 36). In subsequent years the guidance from the Corporation became more constraining, with references to rents being reduced in real terms. At the same time, in a return to the position of the early 1990s, associations were instructed that they should not undercut the published grant rates.

This major change has to be seen in terms of the intersection of development and pricing as two distinct aspects of policy. From the point of view of the government competition for grant had certain advantages, in that it maximised output from the ADP and it put pressure on associations to be more efficient and businesslike in their approach. In the mid-1990s the emphasis was unequivocally on stretching the ADP as far as possible, and if associations subsidised their bids by increased private borrowing which led to higher rents then this was accepted as a price worth paying. However, there were two consequences of this approach which made it unsustainable in the longer run. First, it meant that associations had to draw more heavily on their own resources, with potentially long-term implications. In some cases they diverted revenue income from expenditure on maintenance of the existing stock into subsidising the rents of new houses. Alternatively they raised additional loans, thereby generating heavier loan charges which ate into revenue income. By raising more from private lenders associations were using up their borrowing power at a faster rate, mortgaging more and more of their assets and bringing forward the point at which they encountered difficulties in raising further development loans. Second, higher rents eventually began to be seen as problematic in themselves in terms of affordability, work disincentives and their implications for public expenditure via housing benefit (see Chapter 10).

However, bearing down on rents closes off a degree of freedom previously available to associations in the construction of their bids for grant. By 1998 there were grumbles of discontent among developing associations about the increasing difficulty of producing viable bids that met all the requirements in terms of costs, standards and rents.

Who builds?

At first, the post-1988 system offered the largest and financially strongest actively developing associations an opportunity to combine private finance with a flexible programme of investment at a fixed grant rate; this was known as 'tariff' funding, which meant that they entered into three-year agreements with the Corporation to provide a certain number of dwellings in named local authority areas at amounts of grant set in advance, and determined by the types of accommodation to be built and local costs (represented by a series of Total Cost Indicators (TCIs)). This approach cut out the need to calculate grant on a scheme by scheme basis, and gave associations welcome flexibility about the detailed implementation of their development programmes, but it also exposed them to the full risk of development costs. In practice, tariff agreements were soon disrupted by the Housing Corporation's cash crisis in 1990 (see Chapter 10), but some associations were able to accumulate large surpluses as actual construction costs fell below expectations. Although it did not prove to be viable in all parts of the country (it worked better in areas away from London and the south east) tariff funding did enable some associations (usually the larger ones) greater control over the management of their development programmes. In 1992 tariff funding began to be replaced by cash programme agreements, on similar lines, but these too were overtaken by the drive for competitive bidding for HAG.

Other associations relied on non-tariff mixed funding, and public funding. Dealing with these in reverse order, public funding was available to small associations that could not be expected to raise private finance; thus they carried on with a funding regime that differed least from the old system, receiving HAG plus residual loans from the Corporation or a local authority. Larger associations were encouraged to embark on mixed funding, and this (including mixed funding under tariff arrangements) soon accounted for more than 90 per cent of ADP output (Randolph, 1993: 42; DoE, 1994: 90). As tariff and cash-programme agreements unwound all associations returned to the routine of the annual round of bids and allocations on a scheme-by-scheme basis.

While the largest associations were clearly able to fend for themselves and to contemplate substantial development programmes over a run of years, there was doubt about how far the smaller associations would be able to take advantage of the growth opportunities offered within the new financial regime. In 1991 the Housing Corporation launched an initiative, known as 'Operation Breakthrough', to encourage groups of associations to collaborate in development consortia which could bid collectively for ADP resources to carry out large building programmes with named building contractors. The idea behind such high volume procurement arrangements was that economies of scale would produce significant cost benefits. Examples of consortia set up at that time included the NORVIC group of six northern associations which planned to build up to 2,000 homes over three years, in collaboration with Tarmac Contract Housing as the building contractor, and the South Thames Housing Partnership, which brought together three associations and a building contractor to produce 1,500 homes over three years. However, volume procurement arrangements of this kind have not been continued, and now the Corporation actively discourages proposals involving more than one association building on a given site.

Looking now at the pattern of allocations to individual associations, and bearing in mind the theme of RSLs as agents of central government, it is relevant to refer back to suggestions that the introduction of private finance would tend to squeeze out small associations and result in a small number of large associations becoming even larger and more dominant. The first point to note is that although there are over 2,200 RSLs altogether, most of them are very small and do not have active development programmes. Indeed, half of them have fewer than 50 dwellings and have never received more than £1 million in grant aid (in fact this large group of associations has received an aggregate of under £20 million in grant since 1974 – *Housing Corporation News*, May 1996). Of the remaining 1,100 associations, only 5–600 receive an allocation of grant in any one year, and of these only 3–400 receive grant for increasing their stock of houses. The precise number of associations with a development allocation each year during the 1990s is difficult to calculate from available sources, but it is reasonable to infer that the bulk of the development programme has been carried out by no more than 100 associations. What can be calculated (from data supplied by the Housing Corporation) is that there was considerable stability among the associations receiving the largest allocations in the six years 1993–94 to 1998–99: 25 associations appeared every year in the top 50 by size of allocation, and virtually all of these 25 associations were in the top 50 by total stock in 1998. In 1998–99, the 25 associations with the largest grant allocations accounted for nearly 43 per cent of the total, while the top 50 allocations consumed 55 per cent. This sort of evidence tends to support the commonly held view that there is, in practice, a 'superleague' of top associations regularly absorbing a large share of total grant allocations and accelerating away from the great majority of RSLs. At the end of 1992 there was a brief furore within the movement when a Housing Corporation document leaked to the NFHA appeared to imply that in future financial ratios might become the basis on which ADP allocations were made, thereby favouring the larger and stronger associations. This was swiftly denied and repudiated by the Corporation, but it subsequently emerged that financial indicators form an important part of the information upon which funding decisions are made (Housing Corporation, 1994: 11).

The changing character of the housing association sector

This section looks at the impact of policies and developments over the period since 1988 on the overall stock of housing provided by RSLs and the social composition of the people who occupy those dwellings. The numerical increase in the size of the total stock has been the product of two main strands of activity: new building and acquisitions by established associations and transfers from the local authority sector. Whereas completions of new units have been on a downward curve since 1996, stock transfers have moved sharply upwards since the general election.

Altogether, therefore, more than 352,500 dwellings had been transferred by 86 different local authorities by the end of March 1999 (Table 11.2), and the programme for 1999–2000 contained more than 140,000 dwellings. If transfers continue at this sort of rate (and there are signs, particularly from Scotland, that it may accelerate) then it will not be many years before the RSLs account for more than half of the whole social rented sector, overtaking local authority housing as the second largest tenure category in Britain. This would not only mark an enormous reversal of the position throughout most of the twentieth century, but also a transformation in the character of the sector, for it is clear that growth on this scale would mean that most of the stock would be former council houses, and LSVT associations would be in the majority among the largest RSLs. Indeed, LSVT associations have already begun to have an impact. Over the last decade they have transformed the composition of the largest 100 associations and contributed to an increase in the proportion of the total stock owned by this group. Thus, in 1989 the 45 associations with over 2,500 dwellings owned 54 per cent of the stock in England. By 1997 the largest 116 associations each owned more than 2,500 dwellings, amounting to 74 per cent of the total.

Moving on from the effects of stock transfer to look at the situation from the point of view of tenants, they are now much more likely to be renting from a large organisation, and, as has been pointed out above, from an organisation with a geographically widespread stock of dwellings. They are also more likely to be living in a new build property than a rehabilitated house. In terms of the geographical distribution of housing association properties, there has been a marked decline in the proportion located in London, down from 28 per cent to just under 21 per cent, and an even more marked decline in the proportion in London and the other metropolitan areas, down from 59 per cent to 43 per cent. This is mainly a result of the tendency for stock transfers throughout most of the 1990s to be concentrated in non-metropolitan areas. In future, however, this trend may well be reversed.

Table 11.2   Local authority stock transfers in England, 1988–99

	Large Scale Voluntary Transfers		Estates Renewal Challenge Fund Transfers	
	No. of transfers	*No. of dwellings transferred*	*No. of transfers*	*No. of dwellings*
1988–89	2	11,176		
1989–90	2	14,405		
1990–91	11	45,552		
1991–92	2	10,791		
1992–93	4	26,325		
1993–94	10	30,103		
1994–95	13	40,510		
1995–96	12	44,595		
1996–97	5	22,248		
1997–98	6	24,405	9	8,577
1998–99	12	56,072	12	17,828
Total		326,182		26,405

Source: DETR.

In the first half of the 1990s, when rates of building were high and rising, and when the pressure was on associations to maximise output, evidence began to emerge suggesting that the quality of new dwellings was falling (especially in terms of space standards) (Walentowicz, 1992; Karn and Sheridan, 1994), and that by building large estates associations were in danger of reproducing the same sorts of problems previously experienced by local authorities (Page, 1993). David Page (1993: 8) argued that development consortia were leading to large estates, and he referred to examples of estates of 500–700 dwellings, and claimed that there were at least a dozen more in the pipeline of up to 300 dwellings. Later survey evidence (Farthing *et al.*, 1996: 23) was more reassuring, suggesting that three-quarters of all sites developed by RSLs consisted of fewer than 30 dwellings. Nevertheless, Page was right to highlight the impending residualisation of the housing association sector, for in addition to the size of estates he looked at the socio-economic position of new tenants and at the density of children on estates. He was able to show that new entrants to the sector were changing its social character, reinforcing the wider tendency for social rented housing to become the tenure of the least well-off. Three-quarters of new housing association tenants were not in employment, and more than half relied on benefits for their income. New tenants were more likely than existing tenants to be economically active and to have dependent children, reflecting the policy driven shift away from provision for elderly people and towards statutorily homeless households. Those few new tenants that were in work generally earned very low wages.

Later evidence (MORI, 1996), based on a large sample of tenants confirmed the general picture. Housing association tenants in 1995 were found to have average incomes below those of council tenants, and less than half the average for the population as a whole. Two-thirds of all housing association tenants, but 83 per cent new tenants, relied on housing benefit. Page (1993) warned that this general trend towards housing associations accommodating an increasing proportion of low-income households would lead to growing social problems if they built large estates consisting of family houses and then allocated the dwellings in such a way as to create very high child densities.

Conclusion

The post-1988 funding regime, fuelled initially by increased volumes of ADP funding, and sustained more recently by rising proportions of private finance, has had a major impact not only on the overall scale of housing association provision but also on the shape and character of the sector as a whole. As far as the larger associations, especially those with the most active development programmes, are concerned, the new regime created opportunities for them to grow, diversify and change, to a much greater extent than the considerably more numerous but much smaller management-only associations. Some associations embraced the new opportunities with enthusiasm, revelling in the freedom to grow and expand into new areas, both geographically and in terms of types of service provision. For associations with the right financial and stock profiles it was just so easy to borrow huge amounts of private capital. It was almost too easy, and it took a while for chief executives and development managers, schooled in the old risk-free culture, to realise that it was no longer the case that an allocation of grant guaranteed that a scheme was affordable.

The main points to be brought out in conclusion concern the observation that, on the one hand, actively growing associations have been under pressure to become more businesslike and competitive, while on the other hand they have become ever more obviously and deeply entrenched within the structure of the state apparatus for meeting social needs. Housing associations have been called upon simultaneously to adopt a more commercial approach and to shoulder more of the responsibility for housing the least well-off. The evidence referred to earlier in the chapter has shown how Ministers have steered associations into areas of work that they might not otherwise have undertaken, or not to the same extent, and on occasion (for example the HMP) associations have been quite blatantly used as agents of government policy, as if they were servants of the crown rather than ostensibly independent businesses. Housing associations have long been seen as occupying a somewhat ambiguous position between public and private sectors, but since 1988 the demands on them to have a foot firmly in both camps have resulted in conflicting pressures. For example, under the old regime associations could afford to carry out expensive rehabilitation work in rundown inner-city areas where the post-improvement value of dwellings remained way below cost, because the grant system was designed to bridge the valuation gap. But now associations have to be mindful of the long-term value of their assets, and the fact that they carry responsibility for the full cost of major repairs. Associations that were brought into inner city rehabilitation work as partners to local authorities in housing action areas in the 1970s now find that they have numerous properties in need of further substantial investment, but under the terms of the new regime the government has passed to them the responsibility for funding the work. Associations recognise their social responsibilities to such areas, but they also have to ask themselves whether it is good business to go on investing there. The Housing Corporation has been taking a very firm line with associations, arguing that they should have been making adequate provision for major repairs, but the Corporation was itself implicated in the competition mania just a few years ago, when some imprudent decisions were sanctioned. It is quite possible that the current emphasis on housing associations as partners in the regeneration of council estates will, in due course, produce similar problems of low asset values and high maintenance costs.

12

Governance

Introduction

Although housing associations are nominally independent organisations which have often been accused by their critics of being unaccountable for their actions and for the public money invested in them, Chapters 10 and 11 have shown the extent to which, since 1989, governments have sought to manipulate associations through the grant system and through control of the volume and pattern of development expenditure. The argument underlying this chapter is that the close attention given to debating and modernising the governance of associations and other RSLs during the 1990s is a direct reflection of the impact of the new financial regime and the emergence of housing associations as the main providers of affordable rented housing. Such an interpretation is consistent with other evidence which suggests that as voluntary organisations expand and come under closer public scrutiny they undergo important changes in their organisational structures and accountability systems (Harris, 1998: 178). One way of approaching this chapter is to see it as locating voluntary housing organisations within what might be termed the new governance of housing. This recognises that since 1988 housing associations, and more recently the newly formed local housing companies, have been contributing to a broader transformation of social rented housing as a whole in terms of the pattern of ownership, control and accountability; after decades when most of the stock was owned and managed by local authorities, current trends suggest that within the not too distant future a majority may be in the hands of RSLs. This raises important and interesting questions about the internal control of RSLs, and their accountability to external stakeholders, including tenants, funders, the local authorities in the areas where they operate, and central government.

The governance debates

In the broadest sense governance is about governing; it concerns both the act of governing and the systems and principles within which decisions are taken. Rhodes (1996: 652) has argued that in contemporary usage governance is not seen as a synonym for government, but is used specifically to denote something new, a different way of organising and providing governing. Developments put in train during the 1980s have, during the 1990s, brought debate about aspects of governance to much greater prominence. It is convenient to think in terms of three distinct levels: corporate, local and national (but see also Rhodes, 1996).

First, corporate governance has been variously defined as 'the system by which companies are run' (Cadbury Report, 1992: 7) and 'giving overall direction to the enterprise, ensuring the internal accountability of management to the board, and with meeting the requirements of external accountability and regulation' (Greer and Hoggett, 1997: 1). Corporate governance is about the position and role of boards of directors and the ways in which they discharge their responsibilities for the overall conduct of the business, and as such it is distinct from management, which properly lies in the hands of the executive staff. Public attention was focused on boardroom ethics in the wake of deregulation and restructuring in the financial services industry which heightened concerns about standards of honesty, probity and stewardship, concerns that were brought to a head by a series of high-profile scandals such as the collapse of two banks, BCCI and Barings, and the fraudulent behaviour of the newspaper tycoon Robert Maxwell. This was followed by the emergence of evidence of the fortunes being amassed by directors of privatised utilities and the new rail companies. The sorts of questions raised by these events concerned both internal control and accountability: how could shareholders and non-executive directors limit the behaviour of their executive colleagues? and external regulation: what powers were, or should be, available to the regulatory authorities? At the same time revelations concerning the behaviour of a number of prominent Tory MPs (including cabinet ministers David Mellor and Jonathan Aitken) led John Major to appoint a Committee on Standards in Public Life, under the chairmanship of Lord Nolan (Nolan Committee, 1995).

Second, the fragmentation of services formerly provided by local authorities or bodies on which elected councillors had rights to be represented (Davis and Stewart, 1994: 2) has given rise to a separate debate about local governance. The notion of local governance began to be used by some social scientists as a way of highlighting the significance of the transition from the tradition of direct service provision by elected local government to a new pattern of ownership, control and provision of services by non-municipal organisations (ESRC, 1992; Davoudi and Healey, 1995; Malpass, 1994). Stoker (1995) has suggested that:

> A baseline definition of governance is that it refers to the action, manner or system of governing in which the boundary between organisations and public and private sectors has become permeable. Governance recognises the interdependence of organisations. The essence of governance is the interactive relationship between and within governmental and non-governmental forces.

Local governance implies a more complex and subtle set of arrangements, relying on closer working relationships between local government and ostensibly independent organisations, based partly on formal contracting and partly on informal networks (Reid, 1995, 1997, Rhodes, 1996). Within the academic literature there is a divergence of opinion between those, such as Rhodes (1996), who emphasise the independence of inter-organisational networks, and others (Hoggett, 1996) who interpret the new governance system in terms of mechanisms for increasing the degree of control exercised by the centre.

In health, education, training and social care there has been a proliferation of what the Nolan Committee (1996) called local public spending bodies (LPSBs). These were defined as 'not-for-profit organisations which are neither fully elected nor appointed by Ministers, but which provide public services, often delivered at local level, which are wholly or largely publicly funded' (Nolan Committee, 1996: 9). In its report on LPSBs the Nolan Committee looked at grant maintained schools, further and higher education institutions, Training and Enterprise Councils, Local Enterprise Companies (the Scottish equivalent of TECs) and housing associations; it estimated that there were 4,600 such bodies, spending almost £16 billion in the mid-1990s, and governed by 68,700 board members (Nolan Committee, 1996: 10). Thus housing associations are part of the changing pattern of local governance as a whole (Pollitt *et al.*, 1998). The growth of a range of providers at arm's length from central and local government raised questions about how such organisations could be held to account for the large amounts of tax-payers' money underpinning their activities, and how they could demonstrate sufficient financial probity and business efficiency to attract private investors.

Third, at the national level, the Conservatives' attempts to privatise nationalised industries and utilities and to undermine the powers of elected local government led to the addition of two distinct groups of bodies to the list of governance institutions. The privatisation of natural monopolies and industries where it was difficult to introduce competitive markets required some kind of regulator to ensure improved standards and to limit profits. The result has been the appointment of a series of bodies with names such as OFTEL and OFWAT (regulating the telecommunications and water industries). In the case of grant maintained schools and further education colleges the government set up new national funding councils made up of appointees responsible for the distribution of resources to, and monitoring of, institutions previously managed at the local authority level. These new regulatory and funding bodies moved into positions similar to that already occupied by the Housing Corporation.

This discussion of the notion of governance and its rise to prominence in the 1990s not only sets the subsequent analysis of housing associations in context but also provides a framework for that analysis. Accordingly the next three sections looks at developments in the governance of housing associations since the late 1980s in terms of the three levels identified above, starting from the national level. Although within the housing association movement itself most attention has focused on aspects of corporate governance the theme of gradual incorporation into government policy mechanisms suggests that the national level is the appropriate place to start.

Developments in national-level governance

The first point to note under this heading is that in 1989 the Housing Corporation was restructured into three separate bodies, one for each of the constituent countries of Great Britain. Hitherto the Corporation's offices in Scotland and Wales had had their own budgets and, in effect, their own chief executives, and so in that sense the move to establish independent bodies was little more than rationalisation of existing practice. Scottish Homes was formed from the merger of the Housing Corporation in Scotland with the Scottish Special Housing Association, while Tai Cymru (Housing for Wales) was established in Cardiff. This left the Housing Corporation in London with responsibility for housing associations in England. In 1991 the government published, for the first time, a Management Statement setting out its relationship with the

Corporation (DoE, 1991). This document referred to the extended responsibility and greater freedom being given to the Corporation, but evidence presented to the House of Commons Environment Committee in 1993 indicated that it was generally perceived within the housing association movement that the Corporation was 'in effect an executive arm of the Government' (Environment Committee, 1993: xvi). The fact that every chief executive of the Corporation since its formation in 1964 has been a former civil servant only strengthens this perception. However, on the basis of confidential evidence and the answers given by the Chairman of the Corporation the Committee concluded that this was an inaccurate interpretation and that the board did not see itself in these terms (Environment Committee, 1993: xvii). Nevertheless, the fact remains that the government has responsibility for setting the major policy aims for the Corporation and the detailed priorities for its work in any one year, and there is little the Corporation can do to depart from these. The imposition of the housing market package in 1992, as discussed in Chapter 11, indicates the balance of power, but there are examples of initiatives stemming from the Corporation (for example the promotion of private finance in the mid-1980s).

The next point in relation to the structure of governance at a national level, refers to the recurring debate about whether the regulatory and funding functions of the Corporation would be better carried out by two different bodies – for example, by channelling capital grants through the local authority HIP system, thereby leaving the Corporation free to concentrate on its regulatory role. In support of this view it can be argued that if the Corporation had not been responsible for funding housing associations in the heady, expansionist years of the early and mid-1990s then, acting simply as regulator, it might have counselled associations more firmly about the need to adopt a more cautious approach to borrowing, and a less gung-ho approach to investment. In the early 1990s there was strong support in some quarters (principally the local authority associations and some housing associations) for a dismemberment of the Corporation, and it is possible that if Labour had won the 1992 general election then there might have been some action on the matter (Environment Committee, 1993: xxxix-xli). However, the view was strongly held within the Corporation and the DoE that it was right to retain both functions within one body, on the simple ground that it is easier to ensure compliance with the requirements of the regulator if that body is also responsible for the distribution of grant aid (the same point is still being made by the Housing Corporation itself, 1998c).

The dual role of the Corporation was considered again in a study carried out by the DoE in 1995 (DoE, 1995), and again it was concluded that there were sufficient reasons to retain the status quo. On the argument that capital resources should be distributed through the local authorities the report concluded that this would carry the disadvantage from the government's point of view that, 'Control over programme outputs would be reduced, because programme delivery would depend on 366 [local authorities] rather than one single-purpose organisation' (DoE, 1995: 36). And on the issue of the appropriate distance between the Corporation and the DoE, the report noted that the Corporation had played an important part in implementing national policies on homelessness, tenure diversification and other matters, resulting in the unsurprising conclusion that, 'Moving the Corporation further from government, by recasting the Management Statement to give it greater autonomy, would significantly reduce government's ability to secure such contributions to national policies' (DoE, 1995: 30).

Turning now to the regulatory function itself, there has been a significant tightening of the regime under which associations have been monitored and evaluated. This can be explained partly by the increased volumes of public money flowing into their development programmes in the period up to 1993, but it is also to do with providing reassurance for private lenders, whose representatives said as much in evidence to the Environment Committee in 1993 (page xxxv), and the Corporation itself admitted the value that they derived from knowing that associations were closely monitored:

> The acid test of our regulatory performance is our ability to assure funders, service users and other interested parties that registered housing associations remain managerially and financially viable and conduct themselves in a fit and proper manner. (Housing Corporation, 1994: 24)

Since the introduction of the new financial regime there have been three revisions of the performance monitoring system, in 1992, 1994 and 1998. In 1992 the system was improved by requiring better quality, and more frequently submitted, financial information from associations. All developing associations were required to post quarterly returns on solvency, gearing and efficiency, providing the Corporation with early warning signals about any associations that were facing problems; these financial indicators were also part of the database used by the Corporation to decide annual capital allocations to associations.

In April 1994 the Corporation introduced a new set of refined and tightened performance standards, involving a move away from pre-
arranged, wide-ranging inspectorial visits to a system based on desktop
review of performance measured against a range of indicators. The
objective was to have a wider review of more associations, with visits
to selected organisations, in particular those about which the Corporation had concerns. The Corporation's Annual Report for 1993–94
referred to the way that the further tightening of its requirements of
associations underlined 'the fundamental importance of associations
demonstrating effective committee and management control and financial health'. The message was pressed home later in the same Report:

> Our tighter assessment criteria and the introduction of more benchmarks have...
> made it more demanding for associations to meet our regulatory requirements.

The same message is repeated in the latest three-year strategy document issued by the Corporation (1998c: 13), which refers to a 'culture
of compliance'. This is a phrase that can be read in two ways: the softer
interpretation is to see it encouraging RSLs to adopt patterns and standards of behaviour which mean that their staff naturally adhere to the
Corporation's performance requirements; a stronger interpretation
suggests that the Corporation seeks to establish a situation in which
RSLs unquestioningly follow its lead.

The new set of Performance Standards, issued by the Housing
Corporation in December 1997, runs to 79 A4 pages. As mentioned in
Chapter 1 the Corporation monitors the performance of RSLs in terms
of criteria set out under nine headings, and although it is not appropriate to go through these in any detail, it is important to note that RSLs
are accountable to the Corporation for much more than the proper
expenditure of publicly funded grants and the quality of housing
services provided. There are performance standards relating to aspects
of governance, including the competence of the governing body, openness and equal opportunities, and a series of standards on tenants'
rights. The new Performance Standards took account of changes introduced in the Housing Act 1996, which, it will be recalled, allowed for
the registration of new kinds of registered social landlords that were not
housing associations. Although the 1996 Act did not introduce powers
for the Corporation to register and pay grant to for-profit organisations,
it did make other important changes, including transformation of the
Corporation's power to monitor associations into the much wider
power to obtain information from RSLs. The Act also allowed for the

deregistration of small associations (previously, any association that had received any grant aid from the Corporation, at any time, had to remain on the register) – a move which may be seen as designed to reduce the workload on the Corporation, enabling it to devote more resources to monitoring the larger, more active RSLs. Housing Corporation statistics show that between March 1997 and June 1998 81 small associations deregistered, but the numbers can be expected to increase.

Having discussed the formal performance monitoring system it is important to add that on a day to day basis there is a good deal of informal contact between the Corporation (particularly through its regional office staff) and the more active RSLs. This undoubtedly contributes to the Corporation's ability to steer associations in preferred directions. Over many years the Corporation has been able to shape and mould associations into the sorts of organisations that it wants to work with; reference was made in Chapter 8 to the way in which in the 1970s the Corporation leaned on associations to bring housing management in-house and to rely less on consultants, by making it clear to them that future grant allocations depended on compliance. Other and more recent examples would include pressure on associations to strengthen the composition of their boards, to adopt tenant participation strategies and to move towards devising proper business plans.

All available evidence points towards the conclusion that centralised monitoring and control of RSLs is likely to increase, and the development of the government's 'best value' system to apply to RSLs as well as to local authorities seems certain to add to the pressures on them.

The Housing Corporation not only funds and regulates existing RSLs, but also controls, through the registration process, the creation of new RSLs (although of course anyone can set up a housing association, but only RSLs are entitled to receive grant aid for development). It was noted in Chapter 8 that when the Corporation took over the task of registering housing associations as a whole in 1974 the view was held then that there were too many of them. Over the years the Corporation has pursued a duel strategy of restricting new registrations, and channelling development funds towards a limited number of associations, as discussed in Chapter 11. The policy on registration is that new organisations will be added to the register only where there is clear evidence that there are no existing RSLs operating in the designated area of operation capable of undertaking the sort of work proposed in order to meet identified needs. The numbers of new associations registered in the 1990s have tended to fall, reflecting in part deliberately tighter criteria (Housing Corporation, 1994b: 24). In the period January 1990 to June

1998, 300 new organisations were registered, of which 60 were LSVT associations and a further 8 were formed in connection with the Estates Renewal Challenge Fund (a device for improving conditions on rundown council estates) (data supplied by the Housing Corporation). The pattern of registrations is interesting because the majority are almshouses, local Abbeyfields societies and co-operatives, none of which is likely ever to aspire to great size. In terms of impact on the RSL sector, in the immediate and foreseeable future, it is only the LSVT associations that have the potential to make a significant contribution and to develop into major players.

The main conclusion to be drawn from this is that by its registration and funding policies the Corporation has been able to exert considerable influence on the developing shape of the housing association movement as a whole. One important effect has been to make it very much more difficult than it used to be in the 1960s and 70s for new associations to be formed from scratch and to be built up into large organisations. As mentioned above, the only new associations that are likely to make a measurable impact are LSVTs, springing fully formed from within the public sector. Their immediate entry to the group of the largest 200 RSLs is already changing the overall character of the movement.

A final comment in this section is to acknowledge that although associations often complain about the burdens of monitoring and regulation, there is a view that the system works to their advantage. Mullins (1997) has argued that the regulatory regime has been developed in collaboration with the NFHA/NHF and that it has had the effect of creating a closed group of players, competing with each other but knowing that they were safe from unexpected interventions. This point is reinforced by reference to the expressions of outrage from some housing association chief executives when the LSVT associations began to compete strongly for HAG and to expand into new areas in the early 1990s. While accepting that the regime may be burdensome for small associations, Mullins (1997: 308) suggests that,

> Perhaps the regime has provided greatest benefits to large developing associations with the resources to comply with the requirements and who have maximised their access to public funds while being insulated form external competition.

Local governance

The previous section has shown that in a variety of formal and informal ways RSLs are regularly and directly accountable to the Housing Corporation. Not only must they provide regular information but they are subject to a range of powerful sanctions for non-compliance. But how are they accountable to the communities in which they work? This question arises from the fact that for several decades it was elected, and therefore publicly accountable, local authorities which provided by far the largest proportion of rented housing for people in need. Housing was seen as an important local service and a cherished local responsibility in the sense that it was the main service provided by district councils, it was a service historically associated with a high degree of local autonomy and it generated the majority of the casework dealt with by councillors. The post-1988 emphasis on housing associations as the main providers of new social rented housing, the transfer of existing council owned dwellings to RSLs and the adoption by local authorities of a strategic enabling role represent a fragmentation of the local governance of social rented housing. Fragmentation needs to be seen in terms of both the multiplicity of RSLs and their arm's length (or further) relationship with the local authority. This stands in marked contrast to the established system for managing large stocks of council houses under the control of a unified housing department answerable to a single committee of councillors. Fragmentation raises issues of both political and theoretical significance, about new patterns of power and influence. and about how local councils, as the statutory housing authorities and as the democratically elected representative bodies for the local population, can assert their continuing legitimate interest in the quality and quantity of housing services. Although local authorities are no longer the main providers of new social rented housing they retain an interest in making sure that services are provided at a satisfactory level, and they retain clear overall strategic responsibility for ensuring that the necessary dwellings are provided.

It is important to understand that the restructuring of the local governance of housing (and similar trends in other services) after 1988 was not simply a neutral process of modernisation (or, arguably, post-modernisation); it was pushed through by a Conservative government that continued to be virulently anti-local government. Thus although local authorities were required to produce local housing strategies, it was apparent that Ministers were increasingly assertive about the form and content of those strategies, leading to the conclusion that what emerged in the first half of the 1990s was a system designed to ensure that a wider variety of agencies delivered what Ministers wanted, rather than a system designed to facilitate local responses to local needs. Whereas in principle it would have been possible to construct a system in which accountability to local elected representatives was given priority, in practice the opposite was the case.

It is instructive to look at stock transfer organisations in this context. A question that needs to be asked is, why have virtually all local authorities which have carried out stock transfers opted to set up new associations, and latterly local housing companies, rather than transfer to existing associations? Undoubtedly part of the answer is that in some cases transfers have been pushed through by chief officers who wanted to establish a new organisation, outside the constraints of local government, with themselves in charge, and therefore transfer to an existing association was not an attractive option. But it is also important to remember that by setting up new associations or companies councils have been able to ensure a greater representation for elected councillors than would have been available by transfer to existing associations. In other words, the establishment of LSVT associations and companies reflects an implicit criticism of the lack of accountability in traditional associations, and a search for models of corporate governance that give councillors more influence. Research on early LSVT associations found that all had the maximum permitted number of councillors, and all, initially at least, were chaired by a councillor (Mullins *et al.*, 1992: 29). But, at the same time, it must be recognised that councils have been prevented from setting up new organisations on which councillors filled a majority of board places, and the long debate about various forms of local housing company has to be seen as essentially a product of the obstacles to local council control due to government opposition (Wilcox *et al.*, 1993; Wilcox, 1997).

Another key factor in the way that the fragmentation of the local governance of housing has developed in the 1990s has been the geographical expansion of many associations. As discussed in Chapter 11, after the introduction of the new financial regime the Housing Corporation encouraged greater competition among associations by not only allowing them to bid in new areas but also making it clear to them that they should do so. In some cases this amounted to no more than removing constraints and allowing associations greater freedom to pursue existing ambitions, but in others it was a message received with less enthusiasm. It should also be understood that the Housing Corporation was, at least in certain areas, involved in steering in new associations to stiffen the competition faced by established local organisations. Little detailed research has been carried out to map the way that associations expanded into new areas, although a limited study of the south west showed, for example, that in the first half of the decade a number of large associations moved into the region, and some were able to achieve very large increases in the numbers of districts in the region in which they received grant from the Corporation (Malpass, 1997). The effect of this policy, which was most apparent in the early 1990s (when there was plenty of grant to distribute), was both to reshape and change the character of the movement and to add a further dimension to the fragmentation of the local governance of housing. In addition to its established role in shaping the development of the movement in terms of which associations grew the most, the Corporation became intimately involved in creating new patterns of developing associations in each area, sometimes in spite of the expressed preferences of the local authorities and their existing partners.

Geographical expansionism, especially where incoming associations were in effect imposed on reluctant local authorities, had serious implications for local governance. It introduced new tensions among competing associations and the local authorities, and it increased the numbers of new dwellings being built by large regional or national organisations with dispersed development programmes. It became theoretically possible for situations to arise where such large and financially powerful organisations could completely outbid small and locally-based associations, with the result that all new development would be in the hands of RSLs based far away. Even without invoking such extreme and hypothetical examples, it became clear that, in virtually all areas, expansionism meant that an increasing proportion of new building was being carried out by associations based elsewhere. In the longer run this suggested a further fragmentation of the local governance of housing as a rising proportion of the stock of social rented housing was owned and managed by organisations based far away. It represented a leaking away of local accountability, in that it would appear to be more difficult for elected representatives (or anyone) in an area to have much purchase on the actions of an organisation based up to three hundred miles away and with assets spread over many districts. There is a corporate governance point here too: the more spread out an organisation the less likely it is that the interests of people in any one of its areas will be directly represented on the board.

It is important to understand that developments in the local governance of social rented housing in England in the period since 1988 embrace two distinct processes, reflecting deliberate policy choices. The geographical expansion of housing associations was separate from and overlay the policy of transferring resources from local authority control. It would have been possible, in principle and in practice, to have opted for a strategy which prioritised local connections and local accountability. In this context it may be helpful to distinguish between growth and expansion – associations can grow in terms of the numbers of dwellings in management, without expanding beyond established boundaries. They could have been encouraged to increase their stock holdings in areas where they were already working and where they could demonstrate strong links into the local community. However, in England in the 1990s a particular model of local governance has been developed for social rented housing, based on a dominant role for a relatively small number of large service providers operating across local authority boundaries. This was not the only available model (for examples developed in other service areas see Le Grand and Bartlett, 1993; Greer and Hoggett, 1997; Pollitt *et al.*, 1998), and its adoption required a conscious departure from existing spatial patterns of operation among housing associations. Given that the majority of housing associations in 1989 operated within only one local authority district it would have been possible to develop a model (similar to the one already operating in Scotland) built around locally based and accountable organisations. It is clear that the governance model for RSLs in England reflects deliberate choices made in the late 1980s about weakening the power and influence of local authorities and giving priority to competition and managerialism.

However, having emphasised factors tending to minimise local accountability, it is important to move on to consider ways in which local authorities have been able to retain some influence over RSLs. First, the idea of the strategic enabling role, and the increased weight attached to demonstrable partnership working, meant that, on the one hand, local authorities were under greater pressure to reach mutually acceptable working relationships with associations in their area, and on the other hand, the Housing Corporation came to rely more heavily on the development priorities identified by authorities. As mentioned in Chapter 11, a number of local authorities have adopted a policy of identifying a short-list of designated partner associations for development purposes, and in the process of making their periodic selections they are able to specify certain criteria for participation – such as a local office or a regional committee structure. Second, in addition to the long established system of local authority nomination of a proportion of tenants, some local authorities require participation in their common waiting list, and look for assurances about factors such as rent levels to be set for new dwellings and policies on tenant participation. In these various ways local authorities can exert a not inconsiderable influence over the pattern of housing provision by organisations not under their direct control. Looking at this from the housing association point of view, it can appear that they are effectively agents for the local authorities – building only what they want, letting it to their nominees at rents that they specify.

The corporate level

Housing associations entered the new financial regime in 1989 with management committees that had been recruited in, and were used to, a very different and much less demanding environment. In the past questions had arisen as to the competence and accountability of committee members, but this was generally in relation to allegations of isolated cases of fraudulent or inept behaviour. Now the demands of the new financial regime, alongside a much expanded overall development programme, put a premium on both competence and accountability. As explained in Chapter 10, the new regime meant that associations would take on responsibility for development risk, and for setting rents at levels that would cover expenditure while remaining affordable to the main target groups. These were considerable challenges which required a new approach and different ways of working. At the same time, committee members in the larger and most actively developing associations, had to cope with the implications of organisational growth, accompanied by increasing specialisation, professionalism and managerialism (by 1997 90 per cent of the stock was owned by the 215 RSLs with more than 1,000 dwellings (Housing Corporation, 1998a: 5). In such organisations, operating in a complex legal and regulatory environment, it is reasonable to ask how part-time voluntary board members can make a useful contribution to corporate governance. Could voluntary committee members demonstrate that they had the skills and experience necessary to operate under the new regime? Could they show that they were in control of their organisations, and were the existing structures and procedures such that they could actually exercise that control? Crucially, would the financial institutions be convinced? In terms of accountability, the shifting balance between associations and democratically elected local authorities naturally gave added weight to questions about how committee members were recruited, whose interests they represented (if any), and how they could be held to account, and, if necessary, removed from office.

Management Committees were, and to a large extent still are, rather strange hybrid bodies, reflecting the position of housing associations between the public and private sectors, deeply rooted in the historical traditions of voluntary housing, and arguably ill-suited to the challenges of the present period. The historical account presented in earlier chapters has referred to the diverse origins and varied organisational forms adopted by the antecedents of modern RSLs, but it is clear that there was invariably some sort of committee or board which carried ultimate responsibility for the organisation. In the case of the great charitable trusts the trustees were appointed according to the particular terms of the trust deed, and their role was essentially to ensure that the organisations remained true to the founders' instructions. Their main line of accountability was back to the original trust deed, although they also had to satisfy the requirements of the Charity Commissioners, which in practice acted as a regulator with a light touch. In the majority of housing societies that lacked massive charitable endowment the shareholders were the main source of investment funds and so boards elected by shareholders at annual general meetings could genuinely claim to represent major financial stakeholders. In the days before HAG a key role for the board was raising the necessary capital for property acquisition or development, and so it is probably true that in most cases boards consisted of people who were themselves significant shareholders. Being unpaid for their work was implicit in the philanthropic ethos of voluntary housing, although there is some evidence of directors of some I and P housing societies receiving modest stipends. The top-down nature of philanthropy also meant that tenants were absent from the boards of the great majority of voluntary housing organisations (with the obvious exceptions of co-ops and copartnerships societies).

The reason for this brief historical excursion is to make the point that the advent of high levels of public funding, initially led by the LCC and then taken over by the Housing Corporation after 1974, broke the link between board members and financial stakeholders. Once maximum shareholdings in associations were reduced to a nominal £1 non-tradeable, non-interest bearing share, and the bulk of capital finance came in the form of loans and grants from the public purse it became reasonable to ask what voluntary committee members were there for, whose interests they represented and to what extent they were account-able for their actions, given that the shareholders who elected them were not major financial stakeholders. Another factor at work after 1974 was the policy, implemented by the Housing Corporation, of ensuring that management committee members were people who had no personal financial interest in their association. Initially introduced to root out 'fee grabbing' consultants, this policy also effectively prevented senior staff from being appointed as committee members. Thus the model of corporate governance operating in housing associa-tions to this day resembles a kind of hybrid, with some features remi-niscent of local government (for example the separation between committee members and officers), while others (such as the election of members by shareholders) are derived from the business sector.

It has been shown that English housing associations in the early 1990s had an average of just 64 shareholding members (Kearns, 1994: 5). Here lies the basis for the claim that housing associations have long been unaccountable self-perpetuating oligarchies. Whereas all adults resident in an area can vote at elections for the local council, and anyone can purchase shares in public limited companies, entitling them to take part in elections for non-executive directors, access to the group of shareholding members who alone vote in housing association elections is controlled by the association itself. Thus housing associa-tions can appear to be closed organisations by comparison. This is clearly more of an issue today than it was in the past, given the large amounts of public subsidy channelled in their direction and their key role in the implementation of local housing strategies.

The decision by the NFHA in 1994 to set up a committee, chaired by Sir David Hancock, to carry out an inquiry into the governance of housing associations was a sign of a perceived need to address this and other related issues at that time. Ashby (1997: 68–9) argues that the Federation was aware of the increased demands being placed on volun-tary members, and of the breakdown in the political consensus around the role of associations (in the wake of Tory losses at the 1992 general election some politicians had blamed housing associations for altering the social and political balance within neighbourhoods and constituen-cies). It was beginning to be argued in some circles that housing asso-ciations represented the worst possible combination – neither properly accountable to the taxpayer nor fully exposed to the pressures of market forces (Coleman, 1991). Ashby also refers to the Housing Corporation at that time asserting support for payment for committee members and for senior staff to be appointed to management committees. These were issues about which NFHA members had strong feelings, and 'The NFHA concluded that, if the governance of housing associations was going to be overhauled then it would be better if this was preceded by a much wider debate with more considered proposals' (Ashby, 1997: 69).

The terms of reference of the Hancock inquiry referred explicitly to matters of corporate and financial governance, and the subsequent report (NFHA, 1995) made a series of recommendations addressed to associations, the National Federation, the Corporation and the government on ways of improving the competence and accountability of housing associations. It produced a draft code of governance, which was seen as a way of 'embedding good practice in the wider regulatory framework'. Overall, however, the report was a rather bland document, which discussed key questions about, for example, the rapidly weakening links between associations and localities but then contented itself with the vapid recommendation that geographically dispersed associations should make sure they had area or regional committees. On the question of membership policy, the report took a rather dismissive line, arguing that, 'Much that is attributed to the membership in terms of control and accountability is ineffective in practice. In our view, the accountability impact of membership structures is largely illusory' (NFHA, 1995: 17). Apart from opposing open membership the inquiry team declined to make specific recommendations as to ways to improve the accountability of housing associations through membership policy.

Two topics which attracted much heated debate among committee members themselves were whether they should receive payment for their work, and whether there should be unitary boards of directors, with senior staff sitting as full members alongside non-executives. In the wider context these may seem to be minor issues, but Ashby (1997: 74–5) records that they were subjects of lively debate among the inquiry team members. As he says, those from an industrial background took it for granted that unitary boards were more effective, while those from the voluntary sector wanted to maintain the existing distinction. The message from voluntary committee members themselves was strongly against both payment and unitary boards. The inquiry report took a middle line, recommending that members should be entitled to reimbursement for loss of earnings, and that associations should be empowered to adopt a unitary board system if they wished.

There is no doubt that the Hancock inquiry served a useful purpose in providing a forum for the discussion of critical issues for the rapidly expanding and changing housing association movement. Some real progress has been made, in terms of things such as more open recruitment of board members, but on the really big issues it failed to take a decisive stand. It is possible, of course, that it was never intended to tackle these issues, and that its main purpose was to demonstrate to government and the financial institutions that the movement was taking seriously the need to strengthen its governance arrangements. Overall, though, it is hard to accept the conclusion that the main achievement of the report was that it headed off the more radical aspects of Tory policy towards social rented housing, specifically the extension of grant to commercial developers (Ashby, 1997: 77).

What's left of voluntary housing?

The changes affecting housing associations since 1988 have been as great as those at any time in their history. The three chapters analysing this period have shown how the sector as a whole has virtually doubled in size, and how some associations have grown much more rapidly than the rest, accelerating away from the majority and raising anew questions about the validity of the idea of a unified voluntary housing movement. It has been argued that the price of growth has been loss of autonomy, and that associations have been used as convenient mechanisms for the pursuit of government objectives, which have not always been congruent with those that associations would have set for themselves. The conclusions to be drawn from this are that RSLs at the end of the century are little more than agents of the state, and that the voluntary element has been reduced to only marginal and largely symbolic importance, providing a fig-leaf for those who really hold the power. Far from being unaccountable, there is a case for believing that they are too heavily controlled. The genuine voluntarism of the past has become (since 1974) a form of managed voluntarism, and this is now being joined by what might be depicted as the bogus voluntarism of the LSVT associations and companies.

On the first of these conclusions, Hoggett (1996) has argued that the restructuring of the British public sector has given the appearance of decentralisation and devolution of power, but in fact it has been accompanied by three distinctive strategies of control: managed competition, centralised decentralisation and performance management. Each of these can be found in the foregoing analysis of housing associations. Hoggett points out that in quasi-markets, such as that operating to distribute the ADP, where the state is the sole purchaser it has considerable power to dictate the rules of the game. The notion of centralised decentralisation refers to the way in which across large parts of the public sector there has been a tendency to decentralise operations while control over policy and the allocation of resources has become increasingly centralised. On performance management Hoggett argues that this is a technique for monitoring and shaping behaviour by concentrating on a few key indicators of organisational outputs and outcomes.

Thus it is misleading to think of the voluntary sector in housing as independent of government. But what about the role of volunteers within RSLs? Here the argument is that the growth of large organisations, staffed by fulltime professionals, has inevitably changed the role of voluntary board members in those associations that provide the great majority of the stock. At the same time the separation of board members from major external stakeholders and the failure to address the question of shareholding membership policies has stripped them of authority. It is quite clear that board members have much less at stake in their associations than the staff, whose livelihoods and pensions are tied up in the organisation. The combination of performance monitoring by the Corporation and the employment of professional staff means that in the larger associations board members have very little real work to do. It is fanciful to think that they are in control of strategy in any real sense – it is the government and the Corporation that decide what RSLs will do, and therefore any strategic thinking at the level of individual organisations takes place within narrow and well-defined limits. This is not to imply that board members do not have a role to play; they can be very useful in providing a sounding board for staff, and, on occasion, a sheet anchor to slow down progress on their wilder enthusiasms. On the whole, however, board members probably delude themselves if they think they much difference or represent anyone but themselves.

The question that arises at this point is, does it matter if the cherished traditions of voluntarism in housing have been largely eroded? It could be argued that marginalisation of unelected and unrepresentative voluntary board members is long overdue, and that loss of independence is price well worth paying for the increased levels of output and improvements in organisational practice that have been achieved since 1989. There is much force in this argument. There was a lot wrong with housing associations and good progress has been made in tackling out-moded attitudes and practices. If RSLs are to continue as the main providers of new affordable rented housing and if they emerge as the main alternative to owner occupation then it is right that they should be properly regulated. But important questions need to be asked about, for example, the centralising effect of the growth of the RSL sector, and the continuing co-location of the funding and regulatory roles within the Housing Corporation.

13

Conclusion

This book is an attempt to weave a new thread into the established fabric of historical accounts of housing and housing policy in Britain, and in so doing to create new highlights which help to provide a fresh perspective on the whole pattern. In this final chapter the objectives are to look back over the history of voluntary housing, pulling out the main themes that have run through the book as a whole, and then to look forward, in order to speculate about likely developments in the foreseeable future.

Looking back

The starting point for the project was the observation that although modern housing associations were often said to have deep historical roots there was a dearth of research evidence to substantiate claims of close connections with their putative forebears in the nineteenth century, or earlier. The book was therefore designed to fill in some of the missing history of voluntary housing organisations, and much of what needs to be said at this stage concerns the implications for the historiography of housing and housing policy in Britain. It has been shown that the main reason for the missing history of voluntary housing in the twentieth century is that it has been neglected, not that there is a lack of evidence nor that nothing was happening. There is a fascinating story to be told, not only about the work of some remarkable individuals and the various trusts and societies through which they operated, but also about the long-running dialogue between them and the statutory authorities. The evidence reviewed in earlier chapters points towards conclusions which acknowledge that voluntary housing organisations were closer to active policy debates over a longer period than is implied in much of the existing literature, suggesting a need to augment and re-focus explanations of policy development. Conventional accounts structured around the two world wars and policies designed to meet quantitative targets tend to highlight the contributions of local authorities and to minimise coverage of voluntary organisations, but, as has been shown, a fuller understanding and a different angle can be obtained by recognising that although the postwar periods were times of great difficulty for the voluntary organisations they came back into focus roughly fifteen years after each world war.

Despite the aggregation of evidence of continued activity among growing numbers of organisations, the conclusion has to be that the history of voluntary housing is one in which the discontinuities turn out to be at least as important as the elements of continuity. Indeed, it can be argued that the strength of the voluntary housing movement in Britain is better demonstrated through its dynamism and its ability to recreate itself, rather than through appeals to tradition and historical continuity. It is important to be clear that while it is reasonable to speak of charitable housing having a history stretching back into the middle ages, the origins of contemporary RSLs are much more recent. Over the centuries there has been a series of different responses to the changing problem of how to provide accommodation for those in need: almshouses were a response generated by pre-industrial society to the problem as it was then understood and recognised, in the same way that model dwellings were an attempt to resolve particular aspects of the housing problem of a rapidly urbanising society in the nineteenth century. Modern housing associations should not be seen as having evolved from either almshouses or model dwellings companies; indeed, it is better to highlight the extent to which in the 1920s and 30s, and again in the 1960s, people setting up new associations were careful to distance themselves from pre existing organisations. The same may also be said of the LSVT associations and local housing companies at the present time. Thus successive waves of new formations have served to renew and re-invigorate the sector.

The evidence reported in earlier chapters has shown that only a handful of large, active RSLs at the end of the twentieth century can trace their origins back to before the First World War, and that the majority were set up after 1960. However, it can be argued that there is continuity in the sense that the Industrial and Provident Society model has endured and still provides the basis for the majority of RSLs. It is possible to identify continuity of purpose, in terms of a general orientation towards meeting the housing needs of people on low incomes, but it must be remembered that there was also a strand of activity, represented by the copartnership societies and later by the co-ownership societies, that was designed to provide for a distinctly better off section of the population. This serves to highlight the importance of recognising that the chief characteristic of voluntary housing organisations throughout most of their history was their diversity, in terms of size, constitution, objectives, type of accommodation provided, target groups and, above all, (in the period before the introduction of HAG) methods of funding. Diversity is still celebrated as a strength of the movement today, but historically the differences were much more apparent, and therefore it can be misleading to think in terms of a voluntary housing movement. There is no convincing evidence of any attempt to organise collective action among the plethora of voluntary housing organisations before the early 1930s, and it can be argued that even then nothing happened until the galvanising effect of changes in government policy and the appointment of the Moyne Committee. The fact that the model dwellings companies and charitable trusts did not join the NFHS on its formation in 1935 helps to emphasise the diversity and lack of shared identity at that time.

Another way of looking at this is to see it in terms of debates about some fundamental issues, specifically about how to approach the differing housing needs of distinct fractions of the working class, and the roles to be played by the state and voluntary organisations. As mentioned in Chapter 1, Harloe (1995) has argued that it is appropriate to think in terms of mass and residual models of social rented housing, the first embracing a relatively wide range of income groups while the second concentrates on the least well-off. Debates and struggles around which of these models was to predominate were at the heart of the politics of housing throughout much of the twentieth century, and the diversity among voluntary housing organisations can be seen as reflecting differing perceptions and purposes; on the one hand there was an essentially top-down, philanthropic strand of activity aimed at the poor as targets of middle and upper-class charity, while on the other hand the workers' self-help movement represented a bottom-up initiative involving skilled workers with sufficient income to generate savings that could be invested in co-operative housing ventures. The difficulties implicit in attempts to bring these two strands together in one 'voluntary housing movement' should not be underestimated.

On the debate about the appropriate roles of the state and voluntary organisations, the evidence suggests that over a very long period central government remained unconvinced that housing associations were capable of making a significant contribution to meeting housing needs, and their poor performance in the immediate aftermath of the First World War probably had a long-term impact on government thinking. Local authorities, having rapidly become substantial housing landlords in the early 1920s, were generally either actively hostile or passively resistant to any threat to their status as the main providers of affordable rented housing. They were also, along with officials within the Ministry of Health, dismissive of the capacity of these shoestring organisations to deliver the quantity of accommodation required. For a long time the strength of local government was such that the centre did not openly challenge their stance on housing, leaving it open for councils to co-operate with associations or not. The rise of housing associations in the last quarter of the century has to be seen in the context of the declining strength of local government.

The main theme of the chapters discussing the more recent history of housing associations has been their gradual emergence as instruments of housing policy. Housing associations have provided governments with a convenient test-bed for policy initiatives since the early 1960s. However, it is also important to recognise that the development of voluntary housing organisations in earlier decades was shaped by government. Whereas from the early 1960s they were given a positive part to play, in earlier times they had been influenced in an essentially negative way. This was particularly apparent in the first fifteen years after 1945, when governments concentrated on high levels of local authority output in order to reduce the overall shortage of general needs housing, and the official attitude towards associations was that they must not be allowed to interfere with the important work of the local authorities. In this situation they were tolerated rather than encouraged, and then only if they concentrated on providing for elderly people and other 'special needs' groups that were not high on the list of government priorities; the proliferation at this time of new associations catering specifically for elderly people is evidence of the way that government policy moulded voluntary organisations by default, as is the diversification of established charitable trusts into schemes tailored to elderly people.

One of the most important conclusions to be drawn from the book is that the RSL sector today – in terms of its size, composition, constitution and financial basis – is effectively the creation of successive governments since the early 1960s. This is not to imply that housing associations have been entirely passive and have taken no active part in shaping their development; it has been demonstrated in Chapter 7 that they were actively modernising and renewing themselves before the watershed legislation of 1974. Nevertheless, most associations were set up in response to government policies of one sort or another, and pre-existing organisations have been changed and sent off in new directions by changes in policy. Links to earlier periods are therefore increasingly tenuous and romantic. What, then, is the purpose of writing at length about the more distant past? Part of the answer, of course, is that in order to justify conclusions emphasising discontinuity it is necessary to examine the evidence from previous periods. It is important to challenge and correct taken-for-granted assumptions about the extent to which modern associations are rooted in the nineteenth century. At the same time, it is also necessary to look at the historical evidence in order to be able to argue that existing accounts of the development of housing policy in Britain are incomplete and misleading, being too heavily tilted towards local authority provision and its assumed inevitability. Study of voluntary housing in earlier parts of the century shows that the dominance of local authorities was contested and challenged for much longer than is generally implied.

Housing historians seem to have followed the interests of policy makers, allowing their own research and analysis to be shaped by what was happening in terms of policy developments at any given time, or selected by reference to what is now known to have been important (Daunton, 1983, 1987, Harloe, 1995). They seem to be easily diverted into looking at new developments, following the main currents of government policy, but leading to the neglect of existing institutions and continuing sub-texts. This helps to explain why much more has been written about the growth of council housing after 1890 than about activity among the model dwellings companies and trusts in the same period. An interesting question, which seems to have attracted virtually no attention, is what happened to the Victorian model dwellings companies in the twentieth century? There is evidence, some of which has been referred to in Chapter 3, that a number of them carried on building, albeit not very much nor very often, and that they survived into the 1960s and possibly longer. What was the extent of their contact with the organisations that formed the NFHS, and why did they not join? Other areas that might repay closer investigation include the campaign in the 1930s for a technocratic assault on housing problems, articulated via a national housing corporation, and the not unrelated possibility that the Ministry of Health was considering the development of state-sponsored and controlled housing associations, on the model established in the North Eastern HA and the Scottish Special HA, as a way of outflanking the power brokers in the larger local authorities.

More generally, there is a case for researching relations between housing associations and local authorities in different areas, and at different times, highlighting the differences and seeking to explain why some councils were much more co-operative than others.

Perhaps the most important criticism of the British housing literature arising from this book is its overemphasis on the politics of housing in terms of the mass versus the residual models of social renting, and its failure to come to terms with the emergent transition from one organisational model to another, ie from municipal landlords to RSLs. While it was necessary to account for the changes in the social composition of the tenants of council housing, and for privatisation through the right to buy, it is now equally necessary to provide an explanation for the rise of housing associations in the last quarter of the century and their adoption as the main vehicle for the demunicipalisation of remaining local authority stocks. Housing associations are not just missing from, or underregarded, in most historical accounts, they are also undertheorised in relation to major contemporary trends in the restructuring of both housing and the wider welfare state. The evidence discussed in this book points to the conclusion that it was the rise of the welfare state, especially after 1945, which squeezed them out of the picture, and it has been the retreat from the Keynesian welfare state in the last quarter of the century which has brought them back into focus.

Looking forward

Much of this book has been devoted to a detailed discussion of the growth and development of housing associations and their gradual incorporation into the ambit of state housing policy. Now it is necessary to broaden the focus a little and to ask how they stand in relation to housing problems and policies in the new century, and how they fit into the reformed welfare state. After being seen for so long as essentially conservative (if not actually Conservative) organisations, and having been promoted by Tory governments since 1988, how will they fare with Labour in office for the foreseeable future?

Any attempt to write about the future needs to be heavily qualified and hedged about by references to the difficulties of making accurate predictions. If the past is any guide then the future will turn out to be quite different from what might be expected. Pioneers of voluntary housing such as Octavia Hill, Edward Guinness and Reginald Rowe, who all died in the first half of the twentieth century, were undoubtedly people with some sort of vision of how things might be made better in terms of housing for the poor, but they could not have had the remotest inkling of the kinds of developments that actually occurred. The argument becomes even clearer if one thinks of the stance of the first Thatcher administration as recently as the early 1980s: who then could have envisaged the elevation of housing associations to the status of main providers of new rented housing, the successful introduction of private finance to cover half the cost of their capital programme or the transfer of entire stocks of council housing to new associations?

Given the inevitable uncertainty as to how things are going to turn out, it may be helpful to identify those aspects about which it is possible to be reasonably confident. Problems are generally easier to anticipate than solutions, and it can be said with some confidence that over the next ten or twenty years the population to be housed and the stock of dwellings available for them will change only slowly. Tenure preferences are also unlikely to show much change, with the private market remaining the main source of housing for most people. Over that sort of timescale, and in terms of these variables, the future will be much like the present. Just thinking about the prospects for RSLs:

- a significant proportion of the population will continue to require affordable rented housing;
- there will be a continuing need for new building, more so in some parts of the country than others;
- there will be a need for massive investment in stock regeneration as ageing properties are pressed into prolonged use; and
- there will be increasing numbers of elderly people, a proportion of whom will look to RSLs for accommodation.

In other words, the core business of RSLs looks pretty secure, at least in terms of need. However, the policies that are likely to be adopted are much less predictable, even if it is reasonably safe to assume the continuation of Labour in office beyond the next election. However, Tony Blair's administration has already shown that it has no intention of returning to the sorts of housing policies associated with previous Labour governments. There is to be no return to high levels of new building, and no encouragement to local authorities to invest resources in new council houses. A number of writers (Kleinman, 1996; Bramley, 1997; Hills, 1998; see also Malpass, 1999b) have noted that in recent years housing has slipped down the political agenda, and have argued that housing policy in Britain has ceased to exist, at least in the terms in which it was understood throughout much of the post-1945 period. These commentators refer to the idea that housing problems are now dealt with in distinctly different ways, with the needs of the relatively well-off majority being met through the market for owner occupation, while the needs of the less well-off minority (those who cannot buy) are met through social rented housing and a variety of measures that can be seen as adjuncts of, or nested within, other programme areas, mainly social security. Thus, while it is obvious to all concerned that there is a pressing need to do something about rents in the social rented sectors, it is difficult to make progress until the housing benefit system is reformed, which can really only be done in the context of a wider reform of social security as a whole, and that is a problem that has defeated governments for many years. Another area of concern in the late 1990s has been social exclusion, which provides a good example of a problem that demands the sort of 'joined up' policy approach championed by New Labour. In other words, policies to tackle social exclusion in poor, rundown neighbourhoods favour comprehensive strategies involving action on jobs and access to services as well as improvements to housing and the environment (Great Britain, 1998; Lee *et al.*, 1995).

How will RSLs cope? Housing associations go into the twenty first century far better equipped than they were only ten or twenty years ago to play a significant role in meeting housing need. Together with the newer forms of RSL they have much greater financial and organisational strength than ever before. However, to say that they are stronger and better equipped than they were in the past is not necessarily to say that they are in a good position to meet the demands of the future. One effect of the changes since 1989 has been to demonstrate that associations have reached a stage where they are able to attract private finance, albeit still heavily underwritten by the state. This has allowed them to expand and to achieve a kind of critical mass which might provide the basis for much greater growth in the future. However, it must be added very quickly here that the Conservative governments of Margaret Thatcher and, in particular, John Major, inflicted considerable damage on housing associations. By pushing them into a dog-eat-dog competitive scramble for development resources in the first half of the 1990s the government pursued short-term policy goals at the longer-term expense of associations, causing damage that will take some of them years to repair.

Even if a lasting solution is found to the housing benefit problem, RSLs will still face some intractable problems arising from the tensions and conflicts inherent in their position as private organisations with a social purpose. The vulnerability of RSLs can be illustrated by reference to the way in which housing associations were brought into partnership with local authorities in housing action areas in the 1970s: decisions made at that time, which were justified within the framework of the prevailing funding system, have saddled some associations with stocks of rapidly ageing housing in urgent need of major investment, but which is no longer funded by government. The Conservative government in 1989 abandoned its commitment to fund major repairs, transferring to associations a responsibility which exposed the contradictory position occupied by them in the present period: they are required to shoulder investment risk, but they are also expected to act as responsible social businesses. Thus their social commitment ties them to inner city areas where the need is greatest, even though prudent commercial investment planning might suggest disposal of such low value stock with high long-term maintenance-cost implications. The general point here is that if governments want RSLs to be major and effective players in pursuit of policy objectives, they (governments) must accept responsibility for providing them with adequate funding, and underwrite decisions taken for social reasons where there is a conflict with prudent business strategy.

Turning now to RSLs as organisations within a reformed welfare state, the first point to make is that the fragmentation of the public sector is a permanent feature. The election of a Labour government may have softened the rhetoric and slowed the pace, but, as quoted in Chapter 9, Blair has made it clear that the future lies in partnerships between local authorities and a range of private and not-for-profit service providers. In one sense this is good for RSLs as non-municipal providers of essential services. Housing associations have proved already that they can adapt to new situations and further change seems inevitable as they come to terms with government initiatives of various kinds. The inescapable conclusion coming out of this study of voluntary housing is that it has been transformed from a tiny, insignificant and mostly risible part of the housing system, leading a precarious existence on the margins of viability for three-quarters of the century, into a dynamic, expansionist and highly professional set of social businesses, well-suited to play a key role in the modernised welfare state. Further substantial growth in the total number of dwellings within the sector seems to be inevitable, boosted by stock transfers. But, as has been emphasised earlier, there remains considerable diversity among RSLs. The large majority of very small associations can be expected to make only a negligible impact in the future, and it is reasonable to conclude that the future of the sector lies with a relatively small group of large associations. This may well be seen as a reason for believing that in the next few years there will be many more mergers, in which the smaller associations are absorbed by the larger ones. Evidence has been mentioned at several points in this book to suggest that the Housing Corporation has long held the view that there are too many housing associations, and so a mergers programme that was designed to reduce the number of very small associations would almost certainly find favour from that direction. What is much less likely to be supported by the Corporation is mergers between associations that are already large. There is also a case for a stock rationalisation programme, redistributing stock among associations on a more sensible geographical basis so as to improve the effectiveness of housing management, and, arguably, to strengthen local accountability by vesting ownership in organisations based nearer to where the stock is located.

In the past, when there was even more diversity, it was essentially vertical in character, meaning that there were lots of different sorts of voluntary housing organisations, but now, after a quarter of a century of registration and regulation, it is apparent that the main fault line is horizontal: there are still different kinds of RSLs, but the key variable is size. In contrast to the situation obtaining in the past (including the not so distant past), it is now very much more difficult for small associations to grow into large ones. It is also more difficult to start a new association from scratch and build it up to a size where it could compete with the existing big players. Housing Corporation restrictions on new registrations and its preference for larger associations in the distribution of the ADP mean that in future the only new RSLs with a realistic chance of entering the top 200 are those formed from LSVTs. It was noted in Chapter 10 that the main source of growth in the number of housing association dwellings during the first half of the 1990s was stock transfers, and this may well continue to be the case in the future. Two possibilities then come into view: first, the character of the movement would change, with the prospect of LSVT associations becoming the single most important category, with the potential to act as a cohesive and powerful lobby; and, second, within the next ten or fifteen years it is conceivable that the majority of dwellings remaining in the social rented sector as a whole would be owned by RSLs, with a further marked redistribution of power from local government to the industry regulator and central government. This might well be seen as strengthening the case for re-opening debate about whether it would be

better to split off into separate bodies the regulatory and funding functions currently combined within the Corporation. For the Corporation
to have responsibility for funding and regulating the majority of the
dwellings in the social rented sector as a whole might be seen as an
unwarranted concentration of power.

Voluntary housing has been changed, virtually out of recognition,
transformed to the point where the voluntary element is of symbolic
relevance only, and there is no evidence to suggest that this is likely to
be reversed in the future. The larger associations are, in practice,
controlled by the Housing Corporation and can scarcely make a move
of any real significance without first gaining the approval of the relevant regional office. On a day to day basis their affairs are wholly
managed by their full-time salaried staff, and voluntary board members
are effectively reduced to a largely symbolic role. In the case of stock
transfers it is clear that the new associations are formed within the
public sector and as such are far removed from the traditional notion of
concerned individuals coming together around an issue of mutual
interest. However, LSVT associations and local housing companies are
products of attempts to strengthen democratic accountability by guaranteeing a certain proportion of board places for elected local councillors. To conclude that there is little left of the traditional voluntary
housing movement in England is not to imply a romantic attachment to
unmodernised housing associations. It has to be recognised that there
are real benefits flowing from the transformation that has been
described in this book. In the past they were patently unable to make a
quantifiable impact on the nation's housing needs, they were accused of
displaying patronising attitudes towards their tenants, and there was
undoubtedly a corrupt element in some associations. But times change:
now they can raise the private capital that was so elusive in the past and
the registration and monitoring activities of the Housing Corporation
have brought about a very considerable improvement in their policies
and procedures.

Finally, a personal comment: in writing this book I have tried to
maintain an appropriate degree of academic objectivity and to avoid
taking a partisan position in favour of, or against, housing associations.
However, my feeling is that they are still 'curious entities', and there is
still some force in the argument that they do not do anything that local
authorities could not do better. I deplore the way that the achievements
of local authorities in housing were excoriated by the Thatcherite
Conservatives in the 1980s, but at the end of the twentieth century there
is no point in trying to press the virtues of council housing which were

best displayed in very different social, economic and political circumstance fifty years ago. Now the tide is running too strongly in favour of arm's-length not-for-profit organisations, and the challenge before us is to make them work effectively to provide decent, affordable and safe accommodation that is at least as good as the best council houses of the past. This is a very difficult task, not least because of the greater inequality in modern society, the concentration of poverty in social rented housing, and the unwillingness of the Blairites to countenance robust redistributive social policy. It is undoubtedly a good thing that housing associations have begun to shake off the old taint of paternalism, but it is regrettable that in doing so they have become so closely under the control of central government.

One of the objectives of RSLs in the coming period should be to find a way to establish a greater degree of freedom from the centre, by strengthening their partnerships with local authorities. As I have argued in Chapter 11, the Tories pressed ahead with a model of housing association governance that gave priority to competition over local accountability, and now would be a good time to begin to row back from that position and to re-emphasise the value of links into local communities, demonstrated by more than tokenistic area committees. What is needed is a thoroughgoing stock rationalisation programme, transferring distant, far-flung estates to associations based nearby and re-asserting the value of locality-based social housing organisations. An integral part of such a reshaping of social housing would be the construction of real democratic accountability, which means abandoning elections by tiny, unrepresentative groups of shareholders and facing up to the problem of determining sensible membership policies and open, transparent mechanisms to permit the representation of major stakeholders. An advantage of such a move would be to enable RSLs to shape the parameters of their role, and to avoid being used as convenient vehicles for every passing ministerial whim and enthusiasm. In particular, I believe that it is important that RSLs insist on defining themselves as specialist providers of rented housing, resisting attempts to make them carry responsibility for a wider range of social and economic objectives (that is, it is not their job to have 'anti-poverty' strategies nor to engage in finding employment for their tenants). They should stick to their last, recognising that, as the historical evidence shows, it is the Industrial and Provident Society model and the provision of straightforward rented housing that has proved to be what works in the long run.

References

Addison, P. (1977) *The Road to 1945* (London: Quartet)

Airways Housing Society (1997) *The History of Airways Housing Society: Housing the Generations, 1947–1997* (Stanwell: Airways Housing Society)

AMA/ADC (1995) *Housing Finance Survey 1995–96* (London: Association of Metropolitan Authorities/Association of District Councils)

Ashby, J. (1997) 'The Inquiry into Housing Association Governance: (an inside view)' in Malpass (1997)

Ashmore, B. (1957) 'The Future of Industrial Housing Associations' *NFHS Quarterly Bulletin* (83), October

Ashworth, H. (1957) *Housing in Great Britain* (London: Skinner)

Ashworth, W. (1954) *The Genesis of Modern British Town Planning* (London: Routledge & Kegan Paul)

Bailey, B. (1988) *Almshouses* (London: Robert Hale)

Back, G. and Hamnett, C. (1985) 'State Housing Policy Formation and the Changing Role of Housing Associations' *Policy and Politics*, **13** (4): 393–411

Baker, C. (1975) *Housing Associations* (London: Estates Gazette)

Ball, M. (1986) 'Housing Analysis: Time for a Theoretical Refocus?' *Housing Studies*, **1** (3): 147–65

Banting, K. (1979) *Poverty, Policy and Politics* (London: Macmillan)

Barclay, I. (1976) *People Need Roots* (London: Bedford Square Press)

Barlow, J. and Duncan, S. (1988) 'The Use and Abuse of Housing Tenure' *Housing Studies* **3** (4): 219–31

Barlow, J., Cocks, R. and Parker, M. (1994) *Planning for Affordable Housing* (London: HMSO)

Bartlett, W. and Bramley, G. (eds) (1994) *European Housing Finance* (Bristol: School for Advanced Urban Studies, University of Bristol)

Begg, T. (1996) *Housing Policy in Scotland* (Edinburgh: John Donald Publishers Ltd)

Bell, E. M. (1942) *Octavia Hill: a Biography* (London: Constable)

Best, R. (1991) 'Housing Associations: 1890–1990' in Lowe, S. and Hughes, D., *A New Century of Social Housing* (Leicester: Leicester University Press)

Best, R. (1997) 'Housing Associations: the Sustainable Solution?' in Williams, P. (ed.) *Directions in Housing Policy: Towards Sustainable Housing Policies for the UK* (London: Paul Chapman Publishing)

Beveridge Report (1942) *Social Insurance and Allied Services* (London: HMSO) Cmd 6404

Beveridge, W. (1948) *Voluntary Action: A Report on Methods of Social Advance* (London: Allen & Unwin)

Birchall, J. (ed.) (1992) *Housing Policy in the 1990s* (London: Routledge)

Birchall, J. (1995) 'Co-partnership Housing and the Garden City Movement' *Planning Perspectives*, **10** pp. 329–58

Blair, T. (1998) *Leading the Way: A New Vision for Local Government* (London: IPPR)

Blake, J. (1998) 'Question Time' *ROOF, September/October, pp. 19–21 (interview with Hilary Armstrong)*

Boddy, M. (1980) *The Building Societies* (Basingstoke: Macmillan)

Boddy, M. and Fudge, C. (eds) (1984) *Local Socialism? Labour Councils and New Laft Alternatives* (Basingstoke: Macmillan)

Bogdanor, V. and Skidelsky, R. (eds) (1970) *The Age of Affluence 1951–64* (Basingstoke: Macmillan)

Boleat, M. (1982) *The Building Society Industry* (London: Allen & Unwin)

Bosanquet, N. (1980) 'Labour and Public Expenditure: an Overview' in Bosanquet, N. and Townsend, P. (1980)

Bosanquet, N. and Townsend, P. (eds) (1980) *Labour and Inequality* (London: Heinemann)

Bowley, M. (1945) *Housing and the State 1919–1944* (London: George Allen & Unwin)

Bramley, G. (1990) *Bridging the Affordability Gap* (London: Association of District Councils/House Builders Federation)

Bramley, G. (1993) 'The Enabling Role of Local Housing Authorities: A preliminary evaluation' in Malpass and Means (1993)

Bramley, G. (1994) 'An Affordability Crisis in British Housing: dimensions, causes and policy impact' *Housing Studies*, **9** (1): 103–24

Bramley, G. (1997) 'Housing Policy: A case of terminal decline?' *Policy and Politics*, **25**, (4). 387–407

Bramley, G. and Dunmore, K. (1995) *Do-It-Yourself Shared Ownership: An evaluation* (London: Housing Corporation)

Bramley, G. and Dunmore, K. (1996) 'Shared Ownership: Short-Term Expedient or Long-Term Major Tenure?' *Housing Studies*, **11** (1): 105–31

Brion, M. (1995) *Women in the Housing Service* (London: Routledge)

Brookes, J. (1987) 'St Mellons Joint Finance Scheme' *Housing Review*, May–June, pp. 78–80

Brunskill, R. (1997) *Houses and Cottages of Britain: Origins and Development of Traditional Buildings* (London: Gollancz)

Burnett, J. (1986) *A Social History of Housing 1815–1985* (London: Methuen)

Burrows, R. and Loader, B. (1994) *Towards a Post-Fordist Welfare State?* (London: Routledge)

Byrne, D. and Damer, S. (1980) 'The State, the Balance of Class Forces and Early Working Class Housing Legislation' in Political Economy of Housing Workshop, *Housing, Construction and the State* (London: PEHW)

Cadbury Report (1992) *Committee on the Financial Aspects of Corporate Governance, draft report* (London: Financial Reporting Council)

Centre for Housing Research (1989) *The Nature and Effectiveness of Housing Management in England* (London: HMSO)

Chaplin, R., Jones, M., Martin, S., Pryke, M., Royce, C., Saw, P., Whitehead, C. and Hong Yang, J. (1995) *Rents and Risks: Investing in Housing Associations* (York: Joseph Rowntree Foundation)

Clapham, D. (1997) 'A Woman of her Time' in Goodwin, J. and Grant, C. (eds) *Built to Last? Reflections on British Housing Policy* (London: Shelter)

Clarke, L. (1992) *Building Capitalism: Historical Change and the Labour Process in the Production of the Built Environment* (London: Routledge)

Clarke, P. (1996) *Hope and Glory: Britain 1900–1990* (London: Allen Lane)

Clay, R. M. (1909) *The Mediaeval Hospitals of England* (London: Methuen)

Clinton, A. *et al.* (1989) *The Relative Effectiveness of Different Forms of Housing Management in Wales* (Cardiff: Welsh Office)

Cohen Committee (1971) *Housing Associations* (London: HMSO)

Coleman, A. (1985) *Utopia on Trial* (London: Marion Boyars)

Coleman, D. (1991) 'Backdoor' *Roof*, November/December, p. 40

Connor, J. and Critchley, B. (1986) *The Red Cliffs of Stepney* (Colchester: Connor and Butler)

Cope, H. (1990) *Housing Associations: Policy and Practice* (Basingstoke: Macmillan)

Coulter, J. (1993) 'Financial Structure Needs Reviewing' *Voluntary Housing*, February, pp. 10–13

Cousins, L., Ledward, C., Howe, K., Rock, G. and Taylor, G. (1993) *An Appraisal of Shared Ownership* (London: HMSO)

Crook, A. and Darke, R. (1996) *A New Lease of Life? Housing Association Investment in Local Authority Estates* (Bristol: Policy Press)

Crook, A. and Kemp, P. (1996) 'The Revival of Private Rented Housing in Britain' *Housing Studies*, **11** (1): 51–68

Currie, H. (1996) 'The Governance and Administration of Housing' in Currie, H. and Murie, A. (eds) *Housing in Scotland* (Coventry: Chartered Institute of Housing)

Damer, S. (1980) 'State, Class and Housing: Glasgow 1885–1919', in Melling, J. (1980)

Daunton, M. (1983) *House and Home in the Victorian City* (London: Edward Arnold)

Daunton, M. (1987) *A Property Owning Democracy?* (London: Faber & Faber)

Davis, H. and Stewart, J. (1994) *The Growth of Government by Appointment: Implications for Local Democracy* (Luton: Local Government Management Board)

Davoudi, S. and Healey, P. (1995) 'City Challenge: Sustainable Process or Temporary Gesture?' *Environment and Planning C: Government and Policy*, **13** (1), February, pp. 79–95

Day, M. (1981) 'The contribution of Sir Raymond Unwin and Barry Parker to the development of site planning theory and practice, c. 1890–1918' in Sutcliffe, A. (ed.) *British Town Planning: the Formative Years* (Leicester: Leicester University Press)

Dennis, R. (1989) 'The Geography of Victorian Values: Philanthropic Housing in London, 1840–1900' *Journal of Historical Geography*, **15** (1): 40–54

DETR (1998a) *Modernising Local Government: Improving Local Services Through Best Value* (London: DETR)

DETR (1998b) *Annual Report 1998* (London: Stationery Office)

DETR (1998c) *Housing and Regeneration Policy: A Statement by the Deputy Prime Minister and Secretary of State for the Environment, Transport and the Regions* (London: DETR)

DoE (1987) *Finance for Housing Associations: The Government's Proposals* (London: DoE)

DoE (1988) *New Financial Regime for Local Authority Housing in England and Wales: A Consultation Paper* (London: DoE)

DoE (1991) Management Statement issued to the Housing Corporation by the Secretary of State for the Environment (London: DoE)

DoE (1993) *Housing Associations Rehabilitation and Urban Renewal. Part One, Changes in the Rehabilitation Activity of Housing Associations* (London: DoE)

DoE (1994) *Annual Report 1994* (London: HMSO)

DoE (1995) *Housing Corporation: Prior Options Study* (London: DoE)

Donnison, D. and Ungerson, C. (1982) *Housing Policy* (Harmondsworth: Penguin)

Dorling, D. and Cornford, J. (1995) 'Who has Negative Equity? How House Price Falls in Britain Have Hit Different Groups of Home Buyers' *Housing Studies* **10** (2): 151–78

Dyos, H. and Wolf, M. (eds) (1973) *The Victorian City* (London: Routledge & Kegan Paul)

Emsley, I. (1986) *The Development of Housing Associations* (London: Garland Publishing)

Englander, D. (1983) *Landlord and Tenant in Urban Britain 1838–1918* (Oxford: Clarendon Press)

Environment Committee (1993) *The Housing Corporation*, Second report of the House of Commons Environment Committee, Session 1992–93, **1**, HC 466–I

Environment Committee (1995) *Department of the Environment Memorandum on Provision for Social Housing*, First Special Report, Session 1994–95 (London: HMSO) HC 442

Environment, Transport and Regional Affairs Committee (1998) *Housing*, Tenth Report, Session 1997–98 (London: Stationery Office), HC 495–I

ESRC (1992) *Local Governance: The Purpose of the Proposed Initiative* (Economic and Social Research Council: unpublished briefing paper)

Farthing, S., Lambert, C., Malpass, P., Tetlow, R., Auchincloss, M. and Bramley, G. (1996) *Land, Planning and Housing Associations* (London: Housing Corporation)

Fenter, F. M. (1960) *COPEC Adventure: The Story of the Birmingham COPEC House Improvement Society* (Birmingham: COPEC)

Fishman, R. (1977) *Urban Utopians in the Twentieth Century* (New York: Basic Books)

Fiske, W. (1962) 'Meeting Housing Needs: The Opportunity for Co-operation between Local Authorities and Housing Associations', *Housing Review*, **11** (3) May–June, pp. 80–4

Ford, J. and Wilcox, S. (1994) *Affordable Housing, Low Incomes and the Flexible Labour Market* (London: NFHA)

Forrest, R., Lansley, S. and Murie, A. (1984) *A Foot on the Ladder (Bristol: School for Advanced Urban Studies, University of Bristol)*

Forrest, R. and Murie, A. (1988) *Selling the Welfare State* (London: Routledge)

Forrest, R., Murie, A. and Williams, P. (1990) *Home Ownership: Differentiation and Fragmentation* (London: Unwin Hyman)

Fraser, D. (1973) *The Evolution of the Welfare State* (London: Macmillan)

Fraser, D. (1979) *Power and Authority in the Victorian City* (Oxford: Basil Blackwell)

Gamble, A. (1988) *The Free Economy and the Strong State: The politics of Thatcherism* (Basingstoke: Macmillan)

Garside, P. (1995) 'Central Government, Local Authorities and the Voluntary Housing Sector, 1919–1939' in O'Day, A. (ed.) *Government and Institutions in the Post 1832 UK* (Mellon Press)

Garside, P. and Morris, S. (1994) *Building a Legacy: William Sutton and His Housing Trust* (Tring: William Sutton Trust)

Gaskell, S. M. (1981) ' "The Suburb Salubrious": Town Planning in Practice' in Sutcliffe, A. (1981)

Gaskell, S. M. (1986) *Model Housing: From the Great Exhibition to the Festival of Britain* (London: Mansell Publishing)

Gauldie, E. (1974) *Cruel Habitations* (London: Allen & Unwin)

Gibson, M. and Langstaff, M. (1982) *An Introduction to Urban Renewal* (London: Hutchinson)

Gilmour, I. (1992) *Dancing with Dogma: Britain under Thatcherism* (London: Simon & Schuster)

Glennerster, H. (1995) *British Social Policy since 1945* (Oxford: Blackwell)

Goodlad, R. (1993) *The Housing Authority as Enabler* (Harlow: Longman)

Great Britain (1961) *Housing in England and Wales* (London: HMSO) Cmnd. 1290

Great Britain (1963) *Housing* (London: HMSO) Cmnd. 2050

Great Britain (1965) *The Housing Programme 1965–1970* (London: HMSO) Cmnd. 2838

Great Britain (1966, 1969) *Housing Statistics* (London: HMSO)

Great Britain (1971) *Fair Deal for Housing* (London: HMSO) Cmnd. 4728
Great Britain (1973a) *Widening the Choice: The Next Steps in Housing* (London: HMSO) Cmnd 5280
Great Britain (1973b) *Better Homes: The Next Priorities* (London: HMSO) Cmnd 5339
Great Britain (1976) *Public Expenditure to 1979–80* (London: HMSO) Cmnd 6393
Great Britain (1977) *Housing Policy: A Consultative Document* (London: HMSO) Cmnd 6851
Great Britain (1984) *The Government's Expenditure Plans, 1984–85 to 1986–87* (London: HMSO) Cmnd. 9143
Great Britain (1987) *Housing: The Government's Proposals* (London: HMSO) Cm. 214
Great Britain (1989) *The Government's Expenditure Plans, 1988–89 to 1991–92* (London: HMSO) Cm. 609
Great Britain (1995) *Our Future Homes: The Government's Housing Policies for England and Wales* (London: HMSO) Cm 2901
Great Britain (1998) *Bringing Britain Together: A National Strategy for Neighbourhood Renewal*, Report by the Social Exclusion Unit (London: Stationery Office) Cm 4045
Greer, A. and Hoggett, P. (1997) *Patterns of Accountability Within Local Non-Elected Bodies* (York: Joseph Rowntree Foundation)
Gregg, P. (1965) *A Social and Economic History of Britain 1760–1965* (London: Harrap)
Greve, J. (1964) *London's Homeless* (London: Codicote Press)
Greve, J., Page, D. and Greve, S. (1971) *Homelessness in London* (Edinburgh: Scottish Academic Press)
Hall, S. and Jacques, M. (eds) (1983) *The Politics of Thatcherism* (London: Lawrence & Wishart)
Hardy, D. (1991) *From Garden Cities to New Towns* (London: Spon)
Harloe, M. (1978) 'The Green Paper on Housing Policy' in Brown, M. and Baldwin, S. (eds) *The Year Book of Social Policy in Britain 1977* (London: Routledge & Kegan Paul)
Harloe, M. (1985) *Private Rented Housing in the United States and Europe* (London: Croom Helm)
Harloe, M. (1995) *The People's Home? Social Rented Housing in Europe and America* (Oxford: Blackwell)
Harloe, M., Issacharoff, R. and Minns, R. (1974) *The Organisation of Housing: Public and Private Enterprise in London* (London: Heinemann)
Harris, M. (1998) 'Instruments of Government? Voluntary sector boards in a changing public policy environment' *Policy and Politics*, **26** (2): 177–88
Harrison, M. (1981) 'Housing and Town Planning in Manchester before 1914' in Sutcliffe (1981)

Harvey, D. (1989) *The Condition of Postmodernity: An Enquiry into the Origins of Cultural Change* (Oxford: Blackwell)

Hennessy, P. (1992) *Never Again: Britain 1945–1951* (London: Vintage)

Henslowe, P. (1984) *Ninety Years On: An Account of the Bournville Village Trust* (Bournville: Bournville Village Trust)

Hill, O. (1933) *Letters to Fellow Workers, 1864–1911* (London: Adelphi Book Shop)

Hill, O. (1875) *Homes of the London Poor* (London: Macmillan)

Hills, J. and Mullings, B. (1990) 'Housing: A Decent Home for All at a Price within their Means?' in Hills (1990)

Hills, J. (ed.) (1990) *The State of Welfare* (Oxford: Clarendon Press)

Hills, J. (1998) 'Housing: A Decent Home Within the Reach of Every Family?' in Hills, J. and Glennerster, H. (eds) (1998)

Hills, J. and Glennerster, H. (eds) (1998) *The State of Welfare: the economics of social spending*, 2nd edn (Oxford: Clarendon Press)

Hobsbawm, E. (1987) *The Age of Empire* (London: Weidenfeld & Nicholson)

Hobsbawm, E. (1994) *Age of Extremes: The Short Twentieth Century* (London: Michael Joseph)

Hoggett, P. (1987) 'A Farewell to Mass Production? Decentralisation as an Emergent Private and Public Sector Paradigm' in Hoggett, P. and Hambleton, R. (eds) *Decentralisation and Democracy* (Bristol: School for Advanced Urban Studies, University of Bristol)

Hoggett, P. (1990) 'Modernisation, Political Strategy and the Welfare State' (Bristol: School for Advanced Urban Studies, University of Bristol)

Hoggett, P. (1996) 'New Modes of Control in the Public Service' *Public Administration*, **74**, Spring, pp. 9–32

Hogwood, B. (1992) *Trends in British Public Policy* (Buckingham: Open University Press)

Holmans, A. (1995) *Housing Demand and Need in England, 1991 to 2011* (York: York Publishing Services)

Holmans, A., Morrison, N. and Whitehead, C. (1998) *How Many Homes will we Need?* (London: Shelter)

Holmes, C. (1978) 'The Elusive Panacea' *ROOF*, July, pp. 110–12

House of Commons (1979) *Fifth Report from the Committee of Public Accounts, Session 1978–79: Housing Associations and the Housing Corporation* (London: HMSO) HC 327

House of Commons (1981) *Eleventh Report from the Committee of Public Accounts, Session 1980–81* (London: HMSO) HC 328

Housing Corporation (1976) *Annual Report 1975–76* (London: Housing Corporation)

Housing Corporation (1977) *Annual Report 1976–77* (London: Housing Corporation)

Housing Corporation (1978) *Annual Report 1977–78* (London: Housing Corporation)

Housing Corporation (1980) *Annual Report 1979–80* (London: Housing Corporation)

Housing Corporation (1981) *Annual Report 1980–81* (London: Housing Corporation)

Housing Corporation (1990a) *Housing Associations in 1989* (London: Housing Corporation)

Housing Corporation (1990b) *West Region Policy Statement 1992/93* (Exeter: Housing Corporation)

Housing Corporation (1994a) *The Next Three Years: The Housing Corporation's Plans and Priorities 1994–1997* (London: Housing Corporation)

Housing Corporation (1994b) *Annual Report 1993–94* (London: Housing Corporation)

Housing Corporation (1995) *Housing Associations in 1994: General Report* (London: Housing Corporation)

Housing Corporation (1996a) *Housing for Older People* (London: Housing Corporation)

Housing Corporation (1996b) *The Housing Corporation South West Policy Statement 1997/98* (Exeter: Housing Corporation)

Housing Corporation (1997a) *Performance Standards: Performance Standards and Regulatory Guidance for Registered Social Landlords* (London: Housing Corporation)

Housing Corporation (1997b) *A Housing Plus Approach to Achieving Sustainable Communities* (London: Housing Corporation)

Housing Corporation (1998a) *Housing Associations in 1997: General Report* (London: Housing Corporation)

Housing Corporation (1998b) *South West Policy Statement 1999/2000* (Exeter: Housing Corporation)

Housing Corporation (1998c) *Building a Better Future: Revitalising Neighbourhoods*, The Housing Corporation's Three Year Strategy 1999/2000–2001/2002 (London: Housing Corporation)

Housing Corporation (1999) *Registered Social Landlords in 1998: Profile of the RSL Sector* (London: Housing Corporation)

Housing Corporation (n.d.) *The West Region's Investment Programme: A Review of the Years 1991/92 to 1993/94* (Exeter: Housing Corporation)

Howson, B. (1993) *Houses of Noble Poverty: A History of the English Almshouse* (London: Bellvue Books)

Hulchanski, D. (1995) 'The Concept of Housing Affordability: Six Contemporary Uses of the Housing Expenditure-to-Income Ratio' *Housing Studies*, **10** (4): 471–91

Jackson, A. A. (1973) *Semi-Detached London* (London: Allen & Unwin)

Jones, P. (1985) *National Federation of Housing Associations Jubilee Album 1935–1985* (London: NFHA)

Jordan, W. (1959) *Philanthropy in England 1480–1660* (London: Allen & Unwin)

Karn, V. (1993) 'Remodelling a HAT' in Malpass and Means (1993)

Karn, V. and Sheridan, L. (1994) *New Homes in the 1990s: A Study of Design, Space and Amenity in Housing Association and Private Sector Production* (York: Joseph Rowntree Foundation)

Kavanagh, D. (1987) *Thatcherism and British Politics: The End of Consensus?* (Oxford: Oxford University Press)

Kearns, A. (1992) 'Affordability for Housing Association Tenants. A Key Issue for British Social Housing Policy' *Journal of Social Policy*, **21** (4): 525–49

Kearns, A. (1994) *Going by the Board: The Unknown Facts about Housing Association Membership and Management Committees in England* (Glasgow: Centre for Housing Research and Urban Studies, University of Glasgow)

Kearns, A. (1997) 'Housing Association Committees: Dilemmas of Composition' in Malpass (1997)

Kemp, P. (1993) 'Rebuilding the Private Rented Sector?' in Malpass and Means (1993)

Kendall, J. and Knapp, M. (1996) *The Voluntary Sector in the UK* (Manchester: Manchester University Press)

Kleinman, M. (1996) *Housing, Welfare and the State in Europe* (Cheltenham: Edward Elgar)

Labour Party (1956) *Homes for the Future* (London: the Labour Party)

Lambert, C. and Malpass, P. (1998) 'The Rules of the Game: Competition for Housing Investment' in Oatley (1998)

Langstaff, M. (1992) 'Housing Associations: A Move to Centre Stage' in Birchall (1992)

Lansley, S. (1979) *Housing and Public Policy* (London: Croom Helm)

LCC (1937) *London Housing* (London: LCC)

Lee, P., Murie, A., Marsh, A. and Riseborough, M. (1995) *The Price of Social Exclusion* (London: NFHA)

Le Grand, J. (1990) in Hills, J. (ed.) *The State of Welfare* (Oxford: Clarendon Press)

Le Grand, J. and Bartlett, W. (eds) (1993) *Quasi-Markets and Social Policy* (Basingstoke: Macmillan)

Lewis, J. (1999) 'Voluntary and Informal Welfare' in Page, R. and Silburn, R. (eds) *British Social Welfare in the Twentieth Century* (Basingstoke: Macmillan)

LGA (1997) *Housing Finance Survey 1997/98* (London: Local Government Association)

Lowe, S. (1991) *Introduction: One Hundred Years of Social Housing*, in Lowe, S. and Hughes, D. (1991)

Lowe, S. and Hughes, D. (eds) (1991) *A New Century of Social Housing* (Leicester: Leicester University Press)

Mackintosh, S. and Leather, P. (1993) *Renovation File: A Profile of Housing Conditions and Housing Renewal Policies in the United Kingdom* (Oxford: Anchor Housing Trust)

Macnabb, J. (1956) 'The Housing Associations and Their Contributions to Housing in the Near Future' *Housing Review*, **5** (5), September–October, pp. 153–4

Malpass, P. (1984a) 'Octavia Hill' in Barker, P. (ed.) *Founders of the Welfare State* (London: Heinemann)

Malpass, P. (1984b) 'Housing Benefits in Perspective' in Jones, C. and Stevenson, J. (eds) (1984) *The Year Book of Social Policy in Britain 1983* (London: Routledge & Kegan Paul)

Malpass, P. (1990) *Reshaping Housing Policy: Subsidies, Rents and Residualisation* (London: Routledge)

Malpass, P. (1993) 'Housing Policy and the Housing System Since 1979' in Malpass, P. and Means, R. (1993)

Malpass, P. (1994) 'Policy Making and Local Governance: How Bristol Failed to Secure City Challenge Funding (Twice)' *Policy and Politics* **22** (2): 301–12

Malpass, P. (1996) 'The Unravelling of Housing Policy in Britain' *Housing Studies*, **11** (3): 459–70

Malpass, P. (ed.) (1997) *Ownership, Control and Accountability: The New Governance of Housing* (Coventry: Chartered Institute of Housing)

Malpass, P. (1998) *Housing Philanthropy and the State: A History of the Guinness Trust* (Bristol: UWE, Faculty of the Built Environment)

Malpass, P. (1999a) *The Work of the Century: The Origins and Growth of the Octavia Hill Housing Trust in Notting Hill* (London: Octavia Hill Housing Trust)

Malpass, P. (1999b) 'Housing Policy: Does it Have a Future?' *Policy and Politics*, **27** (2): 217–28

Malpass, P. and Jones, C. (1995) *Home Housing Association: A History* (Newcastle: Home HA)

Malpass, P. and Jones, C. (1996a) 'The Fourth Experiment? The Commissioner for Special Areas, the Ministry of Health and the North Eastern Housing Association' *Planning Perspectives*, **11** pp. 303–21

Malpass, P. and Jones, C. (1996b) *Extending the Hand of Friendship: the first forty years of the Friendship Group* (Birmingham: Friendship Group)

Malpass, P. and Means, R. (eds) (1993) *Implementing Housing Policy* (Buckingham: Open University Press)

Malpass, P. and Murie, A. (1999) *Housing Policy and Practice, 5th edn* (Basingstoke: Macmillan)

Malpass, P., Warburton, M., Bramley, G. and Smart, G. (1993) *Housing Policy in Action: The New Financial Regime for Council Housing* (Bristol: School for Advanced Urban Studies, University of Bristol)

Mantle, J. (1995) *Every Change is a Challenge: The Story of Paddington Churches Housing Association* (London: James & James)

Marsh, D. and Rhodes, R. (eds) (1992) *Implementing Thatcherite Policies* (Buckingham: Open University Press)

Martelli, G. (1956) *A Man of His Time: A Life of the First Earl of Iveagh*, published privately by the Second Earl.

Marwick, A. (1998) *The Sixties* (Oxford: Oxford University Press)

Melling, J. (ed.) (1980) *Housing, Social Policy and the State* (Beckenham: Croom Helm)

Merrett, S. (1979) *State Housing in Britain* (London: Routledge & Kegan Paul)

Merrett, S. (1982) *Owner Occupation in Britain* (London: Routledge & Kegan Paul)

MIH (1988) *Merseyside Improved Houses, Diamond Jubilee 1928–1988* (Liverpool: MIH)

Miller, K. (1993) 'The Let Down' *ROOF*, March–April, pp. 20–1

Miller, M. (1993) *Letchworth: The First Garden City* (Chichester: Phillimore)

Milner Holland (1965) *Report of the Committee on Housing in Greater London* (London: HMSO) Cmnd 2605

Ministry of Health (1921) *Annual Report for 1920–21* (London: HMSO) Cmd 1446

Ministry of Health (1933) *Report of the Departmental Committee on Housing* (London: HMSO) Cmd 4397

Ministry of Health (1935) *Annual Report for 1934–35* (London: HMSO) Cmd 4978

Ministry of Health (1938) *Annual Report for 1937–38* (London: HMSO) Cmd 5801

Ministry of Health (1939) *The Operations of Housing Associations* (London: HMSO)

Ministry of Health (1944) *Private Enterprise Housing* (London: HMSO)

Ministry of Housing and Local Government (1951) *Housing for Special Purposes*, Report of Sub-Committee of the Central Housing Advisory Committee (London: HMSO)

Ministry of Health (1953) *The Cost of House Maintenance* (Report of the Girdwood Committee) (London: HMSO)

Ministry of Health (1955) *Report for 1950/51–1954* (London: HMSO) Cmd 9559

Mole, R. (1987) *Cottage Improvement to Sheltered Housing: Oxford Citizens Housing Association, The First 120 years*, Oxford: OCCHA

Morgan, K. (1984) *Labour in Power, 1945–1951* (Oxford: Clarendon Press)

MORI (1996) *Survey of Housing Association Tenants* (London: Housing Corporation)

Morton, J. (1989) *The First Twenty Five Years* (London: Housing Corporation)

Morton, J. (1991) 'The 1890 Act and its Aftermath – the Era of the 'Model Dwellings" in Lowe, S. and Hughes, D. (1991)

Mullins, D. (1997) 'From Regulatory Capture to Regulated Competition: An Interest Group Analysis of the Regulation of Housing Associations in England' *Housing Studies*, **12** (3), July, pp. 301–20

Mullins, D., Niner, P. and Riseborough, M. (1992) *Evaluating Large Scale Voluntary Transfers of Local Authority Housing* (London: HMSO)

Murie, A. (1975) *The Sale of Council Houses: A Study in Social Policy* (Birmingham: CURS, University of Birmingham) *Occasional Paper no. 35*

NFHS (1964) *National Federation of Housing Associations Annual Report* (London: NFHS)

NFHA (1985) *Inquiry into British Housing: Report* (London: NFHA)

NFHA (1995) *Competence and Accountability: Report of the Inquiry into Housing Association Governance* (London: NFHA)

Noble, D. (1979) 'Policing Voluntary Housing' *ROOF*, July, pp. 122–5

Nolan Committee (1995) *First Report of the Committee on Standards in Public Life* (London: HMSO) Cm 2850–I

Nolan Committee (1996) *Standards in Public Life: Local Public Spending Bodies*, Second Report of the Committee on Standards in Public Life (London: HMSO) Cm 3270-1

Oatley, N. (ed.) (1998) *Cities, Economic Competition and Urban Policy* (London: Paul Chapman Publishing)

Offer, A. (1981) *Property and Politics 1870–1914* (Cambridge: Cambridge University Press)

Orbach, L. (1977) *Homes Fit for Heroes: A Study of the Evolution of British Public Housing, 1915–1921* (London: Seeley, Service)

Owen, D. (1965) *English Philanthropy* (London: Oxford University Press)

Page, D. (1993) *Building for Communities: A Study of New Housing Association Estates* (York: Joseph Rowntree Foundation)

Pawson, H. and Kearns, A. (1998) 'Difficult to Let Housing Association Stock in England: Property, Management and Context' *Housing Studies*, **13** (3): 391–414

Pearman, H. (1985) *Excellent Accommodation: The First Hundred Years of the Industrial Dwellings Society* (London: Industrial Dwellings Society)

Platt, S. (1987) 'Yes Minister, but...' *ROOF*, January–February, pp. 23–5

Pollard, S. (1983) *The Development of the British Economy 1914–1980*, 3rd edn (London: Edward Arnold)

Pollitt, C., Birchall, J. and Putman, K. (1998) *Decentralising Public Service Management* (Basingstoke: Macmillan)

Power, A. (1987) *Property Before People* (London: Allen & Unwin)

Pryke, M. (1994) 'Coping with Some of the New Risks of Social Housing in England' in Bartlett and Bramley (1994)

Quigley, H. and Goldie, I. (1934) *Housing and Slum Clearance in London* (London: Methuen)

Randolph, B. (ed.) (1992) *Housing Associations After the Act* (London: NFHA)

Randolph, B. (1993) 'The Reprivatisation of Housing Associations' in Malpass, P. and Means, R. *Implementing Housing Policy* (Milton Keynes: Open University Press)

Reid, B. (1995) 'Interorganisational Networks and the delivery of Housing Services' *Housing Studies*, **10** (2): 133–49

Reid, B. (1997) 'Interorganisational Relationships and Social Housing Services' in Malpass (1997)

Rhodes, R. (1996) 'The New Governance: Governing Without Government' *Political Studies*, **XLIV**, pp. 652–67

Rowntree, S. (1914) 'How far is it Possible to Provide Satisfactory Houses for the Working Classes, at Rents which they can Afford to Pay?' in Rowntree, S. and Pigou, A. *Lectures on Housing*, reissued by Garland Publishing, London, 1980

Rowntree, S. (1947) *Old People: The Report of a Survey Committee under the Chairmanship of B. Seebohm Rowntree* (London: Nuffield Foundation)

Saunders, P. (1990) *A Nation of Home Owners* (London: Unwin Hyman)

Scott Report (1942) *Report of the Committee on Land Utilisation in Rural Areas* (London: HMSO) Cmd 6378

Seyd, P. (1975) 'Shelter: the National Campaign for the Homeless' *Political Quarterly*, **46**, 418–31

SICLC (1939) *Society for Improving the Condition of the labouring Classes: A Survey* (London: the Society)

Simon, E. D. (1933) *The Anti-Slum Campaign* (London: Longman, Green & Co.)

Skilleter, K. (1993) 'The Role of Public Utility Societies in Early British Town Planning and Housing Reform' *Planning Perspectives*, **8**, 125–65

Smalley, G. (1909) *The Life of Sir Sydney Waterlow, Bart* (London: Arnold)

Smith, M. (1989) *Guide to Housing*, 3rd edn (London: Housing Centre)

Smith, S. (1989) *The Politics of Race and Residence* (Cambridge: Polity Press)

Somerville, P. and Knowles, A. (1991) 'The Difference that Tenure Makes' *Housing Studies*, **6** (2): 112–30

Stack, U. (1967) *The Development of a Housing Association* (Birmingham: University of Birmingham) CURS Occasional Paper no. 1

Stedman Jones, G. (1971) *Outcast London: A Study of Relationships Between Classes in Victorian London* (London: Macmillan)

Stoker, G. (1995) 'Public–Private Partnerships in Urban Governance' (Paper presented to the Housing Studies Association Conference, University of Edinburgh)

Stoker, G. (ed.) (1999) *The New Management of British Local Governance* (Basingstoke: Macmillan)

Survey of London (1973) *Volume XXXVII North Kensington* (London: Athlone Press)

Sutcliffe, A. (ed.) (1974) *Multi-Storey Living: The British Working Class Experience* (London: Croom Helm)

Sutcliffe, A. (ed.) (1981) *British Town Planning: The Formative Years* (Leicester: Leicester University Press)

Swenarton, M. (1981) *Homes fit for Heroes* (London: Heinemann)

Tarn, J. (1966) 'The Peabody Donation Fund: The Role of a Housing Society in the Nineteenth Century' *Victorian Studies*, September, pp. 7–38

Tarn, J. (1968) 'The Improved Industrial Dwellings Company' *Transactions of the London and Middlesex Archaeological Society*, **XXII** (1): 43–59

Tarn, J. (1973) *Five Per Cent Philanthropy: An Account of Housing in Urban Areas Between 1840 and 1914* (Cambridge: Cambridge University Press)

Tarn, J. (1974) French Flats for the English in Nineteenth Century London, in Sutcliffe, A. (1974)

Taylor, I. (1974) *The Insanitary Housing Question and Tenement Dwellings in Nineteenth Century Liverpool*, in Sutcliffe, A. (1974)

Tickell, J. (1996) *Turning Hopes into Homes, A History of Social Housing 1235–1996* (London: National Housing Federation)

Tiltson, J. (1984) *The Gibson Gardens History and Cookery Book* (London: Centerprise Trust)

Uthwatt Report (1942) *Final Report of the Expert Committee on Compensation and Betterment* (London: HMSO) Cmd 6386

Walentowicz, P. (1992) *Housing Standards After the Act* (London: NFHA) Research Report 15

Ward, S. (1988) *The Geography of Interwar Britain* (London: Routledge)

Ward, S. (ed.) (1992) *The Garden City, Past Present and Future* (London: Spon)

Webb, B, (1971) *My Apprenticeship* (London: Penguin)

Webster, D. (1980) 'Housing' in Bosanquet and Townsend (1980)

Weir, S. (1976) 'Associations', Alarm at High Fair Rents' *ROOF*, October, pp. 130–2

Whelan, R. (1998) *Octavia Hill and the Social Housing Debate* (London: IEA)

White, J. (1980) *Rothschild Buildings: Life in an East End Tenement Block 1887–1920* (London: Routledge & Kegan Paul)

White, J. (1997) 'Business out of Charity' in Goodwin, J. and Grant, C. (eds) *Built to Last? Reflections on British Housing Policy*, 2nd edn (London: Shelter)

Whitehead, C. (1991) 'From Need to Affordability: An Analysis of UK Housing Objectives' *Urban Studies*, **28** (6): 871–87

Whitehead, C. and Kleinman, M. (1992) *A Review of Housing Needs Assessment* (London: Housing Corporation)

Wilcox, S. (1993) *Housing Finance Review 1993* (York: Joseph Rowntree Foundation)

Wilcox, S. (1997) 'Local Housing Companies' in Malpass (1997)

Wilcox, S., Bramley, G., Ferguson, A., Perry, J. and Woods, C. (1993) *Local Housing Companies: New Opportunities for Council Housing* (York: Joseph Rowntree Foundation)

Wilcox, S. and Williams, P. (1997) 'Social Housing and Private finance: Prospects for 1997and 1998' *Housing Finance*, no. 34, May, pp. 39–46

Wilding, P. (1972) 'Towards Exchequer Subsidies for Housing 1906–1914' *Social and Economic Administration*, **6** (1): 3–18

Williams, P. and Wilcox, S. (1999) 'Funding Social Housing: A Sustainable Market for Private Finance?' *Housing Finance*, no. 42, May 1999

Wohl, A. (1977) *The Eternal Slum* (London: Edward Arnold)

Wolch, J. (1990) *The Shadow State: Government and the Voluntary Sector in Transition* (New York: the Foundation Center)

Wolfenden Committee (1978) *The Future of Voluntary Organisations* (London: Croom Helm)

Woodward, R. (1991) 'Mobilising Opposition: The Campaign Against Housing Action Trusts in Tower Hamlets' *Housing Studies*, **6** (1): 44–56

Yelling, J. (1992) *Slums and Redevelopment: Policy and Practice in England 1918–1945* (London: UCL Press)

Young, G. (1991) 'Our Shared Commitment' *ROOF*, November–December

Young, K. and Garside, P. (1981) *Metropolitan London: Politics and Urban Change 1837–1981* (London: Edward Arnold)

Young, K. and Kramer, J. (1978) *Strategy and Conflict in Metropolitan Housing* (London: Heinemann)

Name Index

Subject Index